Praise for *Super Fresh*

"The hardest part about leaving Fresh restaurant is knowing that it might be a while
before I can come back. That's why I'm thrilled about the *Super Fresh* cookbook!
Now I can cook my favourite energizing dishes in the comfort of my own kitchen."

ANGELA LIDDON, creator of the award-winning blog *Oh She Glows* and
author of the *New York Times* bestseller *The Oh She Glows Cookbook*

"Living healthy is always in style, and Ruth and Jennifer are experts on getting the most out of what you eat.
I've been going to Fresh restaurant for years and love starting my day with one of Ruth's smoothie recipes.
This book is the perfect way to bring their expertise into your own home every day."

JOE MIMRAN, founder of Joe Fresh

"Ruth and Jennifer make delicious food. I eat at Fresh whenever I'm in Toronto,
and *Super Fresh* is full of recipes I could eat every day."

BRENDAN BRAZIER, international bestselling author of
The Thrive Diet and *Thrive Energy Cookbook*

"Fresh restaurant was doing kale before it was cool, and this gorgeous book proves that
their vibrantly modern approach to eating well is as addictive as ever. Power shakes, immunity shots,
salads for meals, nourishing bowls, and the legendary burgers; I want it all."

LAURA WRIGHT, creator of the *Saveur* award-winning blog *The First Mess*

"We've known Ruth for years and consider her one of our soul sistas! Hands down she makes
the most delicious food ever! The energy and love that she puts in every recipe is pure genius.
This is a vegan BIBLE that everyone must own!"

CAILLI BECKERMAN and **SAM BECKERMAN,** creators of the popular fashion blog *Beckerman Blog*

"The people that I most admire are those who go against the current and create a new path for us to explore.
In *Super Fresh*, Ruth Tal and Jennifer Houston have given us the blueprint to eating and
living to our full potential. They have revealed a world where there are no compromises to eating healthy."

CLAUDIO APRILE, *MasterChef* Canada judge and chef and founder of Orderfire Group

"Since 1999, Ruth and Jennifer have pioneered extraordinary healthy food that tastes so good,
everyone will experience pure pleasure and comfort. They knocked it out of the park again with *Super Fresh*!
Food so decadent it will inspire readers to run to their local farmers' market and health food stores to get started."

JULIE DANILUK, nutritionist and bestselling author of *Meals That Heal Inflammation*

"Jen and Ruth have created such a beautiful way to add life to your kitchen with this cookbook.
Ruth Tal has been such an inspiration to me for so long. Her food is as vibrant and
gorgeous as she is, and this book shows just that."

MARY MATTERN, founder of the popular blog and Instagram *Nom Yourself* and
author of *Nom Yourself: Simple Vegan Cooking*

"Ruth and Jennifer's healthy, hearty and hugely inspiring vegan recipes are golden.
I promise that *Super Fresh* will become one of the most gloriously food-stained cookbooks in your kitchen."

ERIN IRELAND, food reporter and owner of To Die For Fine Foods

SUPER FRESH

Super Natural, Super Vibrant Vegan Recipes

Jennifer Houston · Ruth Tal

PENGUIN

an imprint of Penguin Canada Books Inc., a Penguin Random House Company

Published by the Penguin Group

Penguin Canada Books Inc., 90 Eglinton Avenue East, Suite 700, Toronto, Ontario, Canada M4P 2Y3

Penguin Group (USA) LLC, 375 Hudson Street, New York, New York 10014, U.S.A.
Penguin Books Ltd, 80 Strand, London WC2R 0RL, England
Penguin Ireland, 25 St Stephen's Green, Dublin 2, Ireland (a division of Penguin Books Ltd)
Penguin Group (Australia), 707 Collins Street, Melbourne, Victoria 3008, Australia
(a division of Pearson Australia Group Pty Ltd)
Penguin Books India Pvt Ltd, 11 Community Centre, Panchsheel Park, New Delhi – 110 017, India
Penguin Group (NZ), 67 Apollo Drive, Rosedale, Auckland 0632, New Zealand
(a division of Pearson New Zealand Ltd)
Penguin Books (South Africa) (Pty) Ltd, 24 Sturdee Avenue, Rosebank, Johannesburg 2196, South Africa

Penguin Books Ltd, Registered Offices: 80 Strand, London WC2R 0RL, England

First published 2015

1 2 3 4 5 6 7 8 9 10

Photography by Kyla Zanardi
Photo on page 2 by Stefania Sgambelluri
Prop and food styling by Dara Sutin

Manufactured in China.

LIBRARY AND ARCHIVES CANADA CATALOGUING IN PUBLICATION
Tal, Ruth, author Super fresh : Super natural, super vibrant vegan recipes
/ Ruth Tal and Jennifer Houston. Includes index.
ISBN 978-0-14-319085-1 (pbk.)

1. Vegan cooking. 2. Cookbooks. I. Title.

TX837.T35 2015   641.5'636   C2015-900685-6

eBook ISBN 978-0-14-319615-0

Visit the Penguin Canada website at **www.penguin.ca**

Special and corporate bulk purchase rates available; please see
www.penguin.ca/corporatesales or call 1-800-810-3104.

To our brave and loving mothers,
Vered Tal and Barbara Houston,
who remain an ongoing inspiration.

And to our beloved dads,
David Tal and Wayne Houston,
who are greatly missed.

CONTENTS

at fresh, we're into ...

- veggies as a meal, not a side dish
- rainbows of cold-pressed juices
- giving to charities in our communities
- the planet
- rights for animals
- leafy greens
- craveable veggie burgers
- green smoothies
- women-run businesses
- being strong
- heavenly desserts
- microgreens
- equality for all people
- making vegan food accessible
- working smart
- travel
- eating with your hands
- huge salads that fill you up
- clean food
- comfort food
- chopsticks
- building strong teams
- crunchy, creamy, salty, sweet, and spicy all in the same bite

- our neighbourhoods
- making food from scratch
- decadent, lazy brunches
- fair trade coffee
- food that has a grower, not a manufacturer
- embracing the joys of eating and drinking
- music
- mindfulness
- bright colours
- wood
- freshly ground spices
- sharing our recipes
- not judging other's food choices
- laughing
- singing while you work
- proving that tofu isn't gross
- sitting on the grass in the park after work
- kaleidoscopes of colours on crisp white plates
- eating soup every day
- quinoa
- kindness
- abundance

If you're unfamiliar with our restaurant, Fresh, let us introduce ourselves.

Fresh started out over 20 years ago as a travelling juice bar, and it has now grown into a full-service vegan restaurant with four popular locations in Toronto, two in Moscow, and more on the way in Canada, Mexico, and the United States. We strive to make our restaurants the type of place where, say, a teenaged vegan can bring their parents and grandparents, who have never had a vegan meal before, and everyone leaves feeling happy and satisfied.

We've written four vegan cookbooks over the last few years. This fifth cookbook, *Super Fresh*, has selected recipes from *Fresh at Home*, which was published in 2003. It also includes almost everything from our current menus as well as some things we have planned for upcoming specials and potential new menu items. In short, *Super Fresh* is the quintessential guide to eating and drinking the Fresh way at home.

What is the Fresh way? It's about enjoying a plant-based diet that is satisfying, energizing, and craveable. We make juicing and vegan food approachable and unintimidating. For people who are unfamiliar or even skeptical about eating this way, we make it easier to "lean in" to vegan eating. Whether you're looking for something healthy or just for something delicious, our high-vitality cuisine can fit into your life seamlessly.

Super Fresh is divided into two parts: juice and food, so we can each speak to you directly about our favourite things (Ruth is juice and Jennifer is food). These recipes are exactly the same ones that we use at the restaurants—just with the portions cut down to size—and everything is made with wholesome, natural ingredients that home cooks can easily find in supermarkets and natural food stores.

We hope as you make your way through the book that you will be tempted to join us in the Fresh way of life.

xoxo
Ruth and Jen

RUTH'S STORY

I am snuggled into my window seat at home, witness to a raspberry sunrise on a crisp winter morning in Toronto. Across the street, I watch as our produce guys unload the day's fruit and vegetable supply off the big truck into Fresh on Crawford Street. Deliveries continue to come and go. Familiar faces deliver the staples upon which the Fresh menus have been built. The natural foods purveyor brings pallets of products—almond milk, tofu, buckets of dark maple syrup, quinoa, and 50-pound bags of basmati brown rice. Our van pulls up to drop off the sauces, soup, dressings, and mixes prepared overnight in our central kitchen. Our staff, the charismatic backbone of our operations, quietly arrives for work one at a time, on foot, bicycle, streetcar, or in the occasional taxi. The mystery of how

we do it all is laid bare right here: good intentions, consistency, and hard work.

How did this happen? I'll be turning 50 this May, which puts me square at having spent half my life running my own business, guiding, nudging, and nurturing Fresh into a serious player on the restaurant scene. Having five cookbooks published along the way, I know I am lucky. With no kids of my own, I imagine this is what moms must feel like—such love, pride, and joy when they realize their kids are all grown up and everything is going to be okay.

Twenty-five years ago I was a hungry vegan passionate about turning the world on to the infinite possibilities and pleasures of juicing and a plant-based diet. At the age of 16, I dropped out of high school and moved downtown into my own studio apartment. School was not the right fit for me at that time, and neither was living at home. Naturally rebellious, I was restless to get moving and make my own way. Part-time hours selling jeans at a small independent denim store, Over the Rainbow, evolved into a full-time job. A year later, I took over running one of Toronto's first unisex punk clothing stores at a time when gay pride was coming out and whispers of HIV and AIDS were being heard.

Every day I opened and closed the shop, and on weekends I went on buying appointments with the owner, Andrew Pill. It was an exciting time to be part of the downtown scene, and I remember the many kindnesses extended by local characters who looked out for me. By the good grace of the universe, nothing bad ever happened to me, although I do have quite a few funny anecdotes (and suffice it to say that many people have the right to say that they "knew me when"!).

For my 17th birthday, Andrew Pill gave me a home juicer. It was a massive thing, and I never used it. Looking back, I fancy it was some kind of fore-shadowing. You always remember your first boss, for better or worse, and looking back I marvel at the responsibility that Andrew gave me to run his store. In trusting me, he made me all the more trust-worthy. When I turned 18, I gave my notice, packed up, and bought a plane ticket to California. By then the store was booming. He was not happy I left after investing so much in me, but it was time for me to go. Making difficult choices like this was to become a common theme throughout my life.

My plan was to travel for one year, and it ended up being seven. I spent the first year in Big Sur work-ing in the vegetarian kitchen of the Esalen Institute, a human potential growth centre that specialized in Gestalt therapy. In return for my 30 hours a week, I was given room, board, and the run of the place. At Esalen, I had my first taste of tofu and learned how to be comfortable with naked living in a clothing-optional community. I learned how to say what I mean and mean what I say, because everyone there was in active therapy and eager to call you out if you weren't 100 percent authentic at all times. Tooling around in my best girlfriend's yellow VW bug along the California coast, I felt free and deeply connected to wherever my path would lead me.

That path led me to Israel, where I found I had a weird knack for the physicality and hard work of farming. I spent the next five years in agriculture, specializing in computerized dripper irrigation and driving big tractors. As a pampered city girl I barely understood where my food came from until I had to grow it and harvest it for myself. We grew wheat, mangoes, pink grapefruit, dates, lemons, avocados, olives, alfalfa sprouts, chickpeas, and potatoes—but we used herbicides and pesticides like they were water. Later on, after I had seven miscarriages, I wondered if there was a connection to my early years in the fields.

After that, I spent two years in Australia and the Far East, cleaning hotel rooms on an island, eating pad Thai noodles, enjoying full-moon parties, and trekking in the Himalayas. When I bumped into other travellers, I loved being the one who had no end date to their adventures.

I returned home in time for my first nephew to be born, with a plan to become the kind of professional my parents would be proud of. I got my high-school diploma and was accepted into the University of Toronto, along with being granted a very generous Ontario student loan. Then my life took a serendipitous turn instead.

One day I wandered into a little health-food store. They were cold pressing organic carrot juice. I was blown away by how juicing a simple carrot transformed it into the most alive and nutritious thing I had ever tasted in my life. It was vibrant, creamy, smooth, and sweet. I was instantly hooked. I walked over daily, rain or shine, to get my fix. Soon after I bought a home juicer and began juicing these wildly delicious and exotic combinations of fruits and vegetables, self-prescribing based on the nutritious benefits I was reading about. Overnight, I switched to a plant-based vegan diet. I gave away my leather jackets and quit consuming alcohol, coffee, fried foods, and gluten. It was a radical transformation, but I emerged with an abundance of energy and a deep calm and sense of purpose. I was making a positive impact in the world by treading lightly on the earth, eating low on the food chain, and choosing an eco-friendly and compassionate lifestyle.

Forced to stay at home and cook if I wanted to eat this way, I felt marginalized in my city. But it was also a blessing. I began to develop the core recipes that would evolve into the style of eating later popularized at Fresh: bold flavours, colourful layered salads, life burgers, basmati brown rice bowls, soba noodles, wraps, fruit smoothies, power shakes, and energy elixirs. Like a true Taurus, I was inspired to make these delicious creations by my desire for pleasure, not just health.

I opted out of university and used my student loan to start up Juice for Life, an eight-seat gourmet juice bar and vegan café. My dream was to bring sexy back to healthy eating. Lacking formal training in the kitchen, I broke rules without knowing they existed in the first place. Happy accidents turned into normal operating procedures. During the hardest early years there was no running home to my parents for comfort. Hoping this phase would pass, I had little contact with them until it was an undeniable truth that I was established and well on my path. (Rejecting my mom's Moroccan grilled salmon and chicken didn't help matters much either.)

My original partner in Juice for Life, also my vegan boyfriend, liked to dabble in heroin. His use for wheat grass was to recuperate as quickly as possible from the benders he would go on. The cash in the till became his ATM, and there was not much I could do about it. Unable to keep up with him as his habits spiralled downward, I emerged on the other side of it focussed on getting healthier every day. I wasn't perfect, but I felt a strong obligation to my customers to show up at work and be the change they wished for themselves. I ended the relationship and bought him out in our second year of business. Tragically, he overdosed a few years later. I strongly believe that Juice for Life saved my life.

Deep into 80-hour work weeks, my days started at 4:30 a.m. with runs to the food terminal for fresh produce and didn't stop until 7:00 p.m. when the café closed. I loved every minute of it, but the mountain of paperwork was on the verge of crushing me. Although still gun-shy, I overcame my fear of a new business partnership first with Barry Alper, my accountant, and then a few years later with Jennifer Houston, our head chef. As they dug in and shared the load, the systems improved and the food became more delicious. Everything got easier and better, and we blossomed.

Life mellowed and hummed for another decade or so. I married and divorced. Juice for Life evolved into Fresh, with three busy 80-seat restaurant locations and four national bestselling cookbooks. My parents eventually came around, giddy with pride, loving my vegan ways as though they had discovered the lifestyle themselves back in Morocco. It was great to have them in my corner again.

At year 20 I celebrated the founding of Fresh and went on an extended sabbatical to Mexico. Living by the ocean on a stunning beach in Puerto Escondido, I became part of a community of bohemians, surfers, and yogis. Yet still, after so many years of focus, the freedom unnerved me. Semi-retired at 45, I felt guilty at my good fortune. I gravitated to a beautiful open restaurant on the beach called Guadua. It had the best playlists, Mexican cuisine, and sunsets in the region. I befriended the young owners, three best friends from Mexico City, and soon began designing a daytime juice bar with them in return for my meals and the occasional shot of mescal. We sourced local superfoods—açai, chia seeds, amaranth, and maca—to put in the smoothies. We had a blast and became great friends. We launched a lunch menu loosely based on my favourite Fresh dishes, like the Green Destiny Salad and the Buddha Rice Bowl. I avoided telling Barry and Jennifer what I was up to, not sure how they would feel about it.

Next I accepted an invitation to launch a natural organic restaurant in Mexico City. For $10,000 cash up front I gave it my all. The project took a year to complete. It was the first time I went outside of Fresh to work with other people and got paid for it. I brought the cash home, split into three envelopes, and shared it with my partners. It felt good to contribute to our business again, as Barry and Jennifer were still working in the trenches. I asked for their support as I explored opportunities for us to help like-minded entrepreneurs launch Fresh-inspired concepts abroad.

Do you know the saying "If you take the first step, the universe will always walk the rest of the way with you"? Suddenly the right opportunity presented itself. An entrepreneurial vegan couple from Moscow who were fans of our cookbooks and restaurants reached out to us, looking to bring the Fresh brand to Russia. Introducing beautiful plant-based cuisine and fresh juices to a city starving for it was a romantic notion I eagerly embraced.

Despite my bravado, as I flew to Moscow for the first time, I realized I had no idea what I was doing in a country so foreign. Kale wasn't in vogue yet—there wasn't even a word for it in Russian. Against the current norm, we offered our food in Moscow's first non-smoking full-service architecturally designed restaurant with biodegradable containers for take-out. The first location, five minutes from Red Square, won many awards, and we soon opened a second. Big on promoting our brand, we were featured in *Russian Vogue*, *Elle Russia*, and *InStyle Magazine*.

Fresh's success in Moscow added some sex appeal to our business and inadvertently made us an international brand. It underlined how small the world had become, with a vibrant social media tweeting about having our BBQ Burger on the other side of the planet. It dawned on Barry, Jennifer, and me that if we could make it in Moscow, we could make it anywhere with the right partners. We looked to our own backyard as the next milestone. A friend introduced me to a friend and, before we knew it, we had a Fresh global expansion deal in place with the first stop in Montreal: LOV by Fresh, a nimbler spin-off concept.

All this abundance and yet I had no soul mate to share it with until my life came full circle in 2012. An old friend, a beautiful man and kindred vegan spirit whom I had met 15 years earlier, found me again and reached out. It was magical, and we knew the time was right for our story to begin. Shortly after we fell in love, my dad became very sick with cancer. Before he passed he gave us his blessing to marry.

Dre Wise led me to a life filled to the brim with love, partnership, and family. I began to cook again for the first time in over a decade. Nurturing, making breakfast, packing nutritious lunches, juicing, and blending green smoothies infused the writing of this fifth cookbook with my happy heart.

And then the bonds between Jennifer, Barry, and I—the magic and chemistry of our partnership, the stuff that has kept our brand and business alive all these years—became stronger than ever. After years of Fresh being an alternative option to the mainstream, we are witness to the tidal wave of people finally catching on to the benefits of a plant-based vegan diet all around us, and we are so glad we stayed true to our roots.

Counting my blessings, I am totally stoked for what each day will bring. I have learned through it all that there is always room to grow and stand out when you are passionate and creative about what you do—in life, work, and love—and when you follow your heart.

XO
Ruth Tal
Founder of Fresh Restaurants

JEN'S STORY

I didn't really cook until I was about 25 years old. You always hear about chefs who grew up cooking in the family restaurant or standing alongside their grandmothers while generations of knowledge were passed down to them. Not me. Sure, my mum cooked, but it wasn't the focus of our household by any means. I think I could count on one hand the number of cooking experiences I remember from childhood. I worked in a fast food restaurant when I was a teenager and did something that resembled cooking, but it wasn't until I was older that the little sprout of interest that had always been there finally burst into a fully grown obsession. But still, even though I was constantly reading cookbooks and food magazines, watching cooking shows, and cooking at home, it didn't occur to me to cook for a living until the day I helped out in the kitchen at the pub where I was bartending. I was only in there for a few minutes before I knew that cooking was what I should and would be doing for the rest of my life.

I had graduated from university but was in that phase where you have a degree that you have no interest in pursuing and you really don't know which direction your life is going to take. What a relief when I finally figured out, without a doubt, the job for me. Within a year of that first day in the kitchen I was at cooking school. The year after that, I had a couple of different cooking jobs, and then I moved to Scotland and started working in a vegetarian restaurant. That's when I stopped eating meat.

After a year in Scotland, I came back to Toronto and worked at two very different yet equally uninspiring places, one fancy and one very un-fancy. I had no idea what kind of place was going to be perfect for me because, so far, none of the places were quite right. I was like Goldilocks looking for that perfect fit. I knew I didn't want to work in fine dining, but I also knew that I wanted to be somewhere that was doing things that were different from the norm and

that I could get excited about. I wasn't sure what I was looking for, but I knew that I would recognize it when I found it.

My friend Jojo, who I had worked with at the restaurant in Scotland and who knew I wasn't happy where I was currently working, came to visit me. One day while I was at work she looked in the paper and saw an ad for a vegan restaurant called Juice for Life looking for a sous chef. She convinced me to call them right away. I went for an interview the next day, got along famously with the head chef, and had my first shift the following day. It was all going well until about two weeks after I started, when the head chef took off in the middle of the night and demanded a ransom for the master recipe book from Ruth and Barry, the owners! (Fortuitously, a couple of weeks before this Ruth had awoken in the middle of the night realizing that there was only one copy of the recipes and had come into the restaurant and photocopied the entire book, thwarting that plan!)

With the head chef gone there was much commotion and confusion over the next week or so, and the rest of us were unsure about what was going to happen next. Then Ruth and Barry, who I had barely even met, approached me about taking over the kitchen, all the while assuring me that they were nice people and that it wasn't normally this crazy. I wasn't even fully trained on the menu yet, but I agreed to take over because there was something I loved about the place, even with all the drama that had just occurred. Ruth and I spent time talking over our ideas about where the menu could go, and we knew that creatively we were kindred spirits. Something in me knew that this was the place I had been looking for.

And that is when the work started. The kitchen was not functioning in a very organized way, and I found that there weren't really any systems in place. Luckily it wasn't very busy back then, so we could pretty much get away with it, but it was still unduly stressful. Anyway, I think this was good for me because it gave me the freedom to set things up the way I wanted and to pretty much start from scratch in determining the daily runnings of the kitchen. (And I do love to organize, so that came totally naturally.)

The relationship between Ruth, Barry, and I really solidified as we realized that we formed the perfect triad—each bringing a different viewpoint and set of skills to the table. Ruth and I are the perfect brainstorming partners. Together we come up with ideas that neither of us would come to on our own. And she has taught me to never be afraid of breaking the rules. Whenever there is a problem that I can't solve, Ruth always seems to be able to see a solution, and I admire that so much. She is the queen of thinking outside the box.

Barry is the visionary—always planning the next move for Fresh. He is a numbers guy, but with a spark of creativity and an uncanny ability to always present a side of an issue that you never would have considered before.

After I'd been there for a couple of years, Barry and Ruth decided to make me their partner so no one would steal me away (their words), and for the next 10 years I worked like a madwoman. Some days I would work at one location in the morning and another location at night. I was always on call and could never relax until the restaurant was actually closed for the night. Sometimes I would ride my bike to work thinking "maybe I could just get in a little accident, not too painful, just so I can go to hospital and have a couple of days off." It was pretty crazy.

Those years now seem like a blur, but some-where in there we opened new locations, changed the name of the business, wrote cookbooks, created lots of new menus, and just got busier and busier. What I remember most is the exhausted satisfaction of getting through a busy shift and the thrill of constantly breaking and re-breaking our own records for how many dishes we could put out in a shift.

After years of working day and night, we had three busy locations with systems and management in place, and as a company we were in the position to promote Gillian Mountney, who had been our kitchen manager at a couple different locations, to the position of area kitchen manager (basically taking over the daily runnings of the kitchens and working with the managers to keep everything humming along). Gill is just the best. She is the yang to my yin. She is always calm when I am freaking out. She never lets me get away with anything, which is good for me. She's funny and clever and ethical and intuitive and amazingly hard working. When we opened the new Bloor location in Toronto, I think Gill and I both worked for almost a year straight with barely a day off.

My other favourite girl is Stephanie Weinz, childhood friend of Gill's, and our area general manager. They both came to work at Fresh when they were 20, and we have seen them grow from almost-teenagers into amazing, accomplished women. Stephanie started working in the kitchen, then moved to the front of house, and now oversees the front of house for all of Fresh. At times she has had to stand up to us, the owners, for what she knows to be right for the operations of the business, which is so brave. She is hilarious, kind-hearted, perceptive, courageous, and brilliant. Anyway, I digress, but when I get to talking about these two, I get a little over-excited. I just love them and would be lost without them.

These days I can focus on menu development, supplier relations, social media, and everything else without actually working shifts in the kitchen. It was a hard transition because when you work a shift, as soon as it's over, you're done and you can think to yourself, "I have done enough work for any one human being today, and now I'm just going to relax." When you do more office-y, computer-based work, it's so easy to work all day and feel like you could keep doing it forever and never actually be done. Since I can do most of my work from home now, that happens sometimes, and my work/life balance starts to blur a bit. I'm working on setting some rules for myself (like not checking feedback emails right before I go to bed!).

I recently had an epiphany: I've been waiting for the day when the work would be done, when I would be caught up. Realizing that I'd been thinking this way allowed me to accept that it will never be done … and that's okay. It's not really in my nature—I'm more black and white, and like to finish one thing before moving on to the next—but I am working on letting the fact that the work will always be there flow over me and not stress me out. It's fine that we're constantly under construction, constantly researching, constantly cooking and trying new ideas and predicting what people will like. It's what propels us forward to whatever the future holds for Fresh.

That was and is my Fresh life. I'm thankful that I have partners and colleagues who I love and respect. And I feel so lucky that the work I get to do is in a realm that I am passionate about. I know the word "passion" is chronically overused, but really, without it, I can't imagine having been able to pour myself into this so fully. I'll never forget the time, after my first couple of years at Fresh, I was at a party talking to a girl about work. I guess I was getting pretty fervent about it because she said in a surprised way, "Wow, you really take this seriously, don't you?" I answered, "Duh, of course! It's my life!"

XO
Jennifer Houston
Executive Chef/Partner

**FRESH JUICES,
GREEN SMOOTHIES,
NUT MILKS, AND SHOTS**

JUICING AND BLENDING BASICS

I used to think that being healthy and fit was so complicated, but I have since learned that it's all the little things I do for myself each day that provide the ultimate payoff. For me, juicing and juice cleansing is a big part of that. It all comes down to putting good stuff in, flushing the toxins out, moving my body, and staying positive.

I invite you to embark on your own juice journey. The world can be your juice bar, too! Think of juicing as your daily dose of medicine—pure liquid nourishment that rebuilds cells from the inside out, reboots the immune system, and simply makes you feel amazing. These recipes were created after years of tasting, travelling, and searching for the best ingredients to bring to you. Fresh fruit and vegetable juice, herbal tinctures, and supplements can cleanse and detoxify you, boost your immune system, soothe your nerves, stimulate your brain, and energize your body. Tailoring the individual properties and benefits of each ingredient to suit your needs is where the fun in juicing begins. Play around, don't be shy, and make them your own.

Juicing Basics

Juicing is an acquired skill that is fun, creative, and easy to learn. A working knowledge of basic juicing guidelines, the right equipment, high-quality ingredients, and fresh produce are all that you require. This chapter is full of tips and techniques from our juice bars to help you make great juice.

Juicers

A juicer can unlock the goodness in fresh fruits and vegetables and deliver it quickly and easily. However, just how much of that goodness ends up in your glass depends on your juicer. A high-quality, efficient juicer will extract a smooth, enzyme-rich juice and expel a moisture-free pulp. The drier the pulp, the more juice in the glass.

Today, you can choose from a growing number of good-looking quality home juicers, ranging in price from $125 to $2500. Although it is true that you get what you pay for when purchasing a home juicer, our experience has proven that it is wise to earn your juicing stripes with an inexpensive juicer first before you go for the ultra-deluxe model. Once you are hooked and juicing regularly, then you will probably want to upgrade your home juicer. Keep in mind that an attractive juicer on the kitchen counter is likely to be used more often than one hidden away in the cupboard, where it is out of sight and out of mind.

Citrus attachments are often sold separately from juicers. These attachments are unnecessary, however, if you have a centrifugal juicer. A centrifugal juicer will juice most fruits and vegetables, with the exception of wheat grass. At Fresh, we peel all citrus fruit and run them through the centrifugal juicers. This method produces a creamier, smoother juice and also tends to be faster and less messy than using the citrus attachment.

In our opinion, the true measure of a home juicer is how well it juices fine leafy greens, achieving a high yield of juice and a fine pulp. A new method of juicing that has exploded onto the market recently is the hydraulic cold-press method. It is by far the most efficient.

Juicing Methods

All juicers have their upsides and downsides. Some will save you money, others will save you time; some are quieter, others will make juice with a longer shelf life. The internet is the best method of research for finding the juicer that best suits your needs, including the numerous customer reviews and feedback that can be found. The following are my three top picks.

1. Centrifugal "fast" juicers spin the produce using a shredder disk and a strainer basket. The produce is loaded at the top through the hopper, and the disk shreds and spins at high speeds while juice pours out a spout. It operates at a fast speed, making a glass of juice very quickly. The juice has a shorter shelf life and should be drunk immediately after making it. My top pick: the Breville Juice Fountain Elite.

2. Masticating "slow" juicers chew the produce with one slow-turning gear. The auger breaks down and chews the fibre to form pulp. The machine then squeezes the pulp to extract the juice. It operates at a slow speed, which minimizes oxidation and retains most nutrients. The juice lasts for up to 48 hours when stored in the fridge. My top pick: the Omega 8006 Juicer.

3. Hydraulic cold-press juicers grind the produce into a very fine pulp, releasing it into a mesh bag. The mesh bag with pulp is then pressed hydraulically to extract the juice. No air touches the juice during this process, so the nutrient and live enzyme profile is the highest with this method. It produces no oxidation or foam, extracts 100 percent more juice than a centrifugal juicer and 50 percent more than a masticating juicer. The juice lasts for up to 84 hours when stored in the fridge. My top pick: the Norwalk Model 280 Hydraulic Press.

Sequence of Juicing

Firm fruits and vegetables with a high water content, such as apples, pears, carrots, sweet potatoes, and beets, should generally be juiced, not blended. A juicer will easily separate the water from the fibre in these foods. At Fresh we also prefer to juice our pineapples and all melons, although they are also delicious puréed in the blender.

Leafy greens—such as parsley, cilantro, dandelion, chard, romaine, kale, or spinach—can be juiced or blended whole into green smoothies. Juiced

greens are an important factor in nutrient-rich and enzyme-packed juices. Blending is the right choice if you want both the fibre and the nutrition these ingredients supply.

As a general rule, always juice a higher–water content ingredient after a leafy green vegetable to flush the concentrated juice from the juicer. Start the juicing sequence with the ingredients that have the highest concentration of flavour and end with more neutral ingredients. This method will ensure that strong, pungent flavours (ginger, garlic, beets, peppers, parsley, and spinach, for example) will be flushed out by the more neutral ingredients (such as apple, carrot, or cucumber), guaranteeing that your next juice will not be tainted.

Juicing a neutral ingredient last also allows you to adjust the flavour and potency of the drink. Neutral juices enhance and balance the powerful effects of other, more pungent juices (such as garlic, ginger, beet, and spinach), which should be used in small doses if you have just begun to introduce juicing to your diet.

Juice Prep

We recommend that you use organically grown produce whenever possible to avoid pesticide and herbicide residue and to make the purest juices possible. If you cannot access organic produce, we suggest you peel your fruits and vegetables before juicing. Follow these best practices:

- Before juicing, wash all produce and remove any bruised or mouldy areas. Peel all citrus, melons, and pineapples; these peels are bitter and are very hard on the juicer motor and blades. The skins of most other fruits and vegetables, including garlic and ginger, may be left on. Remove pits from peaches or plums before juicing, as they can damage the delicate blade and screen of the machine. Seeds from lemons, limes, apples, pears, and all melons need not be removed because the juicer will spit them out.

- Cut fruits and vegetables to fit the size of your juicer's hopper (the hole that feeds the juicer).

- Although vegetable and fruit juice will not spoil if refrigerated, the flavour, colour, and potency will decline quickly, depending on the method of juicing you used.

- Be sure to thoroughly clean your home juicer immediately after you use it to avoid clogging the screen with hard, dried bits of pulp.

Blending Basics

When blending smoothies and shakes be sure you have enough of a base liquid to liquefy your other ingredients. Always start on the lowest setting and then switch to a higher setting once the ingredients have been puréed. This will extend the life of your blade and motor. Keep the lid on and use the removable hopper to add ingredients midway through blending, if necessary.

The amount of liquid used in proportion to the amount of whole ingredients will determine the thickness and texture of the drink. There are no hidden ingredients in our drinks—what you see is exactly what you get. We also add ingredients like hemp hearts, nuts and seeds, goji berries, raw cacao nibs, dates, coconut milk, nut butters, spices, pure dark maple syrup, raw agave nectar, or date syrup for additional flavour and depth.

At Fresh, we use digital high-powered Vitamix commercial blenders. All of our blenders have Plexiglas sound enclosures to reduce the noise level. The digital settings allow us to preset the blending times and speeds so we can go on to other things while the juices are blending. Vitamix blenders are available in commercial-use and home-use models. We prefer to use Plexiglas blender jugs because they are lighter in weight and tend to last longer than glass. A stainless-steel jug, while easy to clean, obstructs the view of the juice blending, which is not practical in a busy juice bar setting.

Vitamix and Blendtec are the Cadillacs of high-speed blenders—there are no other brands that can compete, especially when it comes to blending green smoothies. They are both powerful, long lasting, and nice looking. I have owned both at home, and I personally prefer the Vitamix. Not only can you use these for smoothies, but they are also amazing for soups, salad dressings, and making nut milks. Either of these machines is a great investment, in my opinion.

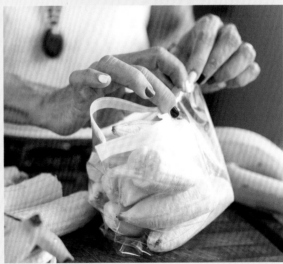

Freezing Bananas

This versatile nutritious fruit can elevate an average juice into a healthy milkshake-worthy smoothie with the flip of a blender switch. Bananas add sweetness and body to blended drinks. They are nature's energy powerhouse. Packed with carbohydrates and potassium, they are ideal before or after workouts. Bananas also help to restore the body's electrolyte balance. They build strong bones by preventing calcium loss and are a natural antacid, providing relief from heartburn.

Using frozen bananas creates even richer, frostier, creamier smoothies. Buy a bunch of bananas, more than you can possibly eat, wait for them to ripen, and then freeze them. Freeze the brownest, ripest bananas—they become truly delicious when frozen.

Before freezing, remove the banana peel, cut the fruit into halves, and lay flat inside a resealable plastic freezer bag (this retains freshness and makes the banana pieces easier to work with). Freeze a big batch so you'll have this awesome smoothie ingredient on hand for weeks to come.

JUICING SUPERFOODS

Incorporating superfoods into our diets is more essential than ever before. Packed with more vitamins, minerals, antioxidants, and phytochemicals than any other foods on the planet, these superfoods clearly live up to their name as nutritional powerhouses. Every superfood has its own unique set of benefits. Becoming more versatile in your use of superfoods will enhance your overall juicing experience.

Açai

The deep purple açai berry contains powerful antioxidants that help defend the body against life's stressors. Antioxidants help protect our bodies' vulnerable cells, reducing the risk of disease and slowing the aging process.

Acerola cherry

Acerola cherry is essential for growth and repair of tissues in all parts of your body. The acerola cherry is considered a superfruit, which possesses the richest known source of natural vitamin C in the world. It is also a good source of vitamin A, riboflavin, and folic acid.

Apple cider vinegar

Apple cider vinegar is capable of so much more than adding flavour to a salad. Organic apple cider vinegar is powerfully antibacterial, antiviral, and antifungal.

- As soon as you feel the prickle of a sore throat, gargle apple cider vinegar to help head off the infection. Most germs can't survive in the acidic environment vinegar creates. Just mix ¼ cup (60 mL) apple cider vinegar with ¼ cup (60 mL) warm water and gargle every hour or so.

- Sip before eating to stoke digestion and avoid heartburn. Add 1 teaspoon (5 mL) apple cider vinegar to a glass of warm water and drink 30 minutes before a meal.

- The next time your sinuses are stuffed up, add 1 teaspoon (5 mL) apple cider vinegar to a glass of water. The vinegar contains potassium, which thins mucus, and the acetic acid it contains prevents bacteria growth, which could contribute to nasal congestion.

Astragalus

Astragalus (*huang qi*) has been a foundational herb in traditional Chinese medicine for hundreds of years. It is sweet, and nourishing, and is often included in recipes designed for convalescence and the general strengthening of the immune system. It is also used to combat fatigue linked to decreased appetite and to strengthen and tone the spleen.

Catnip tincture

Catnip (also known as field balm, catswort, or catmint) has been used for at least 2000 years and is known as strong medicine for the treatment of colds, tension, insomnia, and stomach upsets, yet is gentle enough for children. Catnip herbal extracts are particularly good for relief of insomnia. One of the best ways to control anxiety, catnip is a mild sedative that is said to help you relax. It acts as an overall herbal pain reliever to ease tension headaches, migraines, and cramps.

Chamomile tincture

Chamomile is a naturally calming herb that relaxes nerves and reduces pain. It has been known to settle the stomach, reduce gas, improve sleep, and ease menstrual cramps.

Raw cacao nibs

Cacao nibs are highly antioxidant, and can help to promote cardiovascular health and protect from environmental toxins. They are also said to increase the levels of specific neurotransmitters in our brains, which can promote a sense of well-being.

Raw cacao powder

Cacao powder has been an important food in South America for thousands of years. It is made from cacao beans, which are milled at low temperature to protect the nutrients and flavour, containing a rich source of antioxidants, including an abundance of magnesium and iron. It is a healthy alternative to conventional over-processed "cocoa" used for baking, hot chocolate, desserts, and smoothies.

Raw coconut oil

A heart-healthy fat that keeps your body running smoother, raw coconut oil helps you to resist both viruses and bacteria that can cause illness. Coconut oil boosts thyroid function to increase metabolism, energy, and endurance. It also increases digestion and absorption of fat-soluble vitamins.

Dandelion root tincture

Dandelion has a long history of use as a tonic to the liver and natural diuretic. It has been shown to stimulate the production and release of bile by the liver and gall bladder, helping to break down fats and aid digestion. As a bitter, dandelion stimulates the digestive process, helping to break down all foods more efficiently and thus prevent their stagnation, which often leads to constipation.

Echinacea

Echinacea (also known as a purple coneflower) is a member of the sunflower family. Echinacea extractions have long been used for treating infectious diseases, poor immune function, influenza, colds, chronic fatigue syndrome, and AIDS. Research has shown echinacea stimulates the body's natural immune function. It does so by increasing the activity of white blood cells, raising the level of interferon, and stimulating blood cells to engulf invading microbes. Echinacea also increases the production of substances the body produces naturally to fight cancers and disease.

Ginger

Raw ginger clears the sinuses and eases nausea. It is known to be both antioxidant and anti-inflammatory. Taken before a meal, it stokes the appetite and fires up the digestive juices.

Goji berries

The goji berry is known as one of the most nutrient-rich foods on earth. It is unique among fruits because it contains all essential amino acids and more protein than any other fruit. It is also high in vitamin C, carotenoids, fibre, and iron.

Goldenseal tincture

Goldenseal has been used throughout history as a medicinal herb, partly because of its amazing ability to stimulate the body's own immunity. The bushy plant typically grows wild in rich soils, and has beautiful bright yellow flowers. Its powerful antibiotic properties help to strengthen the immune system, colon, liver, pancreas, spleen, and lymphatic and respiratory systems. Goldenseal also helps to improve digestion, regulate menses, decrease uterine bleeding, and stimulate the central nervous system. Used at the first sign of possible symptoms, it can stop a cold, flu, or sore throat from developing.

Himalayan pink salt

Himalayan pink salt is derived from ancient sea salt deposits, and it is believed to be the purest form of salt available. This salt is recognized for its beautiful pink colour, high mineral content, and therapeutic properties. Regular consumption of Himalayan pink salt provides essential minerals and trace elements, balances electrolytes, supports proper nutrient absorption, eliminates toxins, balances the body's pH, normalizes blood pressure, and increases circulation and conductivity. It can also assist with relief from arthritis, skin rashes, psoriasis, herpes, and flu and fever symptoms.

himalayan
pink salt

raw coconut oil

spirulina
powder

raw maca
powder

turmeric

raw cacao nibs

goji berries

Holy basil

Holy basil (*Ocimum tenuiflorum*) isn't your average basil. It's different from the sweet basil you use to make mama's marinara sauce or the Thai basil you throw into a steaming bowl of pho, although holy basil is used in some Thai dishes. Holy basil is called such because it is considered sacred in Hindu culture, and it's used in the worship of Vishnu and other deities. Extracts made from the root of holy basil have been shown to have mentally stimulating and de-stressing capabilities.

Lucuma powder

Lucuma powder is a subtropical, golden, fleshy fruit from Peru. It's a healthy sweetener with powerful anti-inflammatory and anti-aging benefits. It contains high levels of beta-carotene, B vitamins, and iron.

Raw maca powder

Maca is a root plant and adaptogen. Adaptogens enable the body to increase resistance and adapt to external conditions. Maca powder is believed to have a balancing effect on the endocrine glands and hormone production.

Matcha (green tea powder)

Matcha is a very concentrated form of green tea made from the careful grinding of whole green tea leaves to a fine powder. It has been drunk in Japan as part of the tea ceremony for almost 900 years, and is used by Buddhist monks to keep them awake and focused during long days of meditation. Matcha contains a naturally occurring amino acid called L-theanine. Along with caffeine (also found in green tea), the combination appears to increase alertness and improve concentration. Matcha also contains high doses of antioxidizing flavonoids, which help to protect our bodies from harmful free radicals.

Raw mesquite powder

Raw mesquite powder is ground from the pods of the mesquite tree. It tastes sweet and nutty, with a low glycemic count, and helps regulate cholesterol and sugar levels in the blood. It's an excellent source of fibre, lysine, calcium, magnesium, potassium, iron, and zinc.

Oregano oil

Oregano oil is derived from the leaves and flowers of the herb. Oregano oil can act as an expectorant, which will loosen up or help eliminate the uncomfortable build-up of mucus and phlegm in the respiratory tracts and sinuses, but it is also a soothing balm for inflamed lungs and the throat, which often stimulate coughing fits.

Spirulina powder

Spirulina is a blue-green algae harvested from the sea. It is an easily digested plant protein rich in iron, B vitamins, carotenoids, the essential fatty acid GLA, and other antioxidants.

Turmeric

Turmeric is a rhizome that is part of the ginger family and has been used for centuries as an important anti-inflammatory herbal remedy in ayurvedic medicine.

Uva ursi

Uva ursi (also known as bearberry) is a powerful herb known for its strong astringent and antiseptic properties. It is also a natural diuretic, flushing out the kidneys and often used to treat urinary tract infections.

Vegan protein powder

Vegan protein is a complete multi-source, alkaline-forming, plant-based protein blend that improves strength and exercise performance, repairs and builds muscle, and reduces recovery time between training. We prefer Sun Warrior Protein, Garden of Life, and Vega Performance Protein brands.

Vitamin B12

The body needs a regular supply of this essential vitamin, together with other B vitamins, to maintain a healthy nervous system and maintain energy levels. The main symptoms of vitamin B12 deficiency are feeling tired and lethargic. B-complex vitamins also play an important role in carbohydrate digestion. Vitamin B12 is also critical for the production of red blood cells and is required for the synthesis of DNA during cell division. If there is a lack of B12 during red blood cell formation, DNA production is disrupted and abnormal cells are formed.

The Cold-Pressed Juicing Boom

In 2011, when I was visiting Los Angeles, I frequented an organic juice bar that was cold-pressing and bottling juices. People were coming in and grabbing three or four at a time. If I were a cartoon, you would have seen a light bulb suddenly appear over my head. I found out that juicing technology had advanced far beyond the small painstakingly slow Norwalk Press. There is a new kid on the equipment block, a commercial hydraulic juicer called the X-1 that produces gallons of high-quality cold-pressed juices in a fraction of the time. A game changer.

Cold-pressed juicing has become a big business. The boom has powered small chains into major players vying for the same corners in major cosmopolitan cities like New York City (Juice Press, Organic Avenue, Juice Generation, and Liquiteria), Los Angeles (Beverly Juice Press, Pressed Juicery, Juice Served Here, and Moon Juice), Vancouver (Krocodile Pear, Just Juice, and The Juicery), and Toronto (Village Juicery, Greenhouse Juice Co., and The Good Press).

The major advantage of an organic cold-pressed juice is that it allows the customer to pick up a juice today and drink it within three to four days while still receiving the same nutrients and benefits as a made-to-order freshly squeezed juice. One 16-ounce (454 g) bottle of cold-pressed juice contains approximately 3 pounds, or 10 servings, or 7 salads' worth of raw fresh produce.

A vibrant rainbow of fresh vegetables, fruits, and herbs are crushed and then hydraulically cold-pressed between two steel plates. With no friction, this action does not heat or oxidize the produce, which kills nutrients and enzymes. The end result is a nutritionally packed, mega-amplified live juice created without pasteurizing or processing that is brilliant to taste, is loaded with enzymes, vitamins, and vital trace minerals, and lasts long enough so you can stock up at home.

Many juice providers will use high-pressure processing (HPP) to further extend the shelf life of their cold-pressed juices (this is most often seen in companies who ship across the country). HPP is a cold preservation technology that subjects liquid to intensive pressure—equal to six times the depth of the deepest ocean. This technique inactivates bad bacteria, but it also inactivates good bacteria.

After training on the X-1 Juice Press, I designed our own curated rainbow collection of 12 cold-pressed raw juices made with 100 percent organic fruits, vegetables, spices, herbs, and superfoods, packaged in beautiful glass bottles. Setting ourselves apart from the rest of the pack, our cold-pressed juices utilize the most unique and diverse set of ingredients on the market (goji berries, spirulina powder, maca powder, mesquite powder, lucuma powder, Himalayan pink salt, cilantro, dandelion, and hemp hearts, to name a few). Our organic juices contain nothing but the ingredients listed on the package, including no added sugars.

Cold-pressed juices are now a complementary product to Fresh's made-to-order freshly squeezed juices, power shakes, and smoothies.

FRESH 24-HOUR JUICE CLEANSES

It's in our nature to occasionally fall into routines that don't support us fully, whether it's consuming foods and drinks that irritate our systems or that fatigue rather than fuel us. However, beauty truly does come from within. Taking a break from everyday eating and drinking habits to practise a 24-hour raw juice cleanse is a quick and easy way to reboot our systems while also resetting our relationship to food.

A raw juice cleanse excludes fibre, allowing the entire digestive system to rest. Live nutrients enter the bloodstream rapidly and are assimilated throughout the body in minutes. This rapid absorption is what makes juice a powerful blood alkalizer and detoxifier, boosting immunity and resulting in a rebound of energy, lightness, and mental clarity.

The Fresh 24-hour juice cleanse is about taking it one day at a time, building your confidence as you go. As you complete each 24-hour cycle of cleansing, committing to another day will depend on the demands of your daily life. Small, short cleanses are within everyone's reach. Consuming liquid-only nutrients for just one day—or for as many as three to five days in a row—is an easy, proactive way to regain your equilibrium without having to completely overhaul your life.

Think of a regular juice cleanse as a kick-start to healthy long-term habits. Use it as an occasional tool: at the start of every season, at the end of each year, and even working up to once a week on the same day. (I like Mondays, after the weekend, for my juice-only day of discipline.) Like clocks, our bodies have internal operating systems that respond well to regularity.

Some signs that it is time to cleanse are a weakened immune system, troubled skin, allergies, low moods or anger, sleeplessness, poor digestion, weight gain, low energy, and/or feeling dull and sluggish.

How to Do a Juice Cleanse

The Fresh juice cleanse consists of six juices per day, over 12 hours, including one high-protein nut milk. It is designed to support—not deprive or stress out—your body as you go about your activities.

A few days before your cleanse, to help the transition go more smoothly, do a pre-cleanse by gradually eliminating or cutting out altogether things like nicotine, meat, dairy, refined sugar, fried foods, and wheat.

On your chosen cleanse day, start by consuming your first juice when you would normally eat breakfast. Then continue to drink the juices, about two hours apart, in lieu of regular meals and snacks. Sip them slowly. Because water helps flush waste through your system, be sure to also drink water, lemon water, coconut water, or any herbal tea as desired throughout the day.

Remember: no caffeine or alcohol during your cleanse. Avoiding places that trigger your urges is also a smart move (pick a different day to meet up with friends at your favourite pizza joint or bar).

Some light movement, yoga, or exercise in the morning can improve circulation and really help your digestive system to keep moving and eliminating. Rest is also crucial. Take this time as an opportunity to go to bed early and, if possible, keep your social schedule light. Read more, breathe deeply, and pamper yourself during your cleanse. Dry brushing, scrubs, warm Epsom-salt baths, infrared saunas, and therapeutic massages are all other great ways to support your body during your cleanse day or days.

Ease out of your cleanse for the three days following by eating easy-to-digest, water-plump fruits such as grapefruit, cantaloupe, or watermelon, green leafy salads, and steamed vegetables such as kale, broccoli, and chard.

The goal of a juice cleanse, whether it's for one day or up to five continuous days, is not to lose weight or heal chronic health issues. These goals can best be addressed through a long-term plan of smart nutrition and strategic planning, which you'll want to accomplish slowly and over time with the guidance of a good nutritionist, naturopath, or health coach. A short juice cleanse is simply about rebooting your immune system, detoxifying your liver and kidneys, giving your body's systems a rest, and reclaiming self-control of your negative food habits and urges.

Below we have outlined two kinds of programs: the DIY 24-Hour Cleanse, where you can design your own cleanse, and the Curated 24-Hour Cleanse, which gives you three cleanses to choose from.

The DIY 24-Hour Cleanse

If you're proactive, experienced, and empowered, choose your own do-it-yourself plan. Over your day, include six juices from the following four categories (Deep Green Juices, Light Green Juices, Fruit-Based Juices, and Handcrafted Nut Milks), with an emphasis on green juices for maximum benefits. Greens have the most nutrients to support detoxification. Be mindful of how many fruit-based and root vegetable–based (carrot and beet) juices you consume. You want to *lean into the green* to get the most out of your day-long juice cleanse.

Deep Green Juices

These are low-fruit, low–root vegetable green juices. Ideally, include at least two to four of these in your daily juice cleanse.

- Premium Detox (page 27)
- Urban Detox (page 26)
- Clean Green (page 27)
- Cardio (page 25)
- Serene Green (page 25)
- Antioxidant (page 32)

Light Green Juices

These are the sweeter and lighter green juices, containing slightly more fruits or root vegetables. These are best included in moderation—one or two in your daily juice cleanse.

- Super Cleanse (page 28)
- Easy Green (page 29)
- Green Candy (page 28)
- Multivitamin (page 35)
- Jackpot! (page 33)
- The Daily Dose (page 31)

Fruit-Based Juices

These juices boost vitamins C and D, energize, cleanse, and purify. They are best limited to one per day, preferably in the morning so you have the rest of the day to burn off the naturally occurring fruit sugars.

- Vitamin C Elixir (page 37)

Handcrafted Nut Milks

Almond milk has become a staple of cleanse programs because it's packed with protein, fibre, and omega-3 and omega-6 fatty acids. Have at least one nut milk a day, consumed in the evening since the fats and proteins gently nourish through the night and help promote a good night's sleep. If you're feeling hunger or planning to be especially active, add a second nut milk during the day.

- Everyday Brazil Nut, Almond, Cashew, or Hemp Heart Milk (pages 71 to 76)
- Green Milk (page 68)
- Pink Milk (page 69)
- Root Milk (page 67)

Curated 24-Hour Cleanses

If you don't have the time for do-it-yourself planning, these curated one-day cleanses are ready to go. Keep in mind that if you choose to extend your cleanse into a multi-day cleanse, you can mix and match, depending on how you feel that day. For instance, one day you might choose the Detox Pro; the next day, the Working Cleanse might be more appropriate for your body and lifestyle.

The Easy Cleanse

This cleanse is for those who are not ready to fully commit to a cleanse but are open to giving it a try. It contains a mixture of citrus, greens, and root veggies to reboot our systems—this goes down easy, yet is still very alkalizing and purifying. One day's supply of this cleanse includes:

- 1 Vitamin C Elixir (page 37)
- 1 Easy Green (page 29)
- 1 Antioxidant (page 32)
- 1 Urban Detox (page 26)
- 1 Multivitamin (page 35)
- 1 Everyday Brazil Nut, Almond, Cashew, or Hemp Heart Milk (pages 71 to 76)

The Working Cleanse

For those who want it all, this is a challenging detox undertaken while maintaining our most-loved daily routines. One day's supply of this cleanse includes:

- 1 Cardio (page 25)
- 1 Clean Green (page 27)
- 1 The Daily Dose (page 31)
- 1 Urban Detox (page 26)
- 1 Antioxidant (page 32)
- 1 Everyday Brazil Nut, Almond, Cashew, or Hemp Heart Milk (pages 71 to 76)

The Detox Pro

This is for those who want an intensive detox cleanse beyond their comfort zone, with major benefits and satisfaction. You've been around the block, you know what you want, and you want it hard. Seven green juices will get you in tip-top shape. One day's supply of this cleanse includes:

- 1 Super Cleanse (page 28)
- 1 Serene Green (page 25)
- 1 Clean Green (page 27)
- 1 Urban Detox (page 26)
- 1 Antioxidant (page 32)
- 1 Green Milk (page 68)

GREEN JUICES

If you are as hardcore about your juice habit as I am, by now you have probably moved on to drinking greens more than any other vegetable. As any one of us whose lives have changed since our first taste of green juice will tell you, it's all about the greens. It's incredible to believe that a bunch of ingredients have the power to kick our health into a greater state of well-being.

A rich, beautiful glass of green juice is one of the key, healthy "must-haves" in my daily life. Greens are nutritional powerhouses that energize, revitalize, detoxify, and restore the pH balance in our systems (see below).

Our ancestors used to cover many miles on the mountains and in the valleys, chasing the rain, searching, gathering, and eating many pounds of plants each day. They understood the life force energy gain that comes with consuming living greens. It was a matter of survival. Most of us cannot imagine eating close to that amount of any type of vegetable every day. The intelligence of juicing is that it makes this level of intake possible. Once the mechanism of juicing separates the fibre from its green liquid, it enables us to take in epic amounts of these nutrients. Like a blood transfusion, green juice instantly detoxifies and infuses the body with countless vitamins, minerals, and enzymes.

When we juice leafy greens such as kale, spinach, parsley, chard, cucumber, celery, and, yes, even romaine lettuce, we activate the earth's best blood cleanser available to us—pure, alkaline, chlorophyll-rich juice. The emerald green tones are a sign of good things to come because the natural chemicals that give veggies their luscious hues also provide antioxidants and phytonutrients that boost our health and protect our immune systems.

It is common to be confused by the fact that some foods, such as lemons, are acidic by nature but become alkaline-forming in our bodies. In order for your vital organs to function properly your body requires an alkaline environment. Addressing an over-acidic system is fundamental to bringing the body back to vitality. Drinking green juice is one of the most alkalizing ways you can achieve this.

pH stands for "power of hydrogen," which is a measurement of the hydrogen ion concentration in the body. The total pH scale ranges from 1 to 14, with 7 considered as neutral. A pH less than 7 is said to be acidic, and solutions with a pH greater than 7 are basic or alkaline. Our ideal pH is slightly alkaline: 7.30 to 7.45.

serene green

The ginger adds a wonderful spiciness to this easy-going refreshing green juice, while the mint and cucumber cools it down. Spinach, an amazing source of protein, has a very subtle flavour.

Ginger contains anti-inflammatory compounds called gingerols. These have been known to reduce joint pain and boost the immune system. Ginger has long been used to treat intestinal problems from nausea to gas. It has also been used in eastern medicine to heat the body, which improves circulation and boosts the metabolism, which aids in weight loss.

serves 1 to 2

2-inch (5 cm) piece fresh ginger
½ cup (125 mL) chopped fresh mint
½ cup (125 mL) chopped fresh parsley
1 cup (250 mL) lightly packed spinach

1 cup (250 mL) lightly packed chopped kale
1 English cucumber
1 lemon
4 green apples

1. Juice all of the ingredients following the order listed. Pour into a tall glass. Enjoy.

cardio

Spicy and sweet, this is a sophisticated juice, taste-wise. Jalapeños are mostly available green, turning red as they mature, and contain a negligible amount of calories, with only 4 calories in one pepper. Like other peppers, jalapeños are a rich source of vitamin C, with almost 17 milligrams in a small pepper. The Scoville scale measures the capsaicin in various peppers. Jalapeños rank as medium on the scale, with 2500 to 8000 Scoville heat units per pepper. Capsaicin has impressive health benefits, particularly as an anti-inflammatory and vasodilator that promotes healthy blood flow.

serves 1 to 2

2 jalapeño peppers
½ cup (125 mL) chopped fresh parsley
½ cup (125 mL) chopped fresh cilantro
2 cups (500 mL) lightly packed spinach
6 romaine lettuce leaves

1 English cucumber
6 stalks celery
2 cups (500 mL) chopped pineapple
2 shakes Himalayan pink salt

1. Juice the jalapeños, parsley, cilantro, spinach, romaine, cucumber, celery, and pineapple.

2. Shake pink salt into a tall glass. Pour in juice. Enjoy.

urban detox

Raw ginger can clear sinuses and ease nausea. It is known to be both antioxidant and anti-inflammatory. Taken before a meal it stokes the appetite and fires up the digestive juices. Romaine lettuce is especially high in vitamins K, A, and C, folic acid, and the minerals manganese and potassium. Vitamin K is essential for blood clotting and bone building. Adding apple makes this green juice a little sweeter and easier to drink.

serves 1 to 2

2-inch (5 cm) piece fresh ginger

½ cup (125 mL) chopped fresh parsley

1 cup (250 mL) lightly packed spinach

1 cup (250 mL) lightly packed chopped kale

1 cup (250 mL) lightly packed chopped Swiss chard

6 romaine lettuce leaves

1 lemon

5 green apples

2 shakes cayenne pepper

1. Juice the ginger, parsley, spinach, kale, Swiss chard, romaine, lemon, and apples.

2. Shake cayenne into a tall glass. Pour in juice. Enjoy.

clean green

Dandelions are more than an unloved weed. They are a nutritionally powerful plant. Dandelion greens are antioxidant and diuretic; they detoxify the liver, kidneys, and digestive systems. We purposely left out apple here to reduce the sweetness. Dandelion, spinach, celery, and parsley taste harsh on their own, but when you juice them they somehow become balanced, refreshing, and delicious. This green combination is a good choice for a detoxifying juice cleanse.

serves 1 to 2

2-inch (5 cm) piece fresh ginger

½ cup (125 mL) chopped fresh parsley

½ cup (125 mL) lightly packed dandelion leaves

2 cups (500 mL) lightly packed spinach

6 romaine lettuce leaves

4 stalks celery

2 lemons

3 English cucumbers

1. Juice all of the ingredients following the order listed. Pour into a tall glass. Enjoy.

premium detox

Leafy green vegetables are awesome for their concentrated amounts of vitamins and minerals. Kale is especially high in vitamins K, A, C, and E, and also contains high levels of the minerals manganese, copper, calcium, potassium, iron, and magnesium. Not to mention that kale is full of fibre and also contains protein and omega-3 fatty acids.

   We like to add a little bit of Himalayan pink salt, our favourite kind of sea salt, to bring out the subtle flavours of the greens. Although we usually shy away from adding salt to our food, our bodies actually need some to survive. Sea salt is a source of magnesium and trace minerals that are essential to our health and well-being.

serves 1

2-inch (5 cm) piece fresh ginger

¼ cup (60 mL) chopped fresh parsley

1 cup (250 mL) lightly packed spinach

1 cup (250 mL) lightly packed chopped kale

6 romaine lettuce leaves

1 English cucumber

4 stalks celery

1 lemon

4 green apples

2 shakes Himalayan pink salt

2 shakes cayenne pepper

1. Juice the ginger, parsley, spinach, kale, romaine, cucumber, celery, lemon, and apples.

2. Shake pink salt and cayenne into a tall glass. Pour in juice. Enjoy.

super cleanse

The smooth, sweet flavours of apple, celery, and spinach combine with the citrus kick of lemon and grapefruit. Celery is best known for its high water content. It is a natural diuretic, delivering tons of vitamins K and A, folate, potassium, and molybdenum. This is one of our favourite daily cleansing juices.

serves 1 to 2

½ cup (125 mL) chopped fresh parsley

1 cup (250 mL) lightly packed chopped spinach

1 cup (250 mL) lightly packed chopped kale

4 stalks celery

1 lemon

2 grapefruits

3 green apples

1. Juice all of the ingredients following the order listed. Pour into a tall glass. Enjoy.

green candy

Because we know that drinking greens is not as exciting for everyone as it is for us, we designed this juice to make drinking your greens an easy task, perhaps even a pleasurable thing to do, not only for your body but also for your taste buds.

serves 1 to 2

2-inch (5 cm) piece fresh ginger

½ cup (125 mL) chopped fresh mint

½ cup (125 mL) chopped fresh cilantro

2 cups (500 mL) lightly packed spinach

6 romaine lettuce leaves

2 cups (500 mL) chopped pineapple

3 green apples

1. Juice all of the ingredients following the order listed. Pour into a tall glass. Enjoy.

easy green

Cilantro and mint were made for each other. Their flavours blend beautifully into a green juice. Cilantro is one of the premier herbs for detoxification and cleansing, which makes it popular among juice lovers. It has also traditionally been used for improving blood sugar levels and improving cholesterol.

serves 1 to 2

½ cup (125 mL) chopped fresh mint

½ cup (125 mL) chopped fresh cilantro

1 cup (250 mL) lightly packed spinach

1 cup (250 mL) lightly packed chopped kale

1 English cucumber

2 cups (500 mL) chopped pineapple

3 green apples

1. Juice all of the ingredients following the order listed. Pour into a tall glass. Enjoy.

VEGETABLE JUICES

Juicing is about more not less. A typical glass of vegetable juice contains 3 pounds (1.5 kg) of fresh organic produce. Enrich your well-being with the broad spectrum of nutrition that juicing accesses. Simplicity trumps luxury. It does not have to be complicated or lavish to be good for you. What counts is that your juice is made fresh, raw, and brimming with live enzymes, vitamins, and minerals.

My very first glass of carrot juice 25 years ago kicked off my lifelong addiction to juicing. I learned a long time ago that you need balance when juicing. Greens are very intense on their own, so you need some milder, possibly sweeter, ingredients to make them more palatable. Try keeping apples and pears on hand. Some juices taste flat without a shot of citrus, so keep lemons or limes handy, too. Taste as you go and find the balance by adding more of one thing or another.

the daily dose

Beets have an earthy sweet taste, and fennel adds a warm licorice flavour to this juice that can deliver daily digestive health benefits.

Goji berries are a very popular superfood energy source of all major macronutrients (complete protein, fat, and carbohydrate) and over 20 vitamins and minerals. Their taste is a cross between a raisin and a dehydrated cranberry. They pair really well with the whole range of fruits and vegetables as well as dark chocolate and nuts.

serves 1 to 2

1 bulb fennel	6 carrots
2 beets, trimmed	2 tbsp [30 mL] dried goji berries
2 lemons	2 shakes Himalayan pink salt

1. Juice fennel, beets, lemons, and carrots.

2. Pour juice into a blender and add remaining ingredients. Blend on high speed until smooth. Pour into a tall glass. Enjoy.

antioxidant

Eating an antioxidant-rich diet is one of the most important things we can do to protect ourselves from the onset of disease as well as to look and feel healthier longer. You can help your body by supplying it with liberal amounts of antioxidants in the form of citrus, carrots, green leafy vegetables, root vegetables, berries, nuts, and seeds.

serves 1 to 2

½ cup (125 mL) chopped fresh parsley

1 cup (250 mL) lightly packed chopped kale

3 lemons

3 beets, trimmed

5 green apples

1. Juice all of the ingredients following the order listed. Pour juice into a tall glass. Enjoy.

brazilian immune boost

Customers returning from their travels often share tales and take-out menus of juice bars from around the world with us. That's how we learned of the unlikely combination of freshly squeezed beet and orange juice being served in juice bars throughout Brazil. Beets and citrus do work very well together. If you're feeling under the weather, this fortifying and cleansing juice is a good choice.

Echinacea is possibly the most widely used herb for boosting the immune system during the beginning stages of colds and flu. A little-known fact is that echinacea also has the ability to rid the body of dead cells and other waste products by stimulating lymphatic drainage.

Goldenseal is effective in fighting a cold or flu once the infection has taken hold, by reducing inflammation and stimulating the immune system's response.

serves 1 to 2

2-inch (5 cm) piece fresh ginger

1 lemon

2 beets, trimmed

4 oranges

2 shakes cayenne pepper

20 drops echinacea tincture

20 drops goldenseal tincture

1. Juice the ginger, lemon, beets, and oranges.

2. Pour juice into a tall glass. Add the cayenne pepper and echinacea and goldenseal tinctures and stir well. Enjoy.

jackpot!

Try this nutrient-dense, fiercely detoxifying healing juice combining greens, roots, citrus, herbs, and spices. This is a great meal replacement, when you're feeling under the weather or cleansing.

Pink salt is sourced from the Himalayan mountains of the Far East. Featuring a precious mix of 84 trace minerals that our bodies need to function, Himalayan pink salt is an ultrapure food source in an extremely absorbable form that is sometimes called "white gold." A bit of Himalayan pink salt catapults the flavours in your vegetable juice to gourmet status.

serves 1 to 2

1 clove garlic	4 stalks celery
1 cup (250 mL) lightly packed chopped kale	1 beet, trimmed
1 cup (250 mL) lightly packed spinach	2 lemons
4 romaine lettuce leaves	6 carrots
½ cup (125 mL) chopped fresh parsley	2 shakes Himalayan pink salt
	2 shakes cayenne pepper

1. Juice the garlic, kale, spinach, romaine, parsley, celery, beet, lemons, and carrots.

2. Shake pink salt and cayenne into a tall glass. Pour in juice. Enjoy.

beta-carotene

This juice is super-alkaline, smooth, and creamy. Coconut milk, combined with carrots and beets, is an intensive body builder. Sweet potatoes are nutritional superstars known to improve blood sugar regulation and digestion and contain high levels of beta-carotene and complex carbohydrates. Eating sweet root vegetables such as beets and sweet potatoes helps calm sugar cravings.

serves 1 to 2

2 jalapeño peppers	1 sweet potato
2-inch (5 cm) piece fresh ginger	6 carrots
2 beets, trimmed	½ cup (125 mL) coconut milk

1. Juice jalapeños, ginger, beets, sweet potato, and carrots.

2. Pour juice into a tall glass. Add coconut milk and whisk to combine. Enjoy.

multivitamin

multivitamin

Carrots are the original juice vegetable from way back when. Used as a base, carrots add sweetness and a rich, creamy texture to more challenging ingredients such as bitter greens.

serves 1 to 2

2-inch (5 cm) piece fresh ginger
1 cup (250 mL) lightly packed spinach
½ cup (125 mL) chopped fresh parsley
4 stalks celery

2 lemons
2 green apples
6 carrots
2 shakes cayenne pepper

1. Juice the ginger, spinach, parsley, celery, lemons, apples, and carrots.

2. Shake cayenne into a tall glass. Pour in juice. Enjoy.

stomach soother

The carrot is a storehouse of nutrients—vitamins A, B, and C; iron; calcium; and potassium—and one of the richest sources of beta-carotene (the antioxidant that protects against cancer). Carrots are alkaline-forming and very helpful in relieving stomach acid and heartburn by reducing irritation and inflammation. Carrot juice is known to be very helpful in increasing the milk supply of nursing moms. Carrots also make a good base for adding other juices; if you find carrot juice too sweet alone, cut it with a vegetable such as cucumber or celery to reduce the sweetness.

Chamomile is a calming herb useful in treating anxiety, insomnia, flatulence, and gastritis. Fennel is renowned for its soothing effect on the digestive system, and catnip eases stomach and intestinal cramps.

serves 1 to 2

6 carrots
15 drops chamomile tincture

15 drops fennel tincture
15 drops catnip tincture

1. Juice the carrots.

2. Pour juice into a tall glass. Add the chamomile, fennel, and catnip tinctures and stir well. Enjoy.

kidney cocktail

This delicious vegetable cocktail is sweet, light, and nourishing. Spinach is considered a blood builder due to its rich iron and chlorophyll content. Nicknamed the "smooth mover," spinach has a mild laxative effect. Apples are a rich source of vitamins, minerals, and trace elements. They aid digestion, help regulate acidity in the stomach, and have a cleansing and detoxifying effect on the liver and kidneys.

Cucumber, a natural diuretic that is 96 percent water, counteracts toxins and purifies the skin. It has a cooling effect on the system and aids in preventing fluid retention. Cucumber skin is also high in silicon and chlorophyll, which benefit the skin, hair, and nails.

Dandelion improves kidney, spleen, and pancreas function. It acts as a diuretic and cleanses the blood and liver. Young dandelion leaves can be juiced or eaten in salads.

Uva ursi, a medicinal herb, promotes excretion of fluids and fights bacteria. It is useful for bladder and kidney infections and prostate disorders.

serves 1 to 2

1 cup (250 mL) lightly packed spinach

1 English cucumber

1 lemon

2 green apples

5 carrots

20 drops dandelion tincture

20 drops uva ursi tincture

1. Juice the spinach, cucumber, lemon, apples, and carrots.

2. Pour juice into a tall glass. Add the dandelion and uva ursi tinctures and stir well. Enjoy.

vitamin c elixir

This is a spicy citrus juice. I could sing the praises of vitamin C all day long! Vitamin C is a ferocious antioxidant. It also helps make collagen, supports the immune system, and helps our bodies absorb iron.

Aside from containing the highest botanical source of vitamin C, cayenne pepper is considered an accentuator medicinal spice, meaning it amplifies the nutritional efficacy of the nutrients it is combined with in a synergistic fashion. So, combined with citrus, it boosts the powerful effects of vitamin C to great new heights. It is also rich in capsaicin and contains vitamin B6, vitamin E, potassium, manganese, and flavonoids.

serves 1 to 2

2 oranges

2 lemons

3 green apples

6 carrots

3 shakes cayenne pepper

1. Juice the oranges, lemons, apples, and carrots.

2. Shake cayenne into a tall glass. Pour in juice. Enjoy.

GREEN SMOOTHIES

Green smoothies can be a fantastic meal replacement, with whole fruits, greens, nuts, seeds, and other ingredients blended with the fibre intact. Blending your fruits and greens retains all that good digestive system–cleaning fibre. Smoothies serve a different purpose than green juices do, keeping you feeling full and satiated until you sit down to eat. When you make these smoothies you are making nutrient-dense drinks your body will use as fuel to draw from and sustain energy.

You might notice that the majority of our green smoothies have kale in them. It's no secret that kale has gone from obscurity to stardom in the last 5 years. A big driver of this popularity is the fact that it contains tons of nutrients that protect the body. One cup of kale has 194 percent of the vitamin A, 302 percent of the vitamin C, 31 percent of the calcium, and 50 percent of the iron needed for your whole day. Vitamin B6, copper, vitamin K, and folate are solidly present as well. These are all potent anti-cancer, anti-inflammatory, pro-wellness nutrients.

You can easily get your daily dose of kale when you blend it into your green smoothie. You'll hardly know it's there. For newcomers and children, start with a higher percentage of fruits and slowly add more and more greens until your palate adjusts and you are ready to turn that sweet tooth into a green tooth.

electrolyte green

Sweet pineapple and pure coconut water add bonus electrolytes, potassium, and hydration to this smoothie. Pineapple gives a vibrant tropical flavour and increases energy levels because of its high manganese and thiamine content. It also contains enzymes that aid digestion.

serves 1 to 2

¼ cup (60 mL) dates, pitted

2-inch (5 cm) piece fresh ginger

½ cup (125 mL) pineapple chunks (fresh or frozen)

½ cup (125 mL) lightly packed chopped kale

1 banana (fresh or frozen)

2 cups (500 mL) coconut water

2 shakes ground cinnamon, plus more for garnish

4 ice cubes (optional)

1. Combine dates, ginger, pineapple, kale, banana, and coconut water in a blender.

2. Shake cinnamon into blender and add ice (if using). Blend on high speed until smooth. Pour into a tall glass. Garnish with additional cinnamon. Enjoy.

green detox

I love making this smoothie. Kale melds with sweet, iron-rich spinach and parsley. Earthy and mineral tasting, this juice detoxifies your body and floods it with a healthy dose of vitamin C and antioxidants. Parsley is antibacterial and helps fight infection. Ginger is warming and energizing. Expect to glow from the inside out!

serves 1 to 2

1 lemon

6 green apples

2-inch (2.5 cm) piece fresh ginger

½ cup (125 mL) blueberries (fresh or frozen)

½ cup (125 mL) chopped fresh parsley

½ cup (125 mL) chopped spinach

½ cup (125 mL) chopped kale

4 ice cubes (optional)

1. Juice the lemon and apples.

2. Pour juice into a blender and add remaining ingredients. Blend on high speed until smooth. Pour into a tall glass. Enjoy.

radiant green

radiant green

The combination of greens and banana is a sweet and savoury, creamy yet earthy, balance of flavours and a great way to consume more greens. Almonds give this smoothie a nutty taste as well as a little more bulk to fill you up. They are rich in essential fatty acids and very good for your brain. Cayenne pepper improves cardiovascular health and is a high botanical source of vitamin C.

serves 1 to 2

2 lemons

5 green apples

2-inch (5 cm) piece fresh ginger

½ cup (125 mL) chopped romaine

½ cup (125 mL) chopped spinach

½ cup (125 mL) chopped kale

2 tbsp (30 mL) raw almonds

1 banana (fresh or frozen)

4 ice cubes (optional)

1. Juice the lemons and apples.

2. Pour juice into a blender and add remaining ingredients. Blend on high speed until smooth. Pour into a tall glass. Enjoy.

c monster

This green smoothie is refreshing and balanced, and has a tangy, spicy finish. Lime brightens up the sweet mineral flavour of kale and adds a shot of vitamin C.

serves 1 to 2

1 lemon

1 lime

4 green apples

½ cup (125 mL) chopped romaine lettuce

½ cup (125 mL) chopped kale

3 stalks celery

¼ tsp (1 mL) Himalayan pink salt

2 shakes cayenne pepper

4 ice cubes (optional)

1. Juice the lemon, lime, and apples.

2. Pour juice into a blender and add remaining ingredients. Blend on high speed until smooth. Pour into a tall glass. Enjoy.

brain boost

Anytime you need help focussing, buzz up this smoothie. Turmeric is thought to protect the brain and stop inflammation throughout the body. The dates do an awesome job at turning the mildly bitter turmeric into sweet bliss.

serves 1 to 2

5 oranges

½ tsp (2 mL) ground turmeric

1 tsp (5 mL) spirulina powder

½ cup (125 mL) chopped spinach

2-inch (5 cm) piece fresh ginger

½ cup (125 mL) dates, pitted

1 cup (250 mL) blueberries (fresh or frozen)

1 banana (fresh or frozen)

4 ice cubes (optional)

1. Juice the oranges.

2. Pour juice into a blender and add remaining ingredients. Blend on high speed until smooth. Pour into a tall glass. Enjoy.

eternal youth

The sweet, tart flavours of the pineapple, cherries, and raspberries brighten this smoothie right up. Magnesium-rich spinach helps you relax, relieves headaches, and gives you a good dose of potassium, which is an important mineral for relaxation.

serves 1 to 2

4 cups chopped pineapple

½ cup (125 mL) chopped spinach

½ cup (125 mL) chopped kale

½ cup (125 mL) raspberries (fresh or frozen)

½ cup (125 mL) cherries (fresh or frozen)

4 ice cubes (optional)

1. Juice the pineapple.

2. Pour juice into a blender and add remaining ingredients. Blend on high speed until smooth. Pour into a tall glass. Enjoy.

energizer

Dream in Technicolor of purple, red, orange, and green for a bright smoothie packed with phytonutrients. Plus, the blueberries work double-time fighting free radicals in the most delicious way.

serves 1 to 2

6 oranges

½ cup (125 mL) chopped spinach

½ cup (125 mL) chopped kale

½ cup (125 mL) strawberries (fresh or frozen)

½ cup (125 mL) blueberries (fresh or frozen)

1 banana (fresh or frozen)

4 ice cubes (optional)

1. Juice the oranges.

2. Pour juice into a blender and add remaining ingredients. Blend on high speed until smooth. Pour into a tall glass. Enjoy.

alkaline balance

You may never have considered whether the foods you eat are alkaline or acidic, but it's all pretty simple. In general, all meat, white flour, sugar, and most processed foods are acidifying in your body. Most plants are alkalizing, so they help balance and neutralize the acidic state of your own pH. In this juice, cucumber is cooling and alkalizing, reduces water retention, and helps balance blood sugar. The pear offers a unique hint of sweetness.

serves 1 to 2

1 lemon

2 pears

4 green apples

½ cup (125 mL) chopped spinach

½ cup (125 mL) chopped kale

½ cup (125 mL) chopped romaine lettuce

1 cup (250 mL) strawberries (fresh or frozen)

1 English cucumber

1 banana (fresh or frozen)

4 ice cubes (optional)

1. Juice the lemon, pears, and apples.

2. Pour juice into a blender and add remaining ingredients. Blend on high speed until smooth. Pour into a tall glass. Enjoy.

emerald girl

This smoothie has a sweet, creamy texture. When you are looking for a super-food smoothie that is brimming with plant protein but also want to get your daily greens in, this is for you. Dates sweeten the deal, and coconut water seals it. The sunflower sprouts add tremendous antioxidants and detox power.

serves 1 to 2

½ cup (125 mL) sunflower sprouts

½ cup (125 mL) chopped romaine lettuce

½ cup (125 mL) chopped spinach

½ avocado

½ cup (125 mL) dates, pitted

2 tbsp (30 mL) raw hemp hearts, plus more for garnish

3 cups (750 mL) coconut water

4 ice cubes (optional)

1. Combine all of the ingredients in a blender. Blend on high speed until smooth. Pour into a tall glass. Garnish with additional hemp hearts. Enjoy.

in the raw

Apple juice and sunflower sprouts may sound like an unlikely combination for a blended drink, but the result is truly wonderful, extremely energizing, and rejuvenating. These two ingredients are a good foundation for many more ingredients.

Sweet and tasty sunflower seeds are at the peak of their nutritional and enzymatic vitality when sprouted. Although many delicious sprouts are good for eating, the sunflower sprout is the best for blending into juices.

Hemp hearts have a delicious nutty flavour. They are second only to soybeans as a source of complete vegetable protein. Hemp seeds contain all eight essential amino acids that humans need, in the right proportions. They also contain a generous amount of omega-3 and omega-6 essential fatty acids.

Hemp hearts are the best for making smoothies. Unhulled hemp seeds make the drink gritty and the shells often get caught between your teeth.

serves 1 to 2

5 green apples

1 cup (250 mL) sunflower sprouts

1 banana (fresh or frozen)

2 tbsp (30 mL) raw hemp hearts, plus more for garnish

4 ice cubes (optional)

1. Juice the apples.

2. Pour juice into a blender and add remaining ingredients. Blend on high speed until smooth. Pour into a tall glass. Garnish with additional hemp hearts. Enjoy.

deep green

The apple juice and banana add sweetness and more body to counter the deep, dark abundant greens in this smoothie. Romaine lettuce is a great source of everything leafy greens are famous for, including lots of vitamin A. Spinach is the mildest of greens, but it still packs plenty of green nutrition.

serves 1 to 2

6 green apples

2-inch (5 cm) piece fresh ginger

½ cup (125 mL) chopped romaine lettuce

½ cup (125 mL) chopped spinach

½ cup (125 mL) chopped kale

2 tbsp (30 mL) raw sunflower seeds

1 banana (fresh or frozen)

4 ice cubes (optional)

1. Juice the apples.

2. Pour juice into a blender and add remaining ingredients. Blend on high speed until smooth. Pour into a tall glass. Enjoy.

coco green

Coconut is one of the most delicious healthy fats available. The banana increases the potassium content of the spinach and adds a creamy pie-like texture. Cinnamon is delicious and has been found to lower blood sugar and help lower cholesterol levels.

serves 1 to 2

1 tsp (5 mL) spirulina powder

1 cup (250 mL) chopped spinach

½ cup (125 mL) dates, pitted

½ cup (125 mL) coconut milk

½ cup (125 mL) unsweetened coconut flakes

2 cups (500 mL) coconut water

1 banana (fresh or frozen)

¼ tsp (1 mL) ground cinnamon, plus more for garnish

4 ice cubes (optional)

1. Combine all of the ingredients in a blender. Blend on high speed until smooth. Pour into a tall glass. Garnish with additional cinnamon. Enjoy.

FRUIT SMOOTHIES

When you drink a smoothie instead of a juice, you get added fibre from the raw ingredients that is lost in the juicing process. Smoothies are generally more filling too, and work better as a meal replacement. I juice a lot less than I blend. It's a time thing. Juicing takes a lot of cleaning, assembling, and disassembling, while blending is quick and easy. This comes into play even more so if you have kids. The fruit smoothies I create are mostly with kids and young adults in mind. This is the section they gravitate to when they are ordering off our menus.

There are so many ways to make smoothies. A liquid-fuelled, energizing, fruit-based smoothie can also include spices, herbs, nuts, seeds, vegetables, coconut milk or water, and nut milks. Using a variety of bases gives you a lighter or denser smoothie. Using frozen berries and bananas makes for creamier, thicker smoothies. If you prefer fresh fruit, just replace the frozen fruit with fresh fruit and use a scoop of ice to chill your smoothie instead.

My DIY smoothie routine in the morning goes like this: Fill the blender one-quarter full of coconut water or apple juice. Add some frozen berries (whatever I have in the freezer). Grab a frozen banana and a big chunk of raw ginger. Add a couple superfoods like spirulina powder, raw hemp hearts, or greens. Sweeten with dates and blend.

Smoothies always taste best right after being blended, when their flavour, texture, and even nutrition is at its peak. Blending ingredients mimics the start of the body's process for breaking down food, just like chewing, which sets up the food to decompose at a faster rate. I like to drink my smoothies right away, but you can keep them in an airtight container in the refrigerator for up to 72 hours if you wish.

Always taste your smoothie before pouring it to make sure it's what you want in terms of sweetness, flavour, and consistency. Don't be afraid to make adjustments; often the best smoothies are the ones you've improved to suit yourself. If a smoothie is too sweet for your taste buds, add water, lemon, ice, greens, coconut water, a nut milk, or a healthy fat (like nuts or seeds) to bring it back into balance.

lucky charm

Mangoes are full of relaxing vitamin C as well as healthy digestive enzymes. Three kinds of berries thicken this smoothie. It's bursting with bright flavour and antioxidants.

serves 1 to 2

½ cup (125 mL) strawberries (fresh or frozen)

½ cup (125 mL) blueberries (fresh or frozen)

½ cup (125 mL) raspberries (fresh or frozen)

2 cups (500 mL) mango juice

4 ice cubes (optional)

1. Combine all of the ingredients in a blender. Blend on high speed until smooth. Pour into a tall glass. Enjoy.

treehouse

This classic fruit smoothie is named after the television channel. Ruth appeared on an episode of the Treehouse kids' show *This Is Emily Yeung*, during which she makes smoothies with Emily, a curious 7-year-old pixie. It seems Ruth's a bit of a local celebrity with the under-10 group.

serves 1 to 2

4 oranges

½ cup (125 mL) strawberries (fresh or frozen)

1 banana (fresh or frozen)

4 ice cubes (optional)

1. Juice the oranges.

2. Pour juice into a blender and add remaining ingredients. Blend on high speed until smooth. Pour into a tall glass. Enjoy.

watermelon cherry smash

Watermelons are excellent thirst quenchers and blend beautifully with cherries and bananas. They contain vitamins A and C, iron, and potassium.

serves 1 to 2

1 cup (250 mL) pitted cherries (fresh or frozen)

1 banana (fresh or frozen)

2 cups (500 mL) watermelon juice

4 ice cubes (optional)

1. Combine all of the ingredients in a blender. Blend on high speed until smooth. Pour into a tall glass. Enjoy.

rainbow

red velvet

This delicious and unique juice combines the inherent sweetness and creaminess of beets, the spiciness of ginger, and the fruitiness of pineapple and strawberries.

serves 1 to 2

2-inch (5 cm) piece fresh ginger

2 beets, trimmed

3 cups (375 mL) chopped pineapple

1 cup (250 mL) strawberries (fresh or frozen)

4 ice cubes (optional)

1. Juice the ginger, beets, and pineapple.

2. Pour juice into a blender and add remaining ingredients. Blend on high speed until smooth. Pour into a tall glass. Enjoy.

fruit loop

This bright juice has heaps of fruity flavour and is very quick to make.

serves 1 to 2

4 green apples

½ cup (125 mL) cherries (fresh or frozen)

½ cup (125 mL) blueberries (fresh or frozen)

1 banana (fresh or frozen)

4 ice cubes (optional)

1. Juice the apples.

2. Pour juice into a blender and add remaining ingredients. Blend on high speed until smooth. Pour into a tall glass. Enjoy.

rainbow

Who doesn't love a good rainbow? These days drinking rainbows of fresh fruits and vegetables is encouraged to get the full spectrum of nutrients your body needs.

serves 1 to 2

5 oranges

½ cup (125 mL) raspberries (fresh or frozen)

½ cup (125 mL) strawberries (fresh or frozen)

½ cup (125 mL) blueberries (fresh or frozen)

1 banana (fresh or frozen)

4 ice cubes (optional)

1. Juice the oranges.

2. Pour juice into a blender and add remaining ingredients. Blend on high speed until smooth. Pour into a tall glass. Enjoy.

goji sunset

The goji berry has a very subtle, mostly sweet yet slightly tart taste. Fruits such as citrus and mango enhance the goji's flavour. Goji have been used in Chinese medicine for thousands of years, and are often referred to as the "longevity fruit."

serves 1 to 2

2 oranges

3 green apples

¼ cup (60 mL) dried goji berries

½ cup (125 mL) mango chunks (fresh or frozen)

1 banana (fresh or frozen)

4 ice cubes (optional)

1. Juice the oranges and apples.

2. Pour juice into a blender and add remaining ingredients. Blend on high speed until smooth. Pour into a tall glass. Enjoy.

the wizard

Sweet and sour at the same time, the citrus, banana, and pineapple work well together in this adult-friendly smoothie with youth appeal.

serves 1 to 2

1 lemon

2 oranges

3 cups (750 mL) chopped pineapple

1 cup (250 mL) strawberries (fresh or frozen)

1 banana (fresh or frozen)

4 ice cubes (optional)

1. Juice the lemon, oranges, and pineapple.

2. Pour juice into a blender and add remaining ingredients. Blend on high speed until smooth. Pour into a tall glass. Enjoy.

purple smoothie

Kids tend to love ordering their smoothies by colour, less concerned by what ingredients are lurking in them. This shade of purple always brings a smile to their cute faces.

serves 1 to 2

5 green apples

½ cup (125 mL) coconut milk

1 cup (250 mL) blueberries (fresh or frozen)

1 banana (fresh or frozen)

4 ice cubes (optional)

1. Juice the apples.

2. Pour juice into a blender and add remaining ingredients. Blend on high speed until smooth. Pour into a tall glass. Enjoy.

POWER SHAKES

Today's power shakes enter the realm of epic superfood smoothies. Incorporating superfood smoothies into your diet is a smart move. When I drink superfood smoothies, I experience a noticeable increase in my energy levels. I am more productive and able to think clearly and be physical with sustained vigour. Sounds like all the reasons we love coffee, right? Well, it's so much better than that.

Many power shakes can be treated as a complete meal because they are so nutritionally dense. With flavours ranging from dark chocolate to exotic açaí, these rich and creamy milkshake-like recipes set the perfect stage for using heavier superfoods such as cashew butter, pecans, hemp hearts, chia, flaxseeds, protein powders, cacao nibs, maca powder, mesquite powder, lucuma powder, goji berries, and avocado, to name a few.

Power shakes abound with minerals, healthy fats, and protein, turning what tastes like a naughty treat into a nutritional powerhouse. Filling yet not heavy, these are excellent lunchtime, snack, breakfast, or even dessert replacements. Many are also perfect for fuelling and refuelling pre- and post-workout.

I am currently in love with these natural whole-food sweeteners: lucuma powder, dates, date syrup, pure dark maple syrup, and mesquite powder.

My most favourite vegan protein powders are Vega Performance Protein, Sunwarrior Raw Classic Protein, Sunwarrior Raw Warrior Blend, Garden of Life, and Greens Plus. These are all 100 percent plant-based and alkaline-forming, and provide a complete balanced array of essential amino acids. As well, they are all gluten-free, non-GMO, and free of chemicals, acids, and solvents. Vanilla flavour blends the best with all of our shakes and smoothies.

power cookie

Even though there's no cookie in this shake, it sure tastes like it! Lucuma powder, which has a natural cookie-like flavour, makes this shake powerfully delicious. Lucuma is a Latin American fruit that looks like an avocado from the outside with a bright orange inside similar to a sweet potato. I've even enjoyed it as an ice cream flavour while travelling throughout Peru. It has a slightly fruity, creamy flavour with notes of vanilla.

Caramel-like dates, nutty pecans, maca root, and the occasional chocolate crunch of raw cacao nibs blend perfectly with the elegant sweetness of pear. Adding a fresh or frozen banana will give this shake more body and the additional fortifying benefits of potassium.

serves 1 to 2

¼ cup (60 mL) raw pecans

1 tbsp (15 mL) maca root powder

1 tbsp (15 mL) lucuma powder

2 tbsp (30 mL) raw cacao nibs

3 dates, pitted

½ cup (125 mL) pear juice

½ cup (125 mL) plain almond milk

½ cup (125 mL) plain hemp milk

4 ice cubes (optional)

1. Combine all of the ingredients in a blender. Blend on high speed until smooth. Taste, and adjust if additional sweetness is desired. Pour into a tall glass. Enjoy.

vital protein

This deep purple–hued potion is beautiful to look at and even better to drink.

Spirulina is a primeval superfood that is among the oldest life forms on earth. It is a nutrient-dense blue-green algae largely made up of protein (amino acids) and an excellent source of energy. It offers a staggering quantity of micronutrients, containing as many as 40 types of minerals (especially high in iron) and incredible stores of vitamins A, B, D, and K. As much as 1 to 2 percent of its weight is composed of chlorophyll, making this algae perhaps the most cleansing food found in nature.

Drinking algae is an acquired taste, and though some people don't mind its "ocean" flavour, most people do. In general, it works best in icy-cold shakes, reducing the ocean flavour. My advice is to combine it with something sweet like bananas or berries.

serves 1 to 2

1 tsp (5 mL) spirulina powder

1 scoop vegan protein powder (page 19)

1 cup (250 mL) blueberries (fresh or frozen)

1 banana (fresh or frozen)

1 cup (250 mL) plain almond milk

½ cup (125 mL) plain hemp milk

4 ice cubes (optional)

1. Combine all of the ingredients in a blender. Blend on high speed until smooth. Taste, and adjust if additional sweetness is desired. Pour into a tall glass. Enjoy.

lightning bolt

Grouping the tropical sweetness of pineapple with the delicious heat of fresh ginger and the nutty creaminess of cashews makes this one of my all-time favourite power shakes. You really can't go wrong with cashews. Not only do they have a lower fat content than most other nuts, but 75 percent of their fat is a heart-healthy monounsaturated fat. Raw unsalted cashews also have generous amounts of protein and fibre, plus B vitamins, magnesium, and other minerals.

serves 1 to 2

2 tbsp (30 mL) raw cashew butter

½ cup (125 mL) pineapple chunks (fresh or frozen)

1 banana (fresh or frozen)

2-inch (5 cm) piece fresh ginger

1½ cups (375 mL) plain almond milk

½ cup (125 mL) apple juice

1 tsp (5 mL) lucuma powder

1 shake ground cinnamon

4 ice cubes (optional)

1. Combine all of the ingredients in a blender. Blend on high speed until smooth. Taste, and adjust if additional sweetness is desired. Pour into a tall glass. Enjoy.

amazon warrior

A rich and luxurious shake, there is nothing quite like the flavour of açai, which is part of the reason it is fast becoming a staple ingredient in juice bars across North America. It is a small purplish-blue berry with a slightly oily and creamy texture that grows on a tall palm tree. It can be easily overwhelmed in flavour by other ingredients, which is why I almost always pair it with berries and a little plant-based fat like coconut milk to enhance its delicate flavour. It is available both frozen and powdered. To get the full effects of the flavour and texture I recommend using frozen berries. Açai is most celebrated for its high levels of antioxidants and EFAs (essential fatty acids), including omega-3, -6, and -9. It is very low in sugars.

serves 1 to 2

1 cup (250 mL) frozen açai berries

½ cup (125 mL) strawberries (fresh or frozen)

1 banana (fresh or frozen)

½ cup (125 mL) coconut milk

1½ cups (375 mL) coconut water

1 tsp (5 mL) raw agave nectar

4 ice cubes (optional)

1. Combine all of the ingredients in a blender. Blend on high speed until smooth. Taste, and adjust if additional sweetness is desired. Pour into a tall glass. Enjoy.

super buff

I adore this gorgeous shake, which was created for our menus many years ago and held on to its popularity for a long time. The time eventually came to update and modernize the ingredients while retaining its original intention. I added the high-protein superfood lucuma, switched from soy to almond milk, and replaced the agave nectar with dates.

serves 1 to 2

1 cup (250 mL) frozen açai berries

½ cup (125 mL) raspberries (fresh or frozen)

1 banana (fresh or frozen)

4 dates, pitted

2 cups (500 mL) plain almond milk

1 tsp (5 mL) chia seeds

1 tsp (5 mL) raw flaxseeds

1 tsp (5 mL) lucuma powder

1 scoop vegan protein powder (page 19)

4 ice cubes (optional)

1. Combine all of the ingredients in a blender. Blend on high speed until smooth. Taste, and adjust if additional sweetness is desired. Pour into a tall glass. Enjoy.

cashew almond

This simply delicious power shake is calcium-rich, protein-rich, energizing, and mood-boosting. It's a spin on the Date Almond, our most popular shake for many years. Here we have substituted the almond milk with the rich creaminess of cashew milk, and added the fortifying superfood benefits of maca root.

serves 1 to 2

1 tbsp (15 mL) maca root powder

2 tbsp (30 mL) raw almond butter

3 dates, pitted

1½ cups (375 mL) cashew milk

1 tsp (5 mL) vanilla bean seeds

1 shake ground cinnamon

1 shake ground nutmeg

1 shake ground cloves

4 ice cubes (optional)

1. Combine all of the ingredients in a blender. Blend on high speed until smooth. Taste, and adjust if additional sweetness is desired. Pour into a tall glass. Enjoy.

pink power

Packed with protein and rich in minerals, this super-scrumptious shake is designed for building the body. It's loaded with luscious pink raspberries and red cherries, and is antioxidizing and mood-boosting.

serves 1 to 2

½ cup (125 mL) raspberries (fresh or frozen)

½ cup (125 mL) cherries (fresh or frozen)

1 banana (fresh or frozen)

2 tbsp (30 mL) raw hemp hearts

3 dates, pitted

1 tsp (5 mL) lucuma powder

1 scoop vegan protein powder (page 19)

2 cups (500 mL) cashew milk

4 ice cubes (optional)

1. Combine all of the ingredients in a blender. Blend on high speed until smooth. Taste, and adjust if additional sweetness is desired. Pour into a tall glass. Enjoy.

strawberry blonde

This gorgeous high-protein shake will make you feel beautiful from the inside out. Just one sip of this sweet strawberry-pear blend will leave you feeling enamoured for the rest of the day.

serves 1 to 2

½ cup (125 mL) strawberries (fresh or frozen)

½ cup (125 mL) raspberries (fresh or frozen)

3 dates, pitted

1 tsp (5 mL) lucuma powder

1 scoop vegan protein powder (page 19)

½ cup (125 mL) pear juice

¾ cup (175 mL) plain almond milk

¼ cup (60 mL) plain hemp milk

4 ice cubes (optional)

1. Combine all of the ingredients in a blender. Blend on high speed until smooth. Taste, and adjust if additional sweetness is desired. Pour into a tall glass. Enjoy.

mad chocolate

Yes, this is a decadent chocolate milkshake, but it's much more nice than naughty! If you love chocolate, you will love this shake. Super-packed with nutrients and overflowing with chocolate flavour, this creamy blend offers the healthy excuse I'm usually looking for to have chocolate for breakfast, lunch, or dinner. This is a calcium-rich, protein-rich, antioxidizing, mood-boosting, endurance-loving power shake.

Adding a malty sweetness is the mesquite powder, which incidentally does not taste like barbecue! Traditionally used by Native Americans, this superfood powder has just recently begun to crop up at supermarkets. Mesquite hardwood is often used to add a smoky sweetness to grilled food. Mesquite powder, on the other hand, is ground from the pods of the mesquite plant and has a subtle malty, nutty sweetness. It is gluten-free, high in protein, low on the glycemic index, and a good source of soluble fibre, meaning it digests slowly and does not cause spikes in blood sugar. An interesting note is that the marketing of mesquite products, both wood and powder, provides a sustainable economic alternative to cutting down trees for grazing or charcoal production.

serves 1 to 2

2 tbsp (30 mL) raw cacao powder

1 tbsp (15 mL) maca root powder

1 tsp (5 mL) mesquite powder

2 tbsp (30 mL) dried goji berries

3 dates, pitted

3 shakes Himalayan pink salt

1 cup (250 mL) plain almond milk

½ cup (125 mL) plain hemp milk

4 ice cubes (optional)

1. Combine all of the ingredients in a blender. Blend on high speed until smooth. Taste, and adjust if additional sweetness is desired. Pour into a tall glass. Enjoy.

smashing pumpkin

Most people think of pumpkins as little more than pie filling or something fun to carve and put a candle in, but what happens when a scoop of pumpkin accidentally falls into the blender? Pumpkins have a ton of surprising health benefits. Being rich in fibre, which slows digestion, they keep you feeling full longer. There's 7 grams of fibre in 1 cup (250 mL) of canned pumpkin. That's more than what you get in two slices of whole-grain bread.

Ironically, although filling, pumpkin is a low-calorie fruit containing nearly 90 percent water, giving it fewer than 50 calories per serving. The pumpkin's brilliant orange comes from a super-high supply of the antioxidant beta-carotene, which is converted to vitamin A in your body. This makes it a healthy food for your eyes. A single cup of pumpkin contains over 200 percent of most people's daily intake of vitamin A, helping your body fight infections and viruses.

Despite its stunning beauty, you can't have pumpkin in your shake without using an ample amount of spices and some natural sweetener, such as dates or maple syrup, otherwise it will taste flat and bland as cardboard.

serves 1 to 2

1 cup (250 mL) pure pumpkin purée

1 banana (fresh or frozen)

5 dates, pitted

1½ cups (375 mL) plain almond milk

½ cup (125 mL) coconut milk

2 shakes ground cinnamon

2 shakes ground allspice

1 shake ground cloves

4 ice cubes (optional)

½ tsp (2 mL) raw hemp hearts, for garnish

1. Combine pumpkin purée, banana, dates, almond milk, coconut milk, cinnamon, allspice, cloves, and ice (if using) in a blender. Blend on high speed until smooth. Taste, and adjust if additional sweetness is desired. Garnish with hemp hearts. Enjoy.

nutty buddy

Cashew butter, strawberries, and maple syrup complement each other perfectly in this pretty pink power shake.

serves 1 to 2

2 tbsp (30 mL) raw cashew butter

1 cup (250 mL) strawberries (fresh or frozen)

1 banana (fresh or frozen)

2 cups (500 mL) plain almond milk

1 tbsp (15 mL) pure dark maple syrup

1 shake ground cinnamon

4 ice cubes (optional)

1. Combine all of the ingredients in a blender. Blend on high speed until smooth. Taste, and adjust if additional sweetness is desired. Pour into a tall glass. Enjoy.

moon milk

In my dreams this is what they like to drink on the moon. It's an incredible deep blue-green, the colour of which I have never seen in a shake before. Designing drinks, I always consider the hue it will be, not only the nutritional benefits or taste. I believe a visually beautiful drink will make you want to drink it again and again.

serves 1 to 2

1 tsp (5 mL) spirulina powder

1 scoop vegan protein powder (page 19)

1 cup (250 mL) blueberries (fresh or frozen)

3 dates, pitted

½ cup (125 mL) apple juice

1 cup (250 mL) plain almond milk

4 ice cubes (optional)

1. Combine all of the ingredients in a blender. Blend on high speed until smooth. Taste, and adjust if additional sweetness is desired. Pour into a tall glass. Enjoy.

chai chiller

In India, chai is a popular blend of aromatic spices such as ginger, cardamom, cinnamon, cloves, fennel, and black tea sweetened generously with honey and hot milk. Traditional chai spices warm the body and greatly improve digestion.

Chai is available in health-food stores as loose tea, tea bags, or liquid concentrate. I like to use the liquid concentrate and prefer Sattwa Chai brand for its high quality. Oregon Chai is also a good brand.

In the Chai Chiller, the traditional spiced chai is given a bit of a shake-up. Coconut milk, thick and sweet, fortifies and strengthens the whole body. In the Far East, it is commonly used to treat weakness, malnutrition, and emaciation due to illness. Coconut milk is a thirst quencher and a good saturated fat. This delicious shake is great to drink any time of the day, but be mindful of the stimulating effects of the black tea too late in the day, if you are sensitive like me.

serves 1 to 2

½ cup (125 mL) vegan spiced chai concentrate

½ cup (125 mL) plain coconut milk

1 banana (fresh or frozen)

1 cup (250 mL) plain almond milk

2 shakes ground cinnamon

4 ice cubes (optional)

1. Combine all of the ingredients in a blender. Blend on high speed until smooth. Taste, and adjust if additional sweetness is desired. Pour into a tall glass. Enjoy.

trail mix

This trio of ingredients—goji berries, raw cacao nibs, and maca root—has been used and revered by people from far-flung locales for their strengthening, energizing, and balancing properties, but only recently have they entered our vocabulary as superfoods.

Cacao has a phenomenal combination of compounds that nourish the body, increase alertness, and raise the serotonin levels in our brains by the bliss chemical known as tryptophan. The cacao nibs also add a fun crunch and a healthy dose of antioxidants, iron, and magnesium.

Maca root is a famed adaptogen, a tonic herb that strengthens the body against stress and delivers endurance and virility. Maca has a delicious, faintly malted taste and is a daily staple food of the high-altitude people of the mountains of Peru and Bolivia.

Goji, a Himalayan berry, has inspired a surge of interest for its use in treating diabetes, hypertension, malaria, fever, cancer, and other ailments. Gram for gram, goji berries pack more vitamin C than some oranges and more beta-carotene than carrots.

serves 1 to 2

2 tbsp (30 mL) dried goji berries

1 tbsp (15 mL) maca root powder

1 tsp (5 mL) mesquite powder

2 tbsp (30 mL) raw cacao nibs

1 cup (250 mL) blueberries (fresh or frozen)

½ cup (125 mL) apple juice

3 dates, pitted

1 cup (250 mL) plain almond milk

½ cup (125 mL) plain hemp milk

4 ice cubes (optional)

1. Combine all of the ingredients in a blender. Blend on high speed until smooth. Taste, and adjust if additional sweetness is desired. Pour into a tall glass. Enjoy.

gingersnap

This brightly flavoured shake is simultaneously spicy and sweet with double the amount of ginger that we normally use. The ginger goes straight to the heart of this combination, leaving you feeling your blood's increased circulation in your body.

serves 1 to 2

1 tsp (5 mL) matcha (green tea powder)

3-inch (7.5 cm) piece peeled fresh ginger

½ cup (125 mL) blueberries (fresh or frozen)

½ cup (125 mL) strawberries (fresh or frozen)

1 banana (fresh or frozen)

2 cups (500 mL) plain almond milk

1 tbsp (30 mL) pure dark maple syrup

4 ice cubes (optional)

1. Combine all of the ingredients in a blender. Blend on high speed until smooth. Taste, and adjust if additional sweetness is desired. Pour into a tall glass. Enjoy.

supersonic

Chia seeds are one of the cutest and tiniest edibles around. Indigenous to Central America, this traditional Inca food has been viewed as a staple energy source for centuries. Today it is rising in popularity with athletes in particular, especially those involved in endurance sports. Chia seeds are magicians of hydration, able to absorb more than 12 times their weight in liquid. They give the body prolonged power while working out. Chia makes an excellent thickener of shakes without adding calories (you can always skip the banana if you already have chia in your shake). It is almost flavourless and goes with just about everything.

Flaxseeds are a great beginner superfood if you are looking for an inexpensive ingredient to boost your shakes. Flax is one of the best sources of essential fatty acids. They help to keep the brain healthy, act as an anti-inflammatory, and are excellent for our hearts and joints. Overflowing with vitamin E, flaxseeds are also an excellent boost for healthy skin.

serves 1 to 2

1 tsp (5 mL) spirulina powder

1 tbsp (15 mL) chia seeds

1 tbsp (15 mL) raw flaxseeds

½ cup (125 mL) raspberries (fresh or frozen)

½ cup (125 mL) strawberries (fresh or frozen)

½ cup (125 mL) blueberries (fresh or frozen)

2 cups (500 mL) mango juice

4 ice cubes (optional)

1. Combine all of the ingredients in a blender. Blend on high speed until smooth. Taste, and adjust if additional sweetness is desired. Pour into a tall glass. Enjoy.

zen energy

Matcha is a staple tea in Okinawa, Japan, where some of the oldest living population resides. It is not an ordinary green tea that you steep in hot water. Matcha is the whole tea leaf ground into a precious concentrated green powder that you combine with water and whisk into a frothy drink that delivers 10 times the antioxidant power and stimulating effects of other green teas. Japanese Zen monks traditionally drink matcha to remain alert but calm during their long hours of meditation. It promotes relaxation with the benefit of L-theanine, an amino acid. It is also high in vitamins and other nutrients and is a powerful cancer fighter and fat burner.

serves 1 to 2

1 tsp (5 mL) matcha (green tea powder)

½ cup (125 mL) cherries (fresh or frozen)

½ cup (125 mL) blueberries (fresh or frozen)

1 banana (fresh or frozen)

2 cups (500 mL) plain almond milk

1 tbsp (15 mL) raw agave nectar

4 ice cubes (optional)

1. Combine all of the ingredients in a blender. Blend on high speed until smooth. Taste, and adjust if additional sweetness is desired. Pour into a tall glass. Enjoy.

promised land

This is a great dessert shake that tastes like halvah, the Middle Eastern delicacy. Tahini comprises hulled sesame seeds ground into butter. High in calories, it's a great ingredient for vegans who want to put on some weight. Add a tablespoonful of raw cacao powder for an antioxidant boost.

serves 1 to 2

1 tbsp (15 mL) raw tahini

1 tbsp (15 mL) raw agave nectar

1 banana (fresh or frozen)

1¼ cups (300 mL) plain almond milk

2 shakes ground cinnamon, plus more for garnish

4 ice cubes (optional)

1. Combine all of the ingredients in a blender. Blend on high speed until smooth. Taste, and adjust if additional sweetness is desired. Pour into a tall glass. Garnish with additional cinnamon. Enjoy.

hot banana oat milk

The high starch content and nutritious qualities of bananas make a delicious breakfast shake. The combination of oats and banana has a calming effect. Originally from Eastern and Southern Europe, oat drinks and porridge were prescribed for insomnia, loss of appetite, and constipation. At one time oats were eaten more than any other food in Italy (Leonardo da Vinci apparently loved to eat oats). Today, herbalists often use oat tea to help alleviate the symptoms of drug addicts suffering from withdrawal. The complex carbohydrate content of oats provides energizing fuel for the body. Cinnamon warms the body and enhances digestion, especially the metabolism of fats.

serves 1 to 2

3 tbsp (45 mL) quick-cooking steel-cut oats

1 fresh banana

1¼ cups (300 mL) hot filtered water

1 tbsp (15 mL) pure dark maple syrup

2 shakes ground cinnamon

1. Combine the oats, banana, and hot water in a bowl. Let soak for 5 minutes.

2. Transfer oat mixture to a blender and add maple syrup. Blend on high speed until smooth. Taste, and adjust if additional sweetness or a thinner consistency is desired. Pour into a mug and garnish with cinnamon. Enjoy.

swoosh

Peanut butter and bananas is a classic combination that's almost irresistible. Throw in raw cacao powder and it's a done deal. I will often also add a tablespoonful of spirulina powder to ramp up the nutritional value of this decadent high-protein shake. With steady use, spirulina will increase energy, improve stamina, sharpen mental alertness, and cleanse toxins from the blood.

serves 1 to 2

2 tbsp (30 mL) natural peanut butter

1 banana (fresh or frozen)

1 tbsp (15 mL) raw cacao powder

1¼ cups (300 mL) plain almond milk

1 tbsp (15 mL) pure dark maple syrup

2 shakes ground cinnamon

4 ice cubes (optional)

1. Combine all of the ingredients in a blender. Blend on high speed until smooth. Taste, and adjust if additional sweetness or a thinner consistency is desired. Pour into a tall glass. Enjoy.

SUPERMILKS

My first sip of green milk was as ground-breaking to me as the first glass of carrot juice I had nearly 25 years ago. It just never occurred to me to combine green juice with nut milks. It was as if I had broken some unwritten cardinal rule to never mix vegetables with milk. It may have been wrong, but wow it just tasted so right. It got me thinking about how many beautiful, unlikely combinations of juice and nut milks there were to choose from if you wanted to be a little creative. Easy to drink, supermilks give you the benefit of the intensely nourishing ingredients against the liquid backdrop of creamy nut and seed milks.

Our base milks for the following supermilks are often a blend of almond and hemp. The light, easy-going flavour of almond milk combines gorgeously with the natural grassy taste of hemp milk. Other great nut and seed milks to choose from include Brazil Nut Milk (page 71) or Cashew Milk (page 75).

turmeric gold milk

root milk

The juice of raw sweet potato has more general nutritional value than your average white potato. Along with parsnips, they contain easily digestible carbohydrates, which convert into natural sugars, an excellent high-performance fuel source for your brain and body. These beautiful grounding roots are also very rich in potassium, calcium, sodium, and silicon. The delicious addition of a protein- and calcium-rich almond milk makes this my top choice, especially in the winter.

serves 1 to 2

1 sweet potato

3 parsnips

2-inch (5 cm) piece fresh ginger

1 cup (250 mL) plain almond milk

1 tbsp (15 mL) lucuma powder

2 shakes ground cinnamon

4 ice cubes (optional)

1. Juice the sweet potato, parsnips, and ginger.

2. Pour into a tall glass. Add almond milk, lucuma, cinnamon, and ice cubes (if using) and whisk to combine. Enjoy.

turmeric gold milk

This beautiful milk is the colour of a Buddhist monk's saffron robes. Exotic and spicy, with citrus notes, it is designed to soothe your soul and tummy.

serves 1 to 2

1-inch (2.5 cm) piece fresh turmeric

2-inch (5 cm) piece fresh ginger

1 orange

1 tbsp (15 mL) pure dark maple syrup

½ cup (125 mL) plain almond milk

½ cup (125 mL) plain hemp milk

2 shakes cayenne pepper

2 shakes ground cinnamon

4 ice cubes (optional)

1. Juice the turmeric, ginger, and orange.

2. Transfer juice to a blender and add remaining ingredients. Blend on high speed to combine. Pour into a tall glass. Enjoy.

green milk

This super-green milk is the colour of freshly mowed grass, tasting green, milky, and sweet all at once. I love it for how it fills me up with the fortifying benefits of almond milk while simultaneously delivering the alkalizing and detoxifying benefits of juiced leafy greens.

serves 1 to 2

1 cup (250 mL) lightly packed chopped kale

1 cup (250 mL) lightly packed spinach

4 romaine lettuce leaves

1 tbsp (15 mL) pure dark maple syrup

1 cup (250 mL) plain almond milk

2 shakes Himalayan pink salt

4 ice cubes (optional)

1. Juice the kale, spinach, and romaine.

2. Transfer juice to a blender and add remaining ingredients. Blend on high speed to combine. Pour into a tall glass. Enjoy.

lavender milk

This stunning, delicate, and sweet floral-flavoured milk has a soft lavender hue. Dried lavender can help digestive issues such as vomiting, nausea, intestinal gas, upset stomach, and abdominal swelling.

serves 1 to 2

3 tbsp (45 mL) dried lavender herb, plus more for garnish

1 tsp (5 mL) raw coconut oil

½ cup (125 mL) plain coconut milk

1 cup (250 mL) plain almond milk

1 tbsp (15 mL) lucuma powder

1 tbsp (15 mL) raw agave nectar

4 ice cubes (optional)

1. Combine all of the ingredients in a blender. Blend on high speed until smooth. Garnish with additional dried lavender herb. Enjoy.

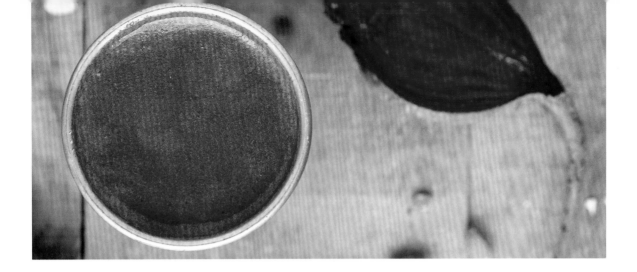

pink milk

This pink milk is the prettiest colour in the rainbow of juices and milks that we make. It tastes just like Strawberry Nestlé Quik. The fruitiness of strawberries completely masks the earthy flavour of the beet juice. Drink up the antioxidizing, liver-cleansing, and muscle-building benefits of this unique combination.

serves 1 to 2

2 beets, trimmed

1 cup (250 mL) strawberries (fresh or frozen)

1 tsp (5 mL) acerola cherry powder

1 tbsp (15 mL) pure dark maple syrup

1 cup (250 mL) plain almond milk

2 shakes Himalayan pink salt

4 ice cubes (optional)

1. Juice the beets.

2. Transfer juice to a blender and add remaining ingredients. Blend on high speed until smooth. Pour into a tall glass. Enjoy.

deep chocolate milk

This deep, dark chocolate milk is tailored to satisfy your cravings. The nourishing yet decadent combination of coconut oil and maple syrup make this the ultimate chocolate milkshake. Coconut oil is a heart-healthy fat that keeps your body running smoother, boosting thyroid function to increase metabolism, energy, and endurance. It also increases digestion and absorption of fat-soluble vitamins.

serves 1 to 2

1 tbsp (15 mL) maca root powder

1 tsp (5 mL) mesquite powder

2 tbsp (30 mL) raw cacao powder

1 tsp (5 mL) raw coconut oil

¾ cup (175 mL) plain almond milk

¾ cup (175 mL) plain hemp milk

1 tbsp (15 mL) pure dark maple syrup

4 ice cubes (optional)

1. Combine all of the ingredients in a blender. Blend on high speed until well incorporated. Pour into a tall glass. Enjoy.

NUT MILKS

When rice milk first hit the market I remember momentarily thinking, "How do you milk a grain of rice?" Even as a vegan, I had trouble wrapping my head around the concept. Rice milk and other milk alternatives have come a long way since those early days. Now multiple brands can be found, and more are appearing every day on grocery store shelves. People are recognizing that they are not just for the lactose intolerant or vegans. However, most boxed nut milks are pasteurized and contain significant added sugars and stabilizers. When you make your own, you get to experience the true taste of the nut in a totally raw beverage that is full of life!

Handcrafted nut milks are a non-dairy rich source of protein, fibre, and fatty acids. Each nut and seed brings a unique nutritional gift. They have a different texture and creaminess that add more depth of flavour than soy milk. With the growing debate about GMOs, the world is shifting toward almond milk as the new non-dairy substitute of choice. Local hipster indie coffee shops have helped push this trend to new mainstream heights by the act of frothing a variety of alternative earthy rich nut milks to top their beautiful coffee drinks.

For a lower-calorie milk, increase the ratio of water to nuts by blending in more water. You will need a blender, metal strainer, cheesecloth or nut milk bag, and a couple 33.8-ounce (1 L) glass jars.

I get bored easily and like to mix things up, so I combine different milks to get the nutritional and taste diversity I need on a particular day. Each nut and seed brings a unique gift. Once you see for yourself how easy these milks are to make and even more delicious to drink, you can experiment with other raw nuts and seeds such as hazelnuts, pecans, walnuts, cashews, and pumpkin seeds.

everyday brazil nut milk

Brazil nut milk is a fabulous dairy-free alternative. I especially enjoy it over a hot bowl of oatmeal, garnished with cinnamon and hemp hearts. Brazil nut milk not only tastes amazing, but also is super-healthy and loaded with vitamins, minerals, and antioxidants. Brazil nuts are a fantastic source of selenium, which protects cells from damage and can lower the risk of some cancers.

makes 3 servings (1 cup/250 mL each)

1 cup (250 mL) raw Brazil nuts

6 cups (1.5 L) filtered water, divided

½ tsp (2 mL) Himalayan pink salt, divided

Seeds from 1 vanilla bean or ½ tsp (2 mL) pure vanilla extract

1 tsp (5 mL) pure dark maple syrup

1. Place the Brazil nuts in a small bowl and cover with 3 cups (750 mL) filtered water. Add ¼ tsp (1 mL) pink salt and stir to combine. Cover and let soak for at least 8 hours.

2. Strain Brazil nuts in a fine-mesh sieve and rinse under cool running water until water runs clear. Drain.

3. Combine the soaked Brazil nuts, vanilla, maple syrup, and remaining ¼ tsp (1 mL) pink salt in a blender. Add remaining 3 cups (750 mL) filtered water.

4. Blend on high speed for 1 to 2 minutes or until completely smooth and creamy.

5. Taste, and adjust the salt and maple syrup (for sweetness) as desired.

6. Using cheesecloth or a nut milk bag placed over a fine-mesh sieve, strain the milk into a large bowl. Use the back of a spoon or a spatula to press down and move the solids around to help the milk drain; discard solids.

7. Transfer milk to a resealable glass jar and refrigerate for up to 4 days.

everyday almond milk

Made by simply blending almonds with pure water and straining, almond milk contains roughly the same amount of calcium as dairy milk, but with no mucous-forming lactose and just a fraction of the calories. Almond milk has become a staple of cleanse programs because almonds are packed with protein, fibre, and omega-3 and -6 fatty acids. A glass of it also contains significant B vitamins, iron, magnesium, zinc, and vitamin E.

Almonds need to be soaked. This softens them and makes them much easier to blend, and easier to digest. The longer the almonds are soaked the creamier the results will be. This is a key element to making a great-tasting and healthy milk. I like to use whole blanched almonds because they have the skins removed, which also makes straining your milk quicker and easier.

makes about 3 servings (each about 1 cup/250 mL)

1 cup (250 mL) raw whole blanched almonds

6 cups (1.5 L) filtered water, divided

½ tsp (2 mL) Himalayan pink salt, divided

Seeds from 1 vanilla bean or ½ tsp (2 mL) pure vanilla extract

3 dates, pitted

1. Place the almonds in a small bowl and cover with 3 cups (750 mL) filtered water. Add ¼ tsp (1 mL) pink salt and stir to combine. Cover and let soak for at least 4 hours.

2. Strain almonds in a fine-mesh sieve and rinse under cool running water until water runs clear. Drain.

3. Combine the soaked almonds, vanilla, dates, and remaining ¼ tsp (1 mL) pink salt in a blender with the remaining filtered water.

4. Blend at low speed for 1 to 2 minutes or until completely smooth and creamy (the mixture will expand).

5. Taste, and adjust the salt and dates (for sweetness) as desired.

6. Using cheesecloth or a nut milk bag placed over a fine-mesh sieve, strain the milk into a large bowl. Use the back of a spoon or a spatula to press down and move the solids around to help the milk drain; discard solids.

7. Transfer milk to a resealable glass jar and refrigerate for up to 4 days.

everyday cashew milk

Cashew milk is my new favourite. I use it in power shakes, over granola, or as a simple nutritious glass of creamy goodness. Smooth and naturally sweet, it offers a delicious break from my daily habit of almond milk. Of all the nut milks, it has the texture closest to regular whole milk. For a half-and-half consistency for coffee or tea, use only 2 cups (500 mL) of filtered water in the recipe.

Cashews are fairly soft and do not need to be soaked as long as almonds. To save on time they can even be milked directly from their dry state. This cashew milk recipe does not require any straining, although if you prefer to strain you can. It is super-quick and easy to make.

makes about 3 servings (each about 1 cup/250 mL)

1 cup (250 mL) raw cashews

6 cups (1.5 L) filtered water, divided

½ tsp (2 mL) Himalayan pink salt, divided

Seeds from 1 vanilla bean or ½ tsp (2 mL) pure vanilla extract

1 tsp (5 mL) pure dark maple syrup

1 shake ground cinnamon

1. Place the cashews in a small bowl and cover with 3 cups (750 mL) filtered water. Add ¼ tsp (1 mL) pink salt and stir to combine. Cover and let soak for at least 2 hours.

2. Strain the cashews in a fine-mesh sieve and rinse under cool running water until water runs clear. Drain.

3. Combine the cashews, vanilla, maple syrup, cinnamon, and remaining ¼ tsp (1 mL) pink salt in a blender. Add remaining 3 cups (750 mL) filtered water. Blend on high speed for 3 minutes or until completely smooth and creamy. Strain through a fine-mesh sieve, if desired.

4. Taste, and adjust the salt and maple syrup (for sweetness) as desired.

5. Transfer milk to a resealable glass jar and refrigerate for up to 4 days.

everyday hemp heart milk

This elegant, slightly grassy-tasting milk can be drunk unstrained for the most nutritional benefit or you can strain it for a smoother result. As hemp heart milk is lighter than your typical nut milk, I sometimes blend it with almond, cashew, or Brazil nut milk to make a more full-bodied milk. Blending in 1 teaspoon (5 mL) of unrefined coconut butter is another delicious way to add richness to this milk.

Highly nutritious, hemp heart is the buttery meat found at the heart of the seed after the shell has been hulled. The hearts are delicate and do not have to be soaked, so preparation time to make the milk is very short. Hemp is an awesome source of omega-3 and omega-6 essential fatty acids, containing powerful anti-inflammatory properties that help to repair tissues, especially after vigorous exercise. They also contain all 10 essential amino acids, making them a complete protein. Hemp protein is easily digestible and easily absorbed by the body, leaving more energy for muscle regeneration and fat metabolism.

makes 3 servings (1 cup/250 mL each)

3 cups (750 mL) filtered water

1 cup (250 mL) raw hemp hearts

2 dates, pitted

Seeds from 1 vanilla bean or ½ tsp (2 mL) pure vanilla extract

¼ tsp (1 mL) Himalayan pink salt

1. Combine the filtered water, hemp hearts, dates, vanilla, and pink salt in a blender.

2. Blend on high speed for 1 to 2 minutes or until completely smooth and creamy. Taste the milk and adjust the pink salt and dates (for sweetness) as desired.

3. Using cheesecloth or a nut milk bag placed over a fine-mesh sieve, strain the milk into a large bowl. Use the back of a spoon or a spatula to press down and move the solids around to help the milk drain; discard solids.

4. Transfer milk to a resealable glass jar and refrigerate for up to 4 days.

HOT TONICS

A tonic is used to help restore, tone, and invigorate systems in the body or to promote general health and well-being. An herbal tonic is a preparation made from an assortment of plants, herbs, and spices. You can find variations of awesome tonics all over the world, the web, and in books. Using local exotic ingredients, almost every country or region has its own recipes for handcrafted tonics, sometimes passed down from generations past.

Concocting tonics makes me feel like a magician, and these are my favourite potions. Once you understand how to achieve different flavours, it's easy to create your own tonic, building it around two or three star ingredients.

radiator tonic

I grew up breathing in the exotic aromas of turmeric and ginger wafting from my mom's Moroccan kitchen nearly every night. Our meals were always brightly coloured and flavoured thanks to the liberal use of those two ingredients in many of her dishes. Many of the traditional ingredients my mom intuitively used to nourish us also had therapeutic value.

Turmeric has a peppery, warm, and bitter flavour and a mild fragrance reminiscent of oranges and ginger. It is best known as one of the basic ingredients to make curry; it also gives mustard its bright yellow colour. Much of its recent popularity is fuelled by research that has highlighted its therapeutic anti-inflammatory properties. Turmeric comes from the curcuma root and has a tough brown skin and deep orange flesh.

Much like turmeric, fresh ginger has a wonderful warming effect on the body, which causes us to sweat and expel toxins. Ginger is also known to soothe the gastrointestinal tract. It also enhances blood flow and is considered a blood thinner.

serves 1

2-inch (5 cm) piece fresh ginger
2 lemons
1 tsp (5 mL) ground turmeric

2 tbsp (30 mL) pure dark maple syrup
1 shake ground cinnamon, plus more for garnish
1 cup (250 mL) boiling water

1. Juice the ginger and lemons.

2. Combine the turmeric, maple syrup, and cinnamon in a large tempered glass. Pour in the juice and boiling water. Stir until well combined. Garnish with additional cinnamon. Enjoy.

master tonic

This is a spin on the old-school Master Cleanser recipe published by Stanley Burroughs in 1940. I've been drinking the Master Cleanser since my first days of juicing, nearly 25 years ago. Primarily created as a juice fast, it's been a very useful tool for me whenever my health has undergone a dip in vitality and vigour. It provides a healthy amount of calories and nutrients specific to cleansing, while resting the digestive system, allowing me to focus on rebooting my body's systems.

Drinking only this, if even for a day, and overcoming the psychological need to eat, you will feel a growing sense of control that motivates you to take better care of yourself. Fresh basil is a great de-stressor.

serves 1

2-inch (5 cm) piece fresh ginger

1 clove garlic

2 lemons

1 lime

½ bunch fresh basil, leaves only

2 tbsp (30 mL) pure dark maple syrup

¼ tsp (1 mL) cayenne pepper

1 cup (250 mL) boiling water

1. Juice the ginger, garlic, lemons, and lime.

2. Combine the basil, maple syrup, and cayenne in a large tempered glass. Pour in the juice and boiling water. Stir until well combined. Enjoy.

royal tonic

Where to start? Garlic and onions are nature's antibiotic, antiviral, and antifungal soldiers in the war against bacterial invaders in our bodies. They are both rich sources of quercetin and are considered blood thinners, improving blood flow and circulation. Jalapeño peppers contain capsaicin, which is a well-known pain reliever. It's like adding ibuprofen to your tonic. Peppers are also anti-inflammatory, and help with digestion. Apple cider vinegar has many uses and benefits. It helps your body eliminate toxins. It strengthens the immune system, promotes digestion, and relieves sore throats, colds, and sinus infections.

serves 1

1-inch [2.5 cm] piece horseradish
2-inch [5 cm] piece fresh ginger
½ white onion
2 cloves garlic

1 jalapeño pepper
2 lemons
2 shakes Himalayan pink salt
2 shakes cayenne pepper

3 tbsp [45 mL] apple cider vinegar
1 tbsp [15 mL] raw agave nectar
¾ cup [175 mL] boiling water

1. Juice the horseradish, ginger, onion, garlic, jalapeño, and lemons.

2. Combine the pink salt, cayenne pepper, vinegar, and agave nectar in a tempered glass. Pour in juice and boiling water and stir until well combined. Enjoy.

repair tonic

Oats are the original Celtic tonic. Oats contain the antioxidant vitamin E (which protects the body from damaging chemicals invading the body), the B-complex vitamins (vital for a healthy nervous system), and calcium for healthy bones. Oats are also a good source of protein, needed for the repair and renewal of tissues. They provide soluble fibre, which binds to cholesterol in the gut, aiding its removal from the body.

serves 1

1 cup [250 mL] boiling water
¼ cup [60 mL] instant steel-cut oats
3 dates, pitted
1 tsp [5 mL] vanilla bean powder

1 shake Himalayan pink salt
1 shake ground nutmeg
1 shake ground cinnamon, plus more for garnish

1. Combine the boiling water, oats, dates, vanilla, pink salt, nutmeg, and cinnamon in a blender. (Be careful to hold the lid on tight using a kitchen towel.) Blend on high speed until smooth.

2. Pour into a large tempered glass. Garnish with additional cinnamon. Enjoy.

IMMUNITY SHOTS

Immunity shots are small weapons in your daily arsenal of staying well. They deliver an intense, potent, concentrated dose of ingredients designed to boost your body's defences. They can be sipped alone or added to your juices and smoothies, amplifying their benefits.

stress

Optimistic people are often more stress-hardy. They tend to embrace challenges, have a strong sense of humour, and accept that change is a part of life. You can also cope better with the symptoms of stress by strengthening your physical health. Set aside time to relax, breathe fresh air, exercise regularly, drink lots of water, and restore yourself with a boost of B vitamins.

serves 1

2-inch (5 cm) piece fresh ginger	½ tsp (2 mL) spirulina powder
2 lemons	20 drops holy basil tincture
3 large chunks pineapple	20 drops B12 tincture

1. Juice the ginger, lemons, and pineapple.

2. Combine juice, spirulina, holy basil tincture, and B12 tincture in a blender. Pulse to combine.

3. Pour into a short glass. Enjoy.

immunity

Your body has an amazing internal defence mechanism called the immune system that protects you from bacteria and viruses that can lead to illness. To function well, it requires balance and harmony.

Your first line of defence is to choose a healthy lifestyle, the single best step you can take toward keeping your immune system strong and healthy. Every part of your body, including your immune system, functions better when protected from environmental assaults and bolstered by healthy-living strategies such as eating a diet high in fruits, vegetables, and whole grains and low in saturated fat, exercising regularly, maintaining a healthy weight, and getting enough sleep.

serves 1

2 cloves garlic	20 drops echinacea tincture
2-inch (5 cm) piece fresh ginger	2 drops oregano oil
2 lemons	Pinch Himalayan pink salt
½ grapefruit	

1. Juice the garlic, ginger, lemons, and grapefruit.

2. Whisk together juice, echinacea, oregano oil, and pink salt. Pour into a short glass. Enjoy.

detox

This is my favourite immunity shot of all time. I try to have one every day. The warming effects of the apple cider vinegar, turmeric, and cayenne pepper quickly alters stagnation in the body within moments of taking it. The sour and bitter ingredients in this shot reduce toxic accumulations in the blood and liver resulting from a rich diet.

serves 1

2-inch (5 cm) piece fresh ginger

½ orange

2 lemons

2 tbsp (30 mL) apple cider vinegar

1 tsp (5 mL) flaxseed oil

¼ tsp (1 mL) ground turmeric

⅛ tsp (0.5 mL) cayenne pepper

20 drops milk thistle tincture

1. Juice the ginger, orange, and lemons.

2. Whisk together juice, vinegar, flaxseed oil, turmeric, cayenne, and milk thistle. Pour into a short glass. Enjoy.

candida

Candidiasis is the overgrowth of yeast-like fungi in the body, causing feelings of heaviness and sluggishness. Candida tends to exist in high levels in individuals with weakened immune systems. Apple cider vinegar, pau d'arco, and oregano oil excel in controlling candida because of their powerful antibacterial and anti-fungal properties.

serves 1

2-inch (5 cm) piece fresh ginger

2 lemons

2 tbsp (30 mL) apple cider vinegar

Pinch cayenne pepper

20 drops pau d'arco tincture

2 drops oregano oil

1. Juice the ginger and lemons.

2. Whisk together juice, vinegar, cayenne, pau d'arco, and oregano oil. Pour into a short glass. Enjoy.

fire

This is a daily health-building digestive tonic.

serves 1

2 cloves garlic

2-inch (5 cm) piece fresh ginger

½ orange

2 lemons

⅛ tsp (0.5 mL) cayenne pepper

¼ tsp (1 mL) ground turmeric

2 tbsp (30 mL) apple cider vinegar

½ tsp (2 mL) raw agave nectar

1. Juice the garlic, ginger, orange, and lemons.

2. Whisk together juice, cayenne, turmeric, vinegar, and agave nectar. Pour into a short glass. Enjoy.

antibiotic

This antibacterial and antifungal shot is best taken during the change of seasons to support and boost the immune system at the first sign of a cold or flu. It is also super helpful during stressful times or while travelling.

serves 1

2 cloves garlic

2-inch (5 cm) piece fresh ginger

2 lemons

½ orange

2 drops oregano oil

1. Juice the garlic, ginger, lemons, and orange.

2. Pour juice into a short glass. Drop in oregano oil and stir to combine. Enjoy.

killer

This antiviral shot is one of the best preventive immunity shots we have at Fresh. It is deeply useful for improving adrenal gland function and fatigue. It is also helpful in warding off frequent colds and the flu.

serves 1

3-inch (7.5 cm) piece fresh ginger

2 lemons

Pinch Himalayan pink salt

⅛ tsp (0.5 mL) cayenne pepper

10 drops astragalus tincture

20 drops echinacea tincture

1. Juice the ginger and lemons.

2. Whisk together juice, pink salt, cayenne, astragalus, and echinacea. Pour into a short glass. Enjoy.

awake

This recipe was inspired by the Mayan hot chocolate shots I occasionally enjoy at other coffee shops. The difference is that this spicy dark chocolate coffee shot works great not only for improved energy but also for improved circulation and long-lasting stamina due to the high-protein maca and mesquite powders.

serves 1

½ cup (125 mL) brewed espresso

1 tsp (5 mL) pure dark maple syrup

1 tsp (5 mL) raw cacao powder

½ tsp (2 mL) maca root powder

½ tsp (2 mL) mesquite powder

⅛ tsp (0.5 mL) cayenne pepper

1. Combine all of the ingredients in a blender. Blend at high speed until smooth. Pour into a short glass. Enjoy.

FRESH FOOD

KITCHEN EQUIPMENT

These days I do my recipe development at home. The restaurants are just too busy, and there's nowhere for me to work without getting in everyone's way. This means I'm developing recipes with home equipment—just like what you'll be using.

Here are some of my favourite kitchen tools and equipment that I use all the time.

Bowls, bowls, bowls

Having lots of bowls in lots of sizes means you'll have big ones for mixing batters and little ones for mixing spice blends—and all the sizes in between for stirring up anything else.

Cutting boards in various sizes

Wooden boards are great, but I also have a couple cutting boards made of wood fibre and resin that I like because they can go in the dishwasher.

Dry and liquid measuring cups

Dry measures look like an oversized spoon. Liquid measures are generally clear and have a pouring spout. For these recipes, it won't make much of a difference if you use the wrong ones, since you're not baking or doing anything that's overly precise, but it's just easier to use the right cups.

Dry measuring cups are designed to be filled right to the top and then levelled off with a straight edge of some sort. Liquid measuring cups are designed to be filled to the gradations on the side of the cup (¼ cup/60 mL, ½ cup/125 mL, etc.) rather than right to the top. Measuring a liquid by pouring to the very top of a dry measuring cup is just asking for a mess—and trying to level a dry ingredient if it doesn't come right to the top of a liquid measuring cup is next to impossible—so do yourself a favour and use the cup meant for whatever you're measuring.

My favourite liquid measuring cups have numbers that you can read from above—so much easier than having to lean down and look from the side. But I'm most excited about a ¼-cup (60 mL) liquid measuring cup with tablespoon increments! I love it more than anyone should love a measuring cup. I used it all the time when I was working on this book. It's so much nicer to measure a tablespoon of liquid in a little measuring cup than in a measuring spoon. The one I have is OXO brand.

Fine-mesh sieve

Fine-mesh sieves are good for rinsing quinoa and small grains that would fall through the holes of a regular colander. Get an all-metal one so you can wash it in the dishwasher. The one I use the most is 7 inches (18 cm) across.

Garlic press

Buy a good garlic press. I got mine in Scotland almost 20 years ago—we used it at the restaurant there—and it's still as good as new. It is called a Westmark Extracta and is available online. It's more expensive than typical garlic presses, but well worth it. The holes are the perfect size and perfect distance apart so you can just poke out the garlic fragments with a fork, which also makes it so easy to clean. If I didn't have this one, I would just use a knife, since every other press I've used doesn't even come close in performance. When ordering, make sure it's the "Extracta" model, not just the Westmark brand.

High-speed blender

For making smooth dressings, nothing compares to a Vitamix or Blendtec high-speed blender. These powerful machines allow you to blend almost anything without worrying about burning out the motor. They are expensive, but have been known to last for over 20 years and still be as good as new.

Immersion blender

Immersion blenders are great because they allow you to blend foods directly in the container you are working with; for example, you can blend a soup right in the pot or make a mayo in the jar you're going to store it in.

Julienne peeler

The julienne peeler looks similar to a regular Y-shaped peeler, but it has a row of serrated teeth that cuts strips of vegetables quickly and easily. It's good for making zucchini noodles or long carrot strands. At the restaurants, we use a turning slicer (or Spiralizer), but if you don't have one of those, a julienne peeler does the trick—and is much cheaper and smaller.

Kitchen rasp

A kitchen rasp is a fine metal grater and is the best for zesting lemons and limes. I prefer the kind made by Microplane.

Knife sharpener

Various simple home knife sharpeners are now available. I have a sharpening stone and a steel, but do you think I ever reach for them at home? Never. Instead, I grab the $10 sharpener that takes about 5 seconds to use and works every time.

Knives

Three knives are really all you need. *Chef's knife:* For home use, I like knives that are 8 to 10 inches (20 to 25 cm) long. Buy knives that feel nice in your hand and aren't too long to feel comfortable using in your kitchen. I always reach for my Santoku-shaped one, although I have a couple of regular ones as well. *Serrated knife:* An all-metal, as opposed to a plastic-handled, one is best because it feels stronger and will last forever. *Paring knife:* Buy a knife that appeals to you. There are plenty of cheap and cheerful, brightly coloured paring knives available now, and that's what I use.

Lemon squeezers

I have two favourite ways of juicing lemons. First, an old-fashioned wooden lemon reamer—quick, efficient, and simple. But a close second are the ones that are almost always bright yellow with two interlocking half spheres at one end and two handles at the other end—these are great because they catch the seeds for you.

Oil sprayer

I like using a fine sprayer to grease a pan for frying, to prep vegetables for roasting, or anywhere that a light coating of oil is needed. You use way less oil by spraying rather than drizzling. With the sprayer I use at home, I just fill it and pump a few times to build up the pressure to spray. There are good choices for about $10 or so.

Rice cooker

It's definitely nice to let a rice cooker do its thing and cook your rice or quinoa to perfection while you get on with something else.

Salad spinner

I dry my washed kale and other greens in a salad spinner—and then store the whole thing in the fridge until needed.

Small spatulas

I love my mini spatulas. They come in all sorts of colours, and the silicone spatula part is about 1 × 2 inches (2.5 × 5 cm). I always reach for them before my big spatulas. They're nice and bendy, so really pleasant to use.

Small whisk

A small whisk is great for mixing marinades or batters.

Spice grinder or mortar and pestle

These days, I actually use my mortar and pestle more than my electric spice grinder. It's kind of nice to feel connected to your spices by grinding them by hand. But, if you're making a batch of something with a lot of spices that need to be finely ground, like the Berbere Spice Mix (page 188) or Jamaican Curry Powder (page 191), it's much quicker and easier with an electric spice grinder.

Tongs

Go to a proper restaurant supply store and get the kind of tongs that don't have a locking mechanism at the top. The mechanism is supposed to keep the tongs closed when stored, but it's annoying when you're trying to use them. My tongs stay open in my drawer, and it has never caused me a moment's worry. The ones I like are about 10 to 12 inches (25 to 30 cm) long and only cost a couple of dollars. Pinch them together in the store to make sure the tips meet perfectly when you close them.

Wooden spoons

I have a bunch of different sizes, but the wooden spoons I use time and again are about 12 inches (30 cm) long, with a bowl no bigger than an average lime. Variety is nice, but if you can only choose one spoon, that size works best for most things.

And, finally, I wanted to mention a couple of kitchen gadgets that aren't worth spending your money on: (1) *Avocado slicer*. I'm talking about the fan-shaped tool with a bunch of cutting wires strung across. It never works—except to clutter up your utensil drawer. (2) *Quick chopper*. I like to watch those infomercials as much as the next person, but I treat them like a fun show to watch. This product isn't something I actually need in my house! Just use a knife—it is so much easier to clean and will give you much better results.

STOCKING YOUR KITCHEN

Let's be honest here. My pantry is not like that of most people. I have about 110 different spices in small jars on shallow shelves I built myself. I never have to move a spice jar to see what's behind it, which feels so luxurious. When I first built the shelves, I took a picture with my phone so I could look at them periodically during the day—that's how much I love them! But I do all of my recipe development and testing at home, so I like to have every ingredient I can think of there, waiting for inspiration to strike me. You won't need to have as many ingredients as I do, but cooking the Fresh way at home is easy as long as you stock up with some basic ingredients that we use a lot.

As you go through this book, you'll notice that certain ingredients pop up over and over, others are used occasionally, and some only show up once or twice. I've organized the ingredients into three lists: the absolute necessities for cooking the Fresh way, the occasional things that you'll need once in a while, and the specialty items that you'll only need if you want to make a specific recipe.

However, I've put some ingredients that only appear in this book once or twice on the occasional list because they are great to have on hand. Once you get comfortable with this way of cooking, the items on the occasional list make it easy to whip together a quick bowl, salad, or sandwich with some basic items from your fridge. I'm talking about quick bowls like brown rice with tamari, flax oil, hemp seeds, sun-dried tomatoes, and green peas. Not book-worthy recipes, but tasty dishes that fill you up and stop you from reaching for a junk-food meal.

I like to keep all my flours, lentils, and other dry ingredients in large Mason jars that I sticker with white address labels. They look nice, you can see what you have, and it encourages you to buy ingredients in bulk rather than wrapped in tons of packaging, since you know you're going to put it into a jar when you get home.

If you live in Toronto and are having trouble finding any ingredients, just email feedback@ freshrestaurants.ca and I'll let you know where I go.

Everyday Items

Fresh Items

- alfalfa sprouts
- avocados
- carrots
- chilies (jalapeños, serranos, Thai red and green, etc.)
- cucumbers, English
- garlic
- ginger
- green onions
- herbs (basil, cilantro, dill, mint, parsley, etc.)
- leafy greens (bok choy, chard, collards, dandelion, kale, spinach, etc.)
- leeks
- lemons
- lettuce (power greens mix, romaine, spring mix, etc.)
- limes
- microgreens
- mushrooms
- napa cabbage
- onions (cooking, red, and sweet)
- peas (fresh or frozen)
- potatoes
- sweet potatoes
- tempeh
- tofu, extra firm
- tomatoes

Beans and Legumes

- adzuki beans (canned)
- black beans (canned)
- chickpeas (canned)

Grains and Flours

- Bob's Red Mill Gluten Free All Purpose Baking Flour
- brown basmati rice
- light spelt flour
- quinoa
- soba noodles

Herbs and Spices

- cinnamon, ground
- coriander seeds
- crushed red chilies
- cumin seeds
- curry powder
- garlic powder
- Mexican chili powder
- turmeric, ground

Milks

- unsweetened plain soy milk
- vanilla almond milk

Nuts and Seeds (Raw)

- almonds
- cashews
- flaxseeds, ground
- hemp hearts
- peanut butter, natural
- pumpkin seeds
- sesame seeds
- sunflower seeds
- tahini

Seasonings

- black pepper, whole
- Dijon mustard
- miso, light or mild (made from soy)
- nutritional yeast
- sambal oelek
- sea salt
- tamari

Sweeteners

- agave nectar, raw
- dark maple syrup, pure

Vinegars and Oils

- apple cider vinegar
- coconut oil, neutral-flavoured
- extra virgin olive oil, highly flavoured, for drizzling
- olive oil, mildly flavoured, for cooking
- rice vinegar
- sunflower oil

Other

- baking powder
- baking soda
- Earth Balance non-dairy buttery spread
- San Marzano tomatoes (canned)
- vanilla extract, pure
- vegetable stock

Occasional Items

Fresh Items
- apples, green
- asparagus
- baby arugula
- bananas
- bean sprouts
- bell peppers, green and red
- blueberries
- broccoli
- Brussels sprouts
- cauliflower
- celery
- corn
- edamame
- grapefruit
- mushrooms, oyster and shiitake
- peaches
- raspberries
- strawberries
- sunflower sprouts
- zucchini

Grains and Flours
- pearl barley
- red lentils
- millet, hulled
- rolled oats, large flake
- panko crumbs

Herbs and Spices
- allspice, ground
- basil, dried
- bay leaves
- cayenne pepper, ground
- cloves, whole
- dillweed, dried
- fennel seeds
- ginger, ground
- mustard powder
- nutmeg, ground
- onion powder
- oregano, dried
- rosemary, dried
- sage, dried
- smoked paprika
- sumac powder
- thyme, dried

Legumes
- white kidney beans (canned)
- lentils (canned)

Milks
- coconut milk (canned)

Nuts and Seeds (Raw)
- chia seeds
- hazelnuts
- peanuts
- pecans
- pistachios
- walnuts

Dried Fruits
- goji berries
- sun-dried tomatoes

Seasonings
- Bragg Liquid Aminos
- cornstarch
- Engevita yeast (powdered nutritional yeast)
- mirin
- Sriracha sauce
- yellow mustard

Sweeteners
- date syrup

Vinegars and Oils
- balsamic vinegar
- flaxseed oil
- red wine vinegar
- white wine vinegar

Other
- Butler Soy Curls
- chipotles in adobo sauce
- dill pickles
- hot banana chilies (jarred)
- lemon flavouring
- pickled jalapeño peppers
- pineapple (canned)
- pumpkin purée, pure (canned)
- tomato paste

Specialty Items

Fresh Items

- beets
- broccoli slaw mix
- butternut squash
- edible flowers
- jicama
- kohlrabi
- lemongrass
- mandarin oranges (canned)
- Scotch bonnet peppers
- smoked tofu, extra firm

Grains, Noodles, and Flours

- brown rice noodles
- cornmeal, coarse grind
- dried pasta stars
- freekeh
- gluten flour (vital wheat gluten)
- gram (chickpea) flour
- jasmine rice
- kamut udon noodles
- puffed quinoa
- quick-cooking rolled oats
- quick-cooking steel-cut oats

Herbs and Spices

- allspice berries
- anise seeds
- black salt (kala namak)
- cardamom, ground
- Chinese five-spice powder
- chipotle powder
- cocoa powder
- fenugreek seeds
- marjoram, dried
- poultry seasoning
- ras el hanout
- red curry paste
- shichimi togarashi
- Szechuan peppercorns
- wasabi powder

Legumes

- black beans, dried
- black beluga lentils, dried
- sprouted lentils
- white lentils, dried
- yellow split peas, dried

Milks

- chocolate almond milk

Nuts and Seeds (Raw)

- poppy seeds

Dried Fruits

- apricots
- cherries
- coconut chips
- coconut, unsweetened, shredded
- cranberries
- currants
- figs
- golden berries
- raisins

Seasonings

- gochujang
- soy sauce (gluten-free or regular)
- Sriracha salt
- umami paste
- Worcestershire sauce, vegan

Sweeteners

- coconut sugar
- molasses
- organic sugar, vegan

Vinegars and Oils

- 3-6-9 oil
- sesame oil

Other

- açai powder
- capers
- dried arame
- hominy (canned)
- lucuma powder
- nori
- dry white wine
- wild rice

KITCHEN TIPS

Cooking brown basmati rice

The most important thing to remember when cooking brown rice is to rinse it thoroughly. Put your rice in the pot you are going to cook it in or, if you're using a rice cooker, in the bowl of the cooker. Add plenty of water and swish the rice around with your hands. Pour the water off. Repeat two or more times, until the water runs clear. (This method works better than just rinsing the rice in a sieve, because it causes all the little hulls and loose bits to float to the top so you can pour them away. In a sieve, those bits would just get stuck in among the kernels and still be there in your finished rice.)

To cook the rice, add your cooking liquid (water or stock) to the pot. You need 2 cups (500 mL) of liquid for each cup (250 mL) of rice (taking into account that there will be some residual water in the rice from rinsing it). If you don't want to measure the cooking liquid (which we never do at the restaurants), just pour in enough to come about ½ inch (1 cm) above the surface of your rinsed rice. Cover pot with a lid. Bring to a boil, reduce heat to low, and simmer, covered, for about 40 minutes or until the rice is tender and the liquid has been absorbed.

If using a rice cooker, just add the cooking liquid to the rinsed rice and let the cooker do its thing. Let the rice sit in the pot with the lid on until ready to use.

Cooking quinoa

Quinoa must be thoroughly rinsed before cooking because it has a natural coating, called saponin, that can give the cooked grain a bitter or soapy taste. Some quinoa comes pre-rinsed, but it never hurts to rinse it yourself, just in case. You can either put the quinoa in a fine-mesh sieve and rinse it thoroughly under cool running water or put it in a bowl, cover it with cool water, swish it around with your hands, and pour off the water, repeating until the water runs clear.

To cook the quinoa, place it in a pot with water or stock, using a ratio of 1 part quinoa to 2 parts liquid. Bring to a boil, reduce the heat, cover, and simmer for about 15 minutes or until the quinoa is tender and all the liquid has been absorbed. Remove the pot from the heat and let stand with the lid on for a few minutes. Fluff and serve.

If using a rice cooker, use the same ratio of quinoa to liquid, and then let the cooker do its thing.

Grinding spices

The secret to getting good flavour from your spices is to toast and grind them right before use. Place your whole spices in a dry frying pan over medium heat. Cook, stirring or shaking the pan often, until they become fragrant and start to smoke a little. Then transfer them to a bowl and let cool. Grind in a clean spice grinder or with a mortar and pestle. (To remove spice residue from your spice grinder, just grind up some raw rice, dump out the resulting powder, and then wipe the grinder with a clean cloth.)

Preparing beans

Our recipes usually call for canned beans, but of course you can cook dried beans if you like (2 cups/500 mL of cooked beans is equivalent to one 19-ounce/540 mL can). Dried beans are not difficult to cook, but they do require one thing: time. You need to first soak them overnight (soaking helps to reduce the cooking time and makes them cook more evenly), and you may need to simmer them for over 3 hours until they become tender. Only embark on cooking dried beans if you know you'll be home for that long.

To begin, pick through the dried beans and discard any shrivelled beans or pebbles. Give them a rinse under cool running water to remove any dust and then put them in a bowl that's large enough to allow the beans to double in size. Cover and set aside in the fridge to soak overnight.

If you don't have time to soak the beans overnight, use the following quick-soak method: place the beans in a pot of water and bring to a boil. Remove from the heat and let the water and beans sit for an hour before draining. This method results in beans similar to those that have been soaked for 8 hours.

To cook, drain the soaking liquid and rinse the beans. Put them in a large pot with lots of water. Bring to a boil, reduce the heat to low, and simmer until the beans are tender. After about an hour, start checking to see how they're coming along. If you're in doubt about whether they're tender enough, they most likely aren't, so keep cooking them. Be sure to taste more than one bean, since in most batches of beans you'll find that some are tender while others are still a bit hard. Add more water as needed.

When the beans are almost ready, you can add some salt. Don't do this earlier in the process—it stops the beans from getting tender. Continue simmering until all of the beans are tender. Remove from the heat and let cool in their cooking liquid. Drain and use.

Puréeing

At the restaurants, we use a large commercial immersion blender for puréeing, which means we can purée soups while they're still hot. If you don't have an immersion blender and want to use a regular blender, cool any hot liquid before you blend it. No matter how tightly you secure the lid of your blender, if the liquid is hot, it will explode right out of the blender, sending the lid and the contents all over your kitchen—and worse, all over you!

Toasting nuts and seeds

To get more flavour from your nuts and seeds, toast them. You can do this in a dry pan over medium heat, shaking the pan often, or on a baking sheet in a 350°F (180°C) oven. Either way takes only about 3 to 5 minutes, so don't walk away—nuts and seeds tend to go from raw to burnt in the blink of an eye.

Zesting

Zesting means thinly peeling or grating the rind of a citrus fruit, excluding the white fibre called the pith. Although a box grater, zester, or knife will do the job, a kitchen rasp (we prefer the one made by Microplane) is the quickest and easiest way to get beautiful zest. They are available at most kitchen supply stores, and can also be used to grate ginger, nutmeg, and chocolate.

INGREDIENT BASICS

Agave nectar

This sweetener comes from the agave, a large spiky plant that thrives in the volcanic soil of Southern Mexico. (Tequila comes from the same plant.) Agave nectar is comparable to honey in taste and sweetness.

To make agave nectar, a seven- to ten-year-old agave plant is trimmed of its leaves, leaving the core of the plant, called the "pina." The pina resembles a giant pineapple and can weigh from 50 to 150 pounds (22.5 to 68 kg). Sap is extracted from the pina, and is then filtered and heated, which breaks down the carbohydrates into sugars. Lighter and darker varieties of agave nectar are made from the same plants.

Most brands of agave nectar have light and dark versions. Lighter syrups go through less heating and more thorough filtration, resulting in a mild-flavoured product. Darker agave nectars are filtered less and the solids are left in the syrup, resulting in a more intense flavour, sometimes compared to maple syrup. We use a light agave nectar in the restaurants.

Arame

Arame (pronounced ar-a-may) is a sea vegetable that grows in bunches intertwined with other sea vegetables. Dark yellow-brown in colour and tough in texture, it's chopped into string-like strips, then boiled and dried in the sun to a charcoal black. Arame's mild, sweet flavour makes it the most versatile of all the sea vegetables. One of the richest sources of iodine, arame also has highly concentrated doses of iron and calcium.

Arame must be soaked for 5 to 15 minutes before using (see Marinated Arame, page 162).

Bragg Liquid Aminos

This liquid protein concentrate—containing 16 amino acids—is made from soybeans and can be used in place of tamari or soy sauce. It is gluten-free and is not fermented or heated.

Butler Soy Curls

This vegan protein source is made from soybeans. The soy curls are sold in dry form, in bags. Once reconstituted, they look and feel very similar to pieces of sliced chicken. They absorb marinades very well, and can substitute for chicken in any traditional recipes.

Chia seeds

These tiny seeds were previously most famous for sprouting into the fur or hair of a Chia pet. I know that I sing the ch-ch-ch-chia song in my head whenever I think of them!

Chia seeds come from a flowering plant related to mint. In recent years, they have gained popularity because of their health benefits and their ability, when mixed with a liquid, to form a jelly-like substance that can be used as an egg replacement. That action is also why, when you eat chia seeds, you'll feel full for longer. They are loaded with fibre, protein, omega-3 fatty acids, and antioxidants.

Coconut oil

Look for a neutral-flavoured coconut oil so you can use it for cooking without imparting a coconut flavour to your other ingredients. It should specify right on the front of the jar that the oil has no flavour or smell; if not specified, it will probably taste very coconutty.

Coconut oil is extracted from mature coconut meat. It's gaining popularity with the health conscious because, among other health benefits, it helps the body build resistance to viruses, bacteria, fungi, and candida.

Date syrup

Made from dates that have been soaked, strained, and reduced, this dark-brown, sweet syrup is gluten-free and vegan. It can be used as a sweetener in any application. (We prefer Date Lady brand.)

Earth Balance

This creamy spread is vegan, trans fat–free, and gluten-free. It is a great substitute for butter.

Flaxseeds

Flaxseeds have been cultivated since 3000 BC and are now widely regarded as one of the most powerful plant foods on earth. Flax has three main healthy components: omega-3 essential fatty acids, lignans, and fibre. Regular consumption of flaxseeds is said to help control high blood pressure, reduce cholesterol levels, and prevent many types of cancer.

We use both flax oil and raw seeds. For our bodies to absorb their nutrients, the seeds must be ground. Keep ground flax in the freezer to prolong its shelf life. Whole flaxseeds keep almost indefinitely. You can buy pre-ground flaxseeds, or buy whole seeds and grind them yourself in a spice grinder or high-speed blender. Look for flax oil in dark bottles, and always keep it refrigerated since it can go rancid quickly.

Gluten-free flour

We use Bob's Red Mill Gluten Free All Purpose Baking Flour. There are a few different brands and blends out there, but this is the one we like best. It is a blend of garbanzo bean flour, potato starch, whole-grain white sorghum flour, tapioca flour, and fava bean flour. Look for it in better grocers and health-food stores.

Goji berries

These slightly sweet and slightly herbal red berries have been used for centuries in Chinese medicine. Fresh goji berries are available in Asia and Europe, but here in North America, we only see the dried versions. They are low calorie, fat-free, high fibre, and packed with antioxidants.

Golden berries

These chewy, tart, and slightly sweet dried berries have been cultivated for thousands of years in South America. They are a source of beta-carotene, protein, bioflavonoids, antioxidants, and vitamin A.

Hemp hearts (hulled hemp seeds)

Hemp is a distinct variety of the plant species *Cannabis sativa* L. The hemp plant is tall, slender, and fibrous, and similar to flax. It can grow to 14 feet (4.25 m) in height. Civilizations throughout history—including those in India, Babylonia, Persia, Egypt, and South America, and native cultures of North America and Europe—have cultivated the hemp plant.

Hemp seeds contain no THC, the chemical in marijuana that makes you high. Hemp contains 34.6 percent protein, 46.5 percent fat, 11.6 percent carbohydrate, plus omega-3 and omega-6 essential fatty acids and all essential amino acids.

The protective shell on hemp seeds is edible, but it's tough and tends to get stuck between the teeth. Hemp hearts, also called hulled hemp seeds, are soft and have a pleasant nutty taste that is delicious in salads, bowls, and smoothies.

Microgreens

Microgreens are tiny plants that have three basic parts: a central stem; cotyledon leaf or leaves; and, typically, the first pair of very young true leaves. They vary in size depending upon the specific variety grown, with the typical length being 1 to 1½ inches (2.5 to 4 cm). Microgreens are smaller than baby greens but harvested later than sprouts, usually around 1 to 2 weeks after sprouting.

There are many varieties to choose from, offering different colours, textures, and flavours. We use an organic microgreen mix from Greenbelt Greenhouse that contains speckled pea, red daikon radish, arugula, ruby streak mustard, and red choi. These days, you can find many different blends in grocery stores, ranging from sweet to spicy.

Miso

Miso is a fermented soybean paste thought to have originated in China 2500 years ago. Miso consists of cooked soybeans, salt, and various grains (barley or rice) that are fermented from 2 weeks to more than 2 years. Miso varieties differ in formulation, salt concentration, and fermenting time, resulting in ranges of flavour and texture from sweet and delicate to meaty and savoury. The darker varieties—reds and browns—tend to be riper, higher in salt, and stronger in flavour. The lighter varieties—yellows and golds— are sweet and mild. We use a light and mild soy miso.

Miso is considered a living food that contains friendly bacteria as well as traces of vitamin B12 and high levels of protein. The intense flavour that miso brings to any dish reduces the need to season with the usual fats, oils, and salts.

Boiling will kill the enzymes and nutrients in miso that make it good for you, so miso is usually added right at the end of a recipe, when the pot is already off the heat.

Nori

Nori, which is a jade-green colour, is harvested in Japan, Ireland, and Scotland. Its fibres are more tender and delicate than those of other sea vegetables. Once harvested, nori is dried, pressed flat into paper-thin sheets, and then toasted. Its mild flavour makes it the preferred wrap for sushi rolls or addition to soups and rice bowls (just tear the sheets into pieces). Rich in vitamins A, B1, and niacin, nori has the highest protein content and is the most easily digested of all sea vegetables.

Nutritional yeast

Nutritional yeast, often called by its nickname "nooch," is a fungus grown on mineral-enriched molasses and is one of the rare vegetarian sources of vitamin B12. It is harvested, washed, and then dried with heat to deactivate it, so it doesn't have the properties of active baking yeast, such as making doughs rise.

It is not the same as brewer's yeast, so don't buy that by mistake. Brewer's yeast is bitter, whereas nutritional yeast has a strong, savoury, nutty, almost cheese-like flavour. It's great straight—just sprinkled on toast or pasta—but at the restaurants, we use it to give the delicious depth of flavour and umami (savoury) element to our scrambled tofu, "cheese" sauce, miso gravy, and crispy tofu.

It comes in two different forms: powdered (also referred to as Engevita yeast) and flaked. If you can't find the powdered version, go ahead and substitute with flakes, which are available in most grocery stores these days.

Nooch is highly nutritious: it has vitamins, folic acid, selenium, zinc, and protein, along with vitamin B12, which makes it a great addition to a vegan diet.

Olive oil

There are many different grades of olive oil, from the top-level extra virgin to the lowest-grade pomace. Extra virgin is from the first pressing after olives are harvested. Pomace is squeezed out of the olive pulp left after making extra virgin and regular olive oil. For everyday home cooking, a mild-flavoured, mid-range olive oil is fine. Don't waste your money on an expensive extra virgin olive oil for cooking because heat will cause its flavour to be lost. Save the really good stuff for drizzling on salads, vegetables, bread— anywhere that you can fully appreciate its flavour.

Panko

This Japanese-style breadcrumb is made from bread specially baked without crusts. The light, airy flakes form a crispy and crunchy coating for fried foods.

Sambal oelek

Sambal oelek is a bright-red hot sauce made from red chilies, vinegar, and salt. It has no other flavourings, making for a simple taste and a clean way to add heat to a dish without altering the other flavours.

Sprouted lentils

Sprouted grains, legumes, and pulses have three times the nutrients of unsprouted. After sprouting, lentils are dehydrated at the peak of their enzyme levels and nutrient value. They are packed with vitamins, minerals, and amino acids.

Sprouting releases absorbable minerals, making the nutrients more available to the body. Sprouting also breaks down gluten, making the lentils more digestible for some people.

Sunflower oil

Sunflower oil is light in flavour and colour, and is a good choice when you need an oil that doesn't add any flavour.

Tahini

Tahini, or "raw tahini," is simply ground sesame seeds. It's used as the base for many different sauces and dressings, such as our Tahini Dressing (page 174), 3-6-9 Dressing (page 173), and Miso Tahini Sauce (page 257). Its mild flavour makes it very versatile, lending a rich creaminess to any dish.

Tamari

This Japanese form of soy sauce is traditionally a by-product of miso production. Tamari has a darker colour and richer flavour than common Chinese soy sauce. It also has a more balanced flavour and is less salty.

A higher concentration of soybeans causes tamari to ferment differently than soy sauce, so it retains its composition and richer, smooth flavour when heated. Since it doesn't break down or "flash" when exposed to high temperatures, it never gives food an overwhelmingly salty taste. We use gluten-free tamari.

Tempeh

Tempeh (pronounced *tem-pay*) is a fermented high-protein product made from whole soybeans. Created in Indonesia, it's traditionally used in Thai, Indonesian, and Malaysian cooking. To make tempeh, whole soybeans are soaked in water, hulled, boiled, formed into cakes or patties, and left to ferment. Fermentation makes for easier digestion of the soy protein.

Tempeh is often confused with tofu; however, they are actually very different in appearance, texture, and taste. Tofu—smooth, silky, and neutral in flavour—is produced from the curds of fermented soy milk. Tempeh—meaty, chewy, and nutty in flavour—is produced from the whole soybean. Tempeh is comparable to chicken in terms of quantity and quality of protein but has no cholesterol. It's a complete protein, containing all of the essential amino acids.

Tempeh is high in B vitamins, calcium, essential fatty acids, fibre, and healthy enzymes. It contains soy isoflavones, which strengthen bones and reduce risk of coronary heart disease. There are up to 30 varieties of tempeh available; different kinds are made by combining soybeans with other ingredients, such as brown rice, millet, quinoa, sea vegetables, or sesame seeds, and allowing the mixture to ferment for varying lengths of time. We use plain soy tempeh, since we make both tempeh bacon and grilled tempeh with it.

Tempeh is also an excellent source of vitamin B12—a bonus for vegans. The tempeh found in most natural food stores is frozen, but it is available fresh, dried, or pre-cooked. Fresh tempeh is highly perishable, which is why we buy ours frozen. You can either thaw it at room temperature or briefly blanch it before cooking.

Although it can be cooked in any number of ways, at the restaurants we like to cut it into thin strips, and then marinate and grill it.

Tofu

Poor tofu! It gets so much flak from people who think they hate it. But it's actually one of the most versatile ingredients around. It absorbs marinades beautifully and lends itself to almost any cooking method, although it can also be eaten raw. I am confident that preparing tofu in any of the ways described in this book will sway even the most ardent tofu-hater. In an average month at the restaurants, we go through about 6500 pounds (2950 kg) of tofu, and there's no way that would happen if it didn't taste good!

Tofu is made by coagulating soy milk and pressing the resulting curds into blocks. It can be silken, soft, firm, or extra firm. We use the extra firm variety to make our tofu steaks and cubes.

Tofu is low in calories, has a relatively high amount of protein, and is high in iron. It contains B vitamins, calcium, phosphorous, selenium, and all eight essential amino acids.

If you open a package of tofu and don't use it all, put what's left in an airtight container, cover it with water, and store it in your fridge. If you change the water daily, the tofu will keep for up to a week.

BREAKFAST AND BRUNCH

Weekend brunch at the Fresh locations is always busy, fun, and a little bit crazy. As soon as we open, the restaurants fill with young families. Strollers line the aisles. As the rest of the world ventures out, the strollers are replaced by shopping bags, and the day goes by in a blur to the soundtrack of juicers, blenders, and espresso machines. Customers arrive hungry for a hearty breakfast and revitalizing fresh juice. Lines form as people wait to sit on the patios in the warmer months. Sweet and savoury cooking smells waft from the open kitchens, bringing hints of the good food to come. Brunch is one of our busiest times, but it is also the time when our customers are the most relaxed.

To us, brunch is about indulging in yummy comfort foods that make you feel satiated without resorting to the use of old standards like eggs, cheese, cream, and butter. At home, you can capture the Fresh brunch experience with dishes from the restaurants as well as some breakfast items developed especially for this book. From oats to scrambled tofu to pancakes, start your day off right with any of these easy-to-make recipes.

scrambled tofu

This scrambled tofu recipe has formed the cornerstone of our brunch menu for over a decade. We use it in the Asparagus Toast (page 120), Spinach Tofu Wrap (page 108), Green Eggs (page 111), and Nuevos Rancheros (page 111).

You will see that we make the seasonings and spices into a paste with some water before adding to the tofu. This step really wakes up the flavours and helps them to coat every last bit of the tofu, so make sure you don't skip it.

This mixture will keep in the fridge for up to 3 days. To reheat, add a little water and warm in a pan over medium heat until water has evaporated.

We use powdered nutritional yeast (also known as Engevita or inactive yeast) at the restaurants, but if you can't find it, you can substitute flaked nutritional yeast.

makes 2 cups (500 mL)

2 tbsp (30 mL) olive oil

1 cup (250 mL) finely diced onion

1 clove garlic, minced

1 tbsp (15 mL) powdered nutritional yeast

¾ tsp (3 mL) dried dill

1 tsp (5 mL) garlic powder

½ tsp (2 mL) sea salt

½ tsp (2 mL) freshly ground black pepper

Pinch ground turmeric

¼ cup (60 mL) water

2 cups (500 mL) chopped extra firm tofu

1. Heat oil in a large frying pan or wok over medium-high heat.

2. Add onion and garlic and cook for a few minutes, stirring often, until softened.

3. Meanwhile, in a small bowl, combine nutritional yeast, dill, garlic powder, salt, pepper, and turmeric. Add water and stir to make a paste.

4. Using your fingers, crumble tofu into very small pieces and add to pan.

5. Pour paste over tofu mixture and stir until thoroughly combined.

6. Bring to a boil, stirring occasionally, and cook until heated through and liquid has evaporated.

7. Serve immediately or let cool and refrigerate for up to 3 days. To reheat, add a little water and warm in a pan over medium heat until water has evaporated.

spinach tofu wrap

For years, this was one of our most popular breakfast specials. The addition of carrots is a bit unusual for breakfast, but really works with the other elements in this wrap. If you are a fan of alfalfa sprouts, go ahead and add some of those as well.

serves 2

2 tbsp [30 mL] olive oil

2 cups [500 mL] lightly packed chopped spinach

1 cup [250 mL] grated carrots

1 tomato, chopped

½ batch Scrambled Tofu [page 107]

1 tbsp [15 mL] water

2 10-inch [25 cm] spinach tortillas

¼ cup [60 mL] Garlic Mayo [page 268]

1. Preheat oven to 350°F [180°C].

2. Heat oil in a frying pan over medium heat.

3. Add spinach, carrots, and tomato. Cook, stirring often, for a minute or two, until slightly softened.

4. Stir in scrambled tofu and water. Cook until liquid has evaporated.

5. Place tortillas on a baking sheet and warm for 2 minutes in pre-heated oven.

6. Spread garlic mayo over warmed tortillas.

7. Divide tofu mixture evenly between tortillas.

8. Fold edges of tortilla in, and then roll into a cylinder. Using a sharp knife, cut in half on the diagonal.

pumpkin seed and kale scramble

You'll really be set up for the day after eating this protein-packed tofu scramble. For a satiating creaminess, try serving this with either Fresh "Cheese" Sauce (page 251) or sliced avocado on top.

serves 2

2 tsp (10 mL) sunflower oil or neutral-flavoured coconut oil

6 cups (1.5 L) lightly packed thinly sliced kale leaves (thick rib removed, leaves cut into thin strips)

2 tsp (10 mL) tamari

2 tbsp (30 mL) raw pumpkin seeds

2 tbsp (30 mL) raw hemp hearts

1 batch Scrambled Tofu (page 107)

½ cup (125 mL) Fresh "Cheese" Sauce (optional; page 251)

6 slices avocado (optional)

1 cup (250 mL) grape tomatoes, halved

Sea salt and freshly ground black pepper, to taste

1. Heat oil in large frying pan or wok over medium-high heat.

2. Add kale and tamari, and cook for 1 to 2 minutes or until kale is softened. Add pumpkin seeds, hemp hearts, and scrambled tofu. Cook, stirring, for 1 to 2 minutes or until warmed through.

3. Divide mixture evenly between 2 plates and top with either "cheese" sauce or sliced avocado (if using). Serve with tomatoes on the side, seasoned with salt and pepper.

breakfast quesadilla

Tempeh bacon, scrambled tofu, mushrooms, kale, tomato, and cheesy sauce inside a crispy tortilla? How could you say no to that?

serves 1

2 tsp (10 mL) sunflower oil or neutral-flavoured coconut oil, divided

½ cup (125 mL) sliced button mushrooms

2 slices Tempeh Bacon (page 273), chopped

1 cup (250 mL) shredded kale

1 12-inch (30 cm) whole-wheat tortilla or 2 6-inch (15 cm) whole-wheat tortillas

½ cup (125 mL) Fresh "Cheese" Sauce (page 251) or non-dairy cheese (we prefer Daiya)

¼ cup (60 mL) chopped tomato

½ cup (125 mL) Scrambled Tofu (page 107)

Ketchup or hot sauce, for serving (optional)

1. Heat 1 tsp (5 mL) oil in a large frying pan.

2. Add mushrooms and tempeh bacon and cook, stirring occasionally, until browned (use a fork to turn each mushroom slice individually to brown both sides).

3. Stir in kale and cook for a minute, until kale is softened. Remove from heat.

4. Lay tortilla flat on plate. Spread one half of tortilla with "cheese" sauce. Top with kale mixture, followed by tomato and scrambled tofu mixture. Fold other side over fillings.

5. Wipe out pan. Heat remaining 1 tsp (5 mL) oil over medium heat.

6. Carefully place quesadilla into pan and cook until bottom is browned. Flip and cook other side until browned.

7. Serve with ketchup or hot sauce (if using).

green eggs

This scrambled tofu mixture is great served with toast, sliced tomato (either raw or grilled), Home Fries (page 119), baked beans, and vegan sausages or bacon.

serves 2

2 tbsp (30 mL) olive oil

½ red bell pepper, chopped

½ green bell pepper, chopped

1 cup (250 mL) sliced button mushrooms

1 batch Scrambled Tofu (page 107)

1 tbsp (15 mL) water

1. Heat oil in a frying pan over medium heat.

2. Add red and green peppers and mushrooms. Cook for a few minutes, stirring occasionally, until mushrooms are browned.

3. Add scrambled tofu and water. Cook for a minute or so, stirring, until tofu is heated through and liquid has evaporated.

nuevos rancheros

Add some spice to your mornings with our version of this classic Mexican dish. It is an unusual breakfast, perfect for those days when you feel like something a little different.

serves 2

¼ cup (60 mL) olive oil

4 6-inch (15 cm) corn tortillas

Pinch sea salt

2 tomatoes, chopped

1 jalapeño pepper, minced

1 batch Scrambled Tofu (page 107)

1 tbsp (15 mL) water

½ avocado, sliced

1 green onion, sliced

½ batch Spicy Black Beans, warmed (page 236)

1. Heat oil in a frying pan over medium heat. Add corn tortillas and fry for about a minute, until crisp. (You may have to do this one at a time, depending on the size of your pan.) Remove from heat. Sprinkle cooked tortillas with salt, transfer to paper towels to drain, and set aside.

2. Drain out all but 1 tbsp (15 mL) of oil from pan. Return pan to heat. Add tomatoes and jalapeño and cook for 1 to 2 minutes or until jalapeño is softened.

3. Add scrambled tofu and water. Cook, stirring, for 1 to 2 minutes or until tofu is heated through.

4. Place 2 tortillas onto each plate and top with scrambled tofu mixture.

5. Garnish with avocado slices and green onion.

6. Serve with warmed spicy black beans on the side.

tofu omelettes

This omelette mixture can be folded around any fillings you like best. It is quite flavourful, so I like it best with mild fillings. You'll find a few suggestions below, but feel free to try any of your favourites. (This mixture is also used in the Shinto Rice Bowl, page 229.)

The amount of gluten flour required will vary, depending on the day. (As with most doughs, the heat and humidity in the air can affect the consistency, so just add a little more flour if needed; see below.) If you have time, let the mixture sit for a couple of hours in the fridge to make it easier to roll out.

serves 6

2 tsp (10 mL) sunflower oil or neutral-flavoured coconut oil + more for frying

½ cup (125 mL) sliced onion

½ cup (125 mL) grated carrot

½ cup (125 mL) chopped green onions

3 cloves garlic, roughly chopped

3 cups (750 mL) chopped extra firm tofu

2 tbsp (30 mL) flaked nutritional yeast

½ cup (125 mL) gluten flour (vital wheat gluten)

1½ tsp (7 mL) sea salt

1½ tsp (7 mL) freshly ground black pepper

Whole-wheat flour, for dusting

suggested omelette fillings

Tomato, avocado, and vegan sour cream (see recipe on page 275)

Sautéed asparagus

Sautéed mushrooms

Sautéed napa cabbage

Mashed avocado and fresh herbs

1. Heat oil in a frying pan over medium heat. Add onion and cook, stirring occasionally, until browned, 5 to 10 minutes. Remove from heat and set aside to cool.

2. Combine cooked onion, carrot, green onions, and garlic in a food processor. Process until finely minced.

3. Add tofu and process until thoroughly combined.

4. Add nutritional yeast, gluten flour, salt, and pepper and process until combined. (Mixture should be firm, elastic, and easy to handle. If it is sticky, add some more gluten flour, 1 tbsp/15 mL at a time, and process until combined and mixture reaches desired consistency.)

5. Turn mixture out of food processor and divide into 6 equal portions (about ½ cup/125 mL each).

6. Sprinkle a clean work surface with whole-wheat flour. Working with 1 portion at a time, roll or press mixture into a 6-inch (15 cm) circle about ¼ inch (0.5 cm) thick. Repeat with remaining portions.

7. In a large frying pan, heat enough oil to just cover the bottom of the pan over medium-high heat. Working in batches so as not to crowd the pan, cook omelettes for about 3 minutes or until browned on the bottom. Slide onto a plate. Add a little more oil to the pan and return omelette to pan; cook other side until browned.

8. If necessary, keep omelettes warm in a 250°F (120°C) oven while cooking remaining omelettes. Serve with your favourite fillings.

flying saucers

These little discs are an easy grab-and-go when you are on your way out the door in the morning or you need a great mid-afternoon pick-me-up.

This is my favourite combination, but the possibilities are endless. These are a great way to use up any little odds and ends of dried fruits and nuts that you have hanging around. The lucuma in this combination adds a certain caramel nuttiness that I love. The puffed quinoa lightens up the whole mix. If you can't find puffed quinoa, try puffed millet instead.

makes 20

⅔ cup (150 mL) raw cashews

⅓ cup (75 mL) raw hazelnuts

⅓ cup (75 mL) raw almonds, roughly chopped

⅓ cup (75 mL) raw pecans

2 tbsp (30 mL) ground flaxseeds

¼ cup (60 mL) raw hemp hearts

2 tbsp (30 mL) raw pumpkin seeds

⅓ cup (75 mL) dried unsweetened cherries or cranberries

½ tsp (2 mL) ground cinnamon

1 tsp (5 mL) lucuma powder (optional)

¼ cup (60 mL) date syrup

1 cup (250 mL) puffed quinoa

1. Combine cashews, hazelnuts, almonds, pecans, ground flaxseeds, hemp hearts, and pumpkin seeds in a food processor and process just until finely chopped (don't let it turn into nut butter).

2. Add cherries, cinnamon, lucuma powder, and date syrup and process until cherries are finely chopped.

3. Add puffed quinoa and pulse to combine.

4. Transfer mixture to a large bowl and knead with your hands to bring it all together.

5. Roll mixture into small balls (about 1 to 2 tbsp/15 to 30 mL each), and then press between your palms to form into a disc. Stack in an airtight container and refrigerate for up to 2 weeks.

brussels sprout fritters with smoked tofu and hollandaise sauce

My family has been eating Brussels sprouts every Sunday or holiday dinner for years, so it's nice to see them surging in popularity right now. I never understood why they got such a bad rap, so I'm glad those days are over!

The smoked tofu adds an amazing savoury depth of flavour to these fritters. And while the truffle oil is a nice addition, don't go out and buy it just for this dish—use it only if you happen to have some in your cupboard or if you particularly like it.

serves 4 to 6

2 cups (500 mL) Brussels sprouts, shredded (about 10 sprouts)

1 cup (250 mL) shredded smoked extra firm tofu

1 cup (250 mL) gluten-free all-purpose flour (we prefer Bob's Red Mill)

¼ cup (60 mL) raw pumpkin seeds

1 tbsp (15 mL) ground flaxseeds

½ tsp (2 mL) sea salt

½ tsp (2 mL) baking powder

½ tsp (2 mL) baking soda

½ tsp (2 mL) crushed red chilies

1 cup (250 mL) plain unsweetened soy milk

Oil, for frying (sunflower, canola, or neutral-flavoured coconut oil)

garnishes

1 batch Hollandaise Sauce (page 252), warmed

1 avocado, sliced

1½ cups (375 mL) grape tomatoes, halved

Sea salt and freshly ground black pepper, to taste

3 cups (750 mL) assorted microgreens

Truffle oil, to taste (optional)

1. Combine Brussels sprouts, tofu, flour, pumpkin seeds, flaxseeds, salt, baking powder, baking soda, and crushed red chilies in a large bowl and stir well.

2. Add soy milk and stir until a thick batter forms.

3. Heat a little oil in a frying pan over medium-low heat. Drop batter ¼ cup (60 mL) at a time into the hot oil. Cook for 3 to 5 minutes per side or until golden brown and cooked through. Repeat with remaining batter. Keep cooked fritters warm in a 250°F (120°C) oven, if desired.

4. Arrange 2 fritters on each plate. Top fritters with equal amounts of hollandaise sauce, avocado, tomato, and salt and pepper. Mound equal portions of microgreens on top.

5. Drizzle with truffle oil (if using). Serve.

Tip: To prepare the Brussels sprouts, cut off the stem end and remove any yucky-looking outer leaves. Using a food processor, mandoline, or sharp knife, cut them into fine shreds.

tempeh florentine

This breakfast entrée really works because of the smokiness of the tempeh bacon combined with the creamy, lemony hollandaise. Go ahead and add some scrambled tofu if you'd like to make it a bit more substantial.

We use sprouted grain English muffins, but if you can't find them, just use regular whole-wheat ones. We serve this with either a cup of soup, Home Fries (page 119), or a small Superfood Salad (page 156).

serves 2

½ tsp (2 mL) sunflower oil or neutral-flavoured coconut oil

8 cups (2 L) lightly packed baby spinach leaves

½ tsp (2 mL) tamari

2 sprouted whole-grain English muffins, split in half

Non-dairy buttery spread (we prefer Earth Balance)

8 slices Tempeh Bacon, cooked (page 273)

4 large slices tomato

Sea salt and freshly ground black pepper, to taste

½ cup (125 mL) Hollandaise Sauce, warmed (page 252)

2 tsp (10 mL) raw hemp hearts

1. Heat oil in large frying pan or wok over high heat.

2. Add spinach and tamari and cook, tossing constantly, until spinach is wilted, about a minute or less. Remove from heat and set aside.

3. Toast English muffins and spread with non-dairy butter.

4. Place 2 English muffins halves on each plate and top each half with 2 slices of tempeh bacon and 1 slice of tomato. Sprinkle tomatoes with salt and pepper.

5. Divide spinach evenly among muffins.

6. Top spinach with hollandaise and hemp hearts. Serve with side of your choice.

gallo pinto

Gallo pinto means "spotted rooster" in Spanish—the name comes from the appearance of the black beans and rice all mixed together. This is a traditional Nicaraguan and Costa Rican breakfast dish, and it makes a great brunch item, especially when served with a green salad and some sliced avocado. Prepping beans and rice this way really elevates both of them. Serve with Lizano, a traditional Costa Rican condiment, or substitute HP Sauce or vegan Worcestershire sauce.

serves 4

9 cups [2.1 L] water

1 cup [250 mL] dried black beans

½ cup [125 mL] chopped fresh cilantro

1½ tsp [7 mL] dried oregano

2 cloves garlic, whole

1 tbsp [15 mL] olive oil

1½ cups [375 mL] chopped onions

2 cloves garlic, minced

2 tbsp [30 mL] tamari

½ tsp [2 mL] sea salt

3 cups [750 mL] cooked brown basmati rice

1. Combine water, beans, cilantro, oregano, and whole garlic in a large pot and bring to a boil.

2. Reduce heat and simmer until beans are tender, 1½ to 2 hours.

3. Drain beans and discard garlic. Set aside.

4. In a saucepan, heat oil over medium-high heat. Add onions and minced garlic and cook, stirring, until softened, about 5 minutes. Stir in tamari and salt.

5. Add cooked bean mixture, mashing beans into the onions slightly using a wooden spoon or potato masher.

6. Stir in cooked basmati rice and cook, stirring, until mixture is heated through, about 2 minutes.

home fries

The secret to great home fries is blanching them first. Shaking the potatoes around in the pan breaks up the edges and creates lots of little nooks and crannies that get nice and crispy.

serves 2 to 4

6 cups (1.5 L) water

4 cups (1 L) chopped potatoes (cut into bite-size pieces)

3 bay leaves

3 cloves garlic, roughly chopped

1 tbsp (15 mL) sea salt

3 tbsp (45 mL) olive oil

Sea salt, to taste

1. Combine water, potatoes, bay leaves, garlic, and salt in a large saucepan over high heat and bring to a boil.

2. Reduce heat and simmer for 10 to 15 minutes or until potatoes are almost tender.

3. Preheat oven to 400°F (200°C).

4. Drain potatoes. Discard bay leaves.

5. Return potatoes to pot, shaking them around a bit to roughen up the edges.

6. Add oil and toss to coat well.

7. Spread potatoes in a single layer on a baking sheet. Bake in preheated oven until crispy, 20 to 30 minutes, turning halfway through the cooking time.

8. Remove from oven. Sprinkle with salt (if using). Serve.

asparagus toast

This breakfast is so savoury and tempting, and is an easy way to get something green into your day right away. The easiest way to prep asparagus is to take each piece in your hand and bend it in half. It will break at the point where it becomes tough, leaving you with the tender part to use for your recipe.

For the toast, I use a large piece of rye bread, but you can use whatever kind you like. If your bread is small, use two pieces. The scrambled tofu will overflow onto the plate anyway.

serves 2

2 tsp (10 mL) olive oil or neutral-flavoured coconut oil

2 cups (500 mL) chopped asparagus (cut into bite-size pieces)

½ batch Scrambled Tofu (page 107)

2 large pieces bread

Non-dairy buttery spread (we prefer Earth Balance)

½ cup (125 mL) grape tomatoes, halved

½ cup (125 mL) Fresh "Cheese" Sauce (page 251) or Tofu Sour Cream (page 275)

½ avocado, sliced (optional)

1. Heat oil in large frying pan or wok over high heat.

2. Add asparagus and sauté for 1 to 2 minutes or until tender-crisp and starting to brown.

3. Add scrambled tofu and cook, stirring, for a minute or two, until heated through. (It is also good if you leave it undisturbed in the pan for a minute and let the tofu brown.)

4. Meanwhile, toast bread and spread with non-dairy butter.

5. Place 1 piece of toast on each plate and top with scrambled tofu mixture.

6. Top with grape tomatoes and "cheese" sauce or vegan sour cream.

7. Arrange avocado slices (if using) over top.

leek and mushroom toast

Mushrooms on toast is a classic British dish, and is incredibly satisfying when paired with some leeks and scrambled tofu. Sliced button mushrooms work just fine, or use a mix of whichever mushrooms strike your fancy. Serve this with a simple salad on the side, or some sliced tomatoes topped with sea salt and freshly ground black pepper.

serves 2

2 tsp (10 mL) sunflower oil or neutral-flavoured coconut oil

1 cup (250 mL) sliced leeks, white and green parts

4 cups (1 L) sliced button mushrooms

1 cup (250 mL) Scrambled Tofu (page 107)

¼ cup (60 mL) Lemon Garlic Glaze (page 255)

2 large slices bread

Non-dairy buttery spread (we prefer Earth Balance)

2 tsp (10 mL) raw hemp hearts

1. Heat oil in a large frying pan over medium-high heat.

2. Add leeks and mushrooms, and cook until browned, 5 to 10 minutes.

3. Add scrambled tofu and lemon garlic glaze, and cook for 1 to 2 minutes or until heated through.

4. Meanwhile, toast bread and spread with non-dairy butter.

5. Place 1 piece of toast on each plate and top each with half of the mushroom mixture.

6. Sprinkle with hemp hearts.

cauliflower benedict

This is the perfect hangover breakfast. The crispy cauliflower satisfies your desire for a greasy-spoon brekkie, and the greens, tomato, and avocado help you to not feel guilty! If you're really hungry, serve with a side of Tempeh Bacon (page 273) and Home Fries (page 119).

serves 2

½ batch Dosa Batter (page 266)

2 cups (500 mL) chopped cauliflower (cut into small florets)

1 cup (250 mL) panko crumbs

Oil, for frying (sunflower, canola, or neutral-flavoured coconut oil)

Sea salt, to taste

4 cups (1 L) lightly packed chopped kale (thick ribs removed)

1 tsp (5 mL) tamari

4 large slices tomato

⅔ to 1 cup (150 to 250 mL) Hollandaise Sauce (page 252), warmed

8 slices avocado

2 tsp (10 mL) raw hemp hearts

1. Combine dosa batter and cauliflower in a large bowl. Toss until cauliflower is completely coated. Set aside.

2. Place about one-quarter of the panko in a shallow bowl. Working in batches, add battered cauliflower and toss until thoroughly coated. (Discard panko that has become saturated with dosa batter, and add fresh panko to the bowl as needed.) Set aside coated florets.

3. In a large frying pan or wok, heat about ¼ inch (0.5 cm) of oil over medium-high heat.

4. When oil is hot, carefully add prepared cauliflower to pan, working in batches if necessary so as not to crowd the pan.

5. Cook for 2 to 4 minutes, turning cauliflower as needed to brown on all sides.

6. Transfer cooked cauliflower to paper towel to drain excess oil. Immediately sprinkle with salt. Repeat with remaining cauliflower.

7. Once all of the cauliflower is cooked, drain most of the oil out of the pan, leaving just a thin coating on the bottom of the pan. Reduce heat to medium and add kale and tamari. Sauté until kale is bright green and tender. (If kale leaves are particularly tough and you find it necessary, add a little water to the pan and cover with a lid to steam and soften the kale.)

8. Divide cooked cauliflower evenly between plates. Top with tomato and sautéed kale. Garnish with warm hollandaise sauce, avocado, salt, and hemp hearts.

banana walnut polenta with coconut whip

The secret to making good polenta is cooking it long enough. When you make it, you will see that about a minute after you add the cornmeal to the water, the mixture gets really thick and looks as if it's done. But don't be fooled. If you stop cooking it then, it will be grainy and raw tasting. You need to cook it for about 40 minutes, at which point you will see that the colour lightens and each grain of cornmeal softens, so that the whole thing is beautifully smooth. Just be sure to cook it over really low heat, or you'll get a lava-like explosion of polenta all over your kitchen!

You can cook the polenta the day before and keep it in the fridge until you are ready to reheat it. Or you could even buy one of the logs of prepared polenta that are available at most grocery stores. Top with either Coconut Whip or Tofu Whip. Alternatively, you can buy vegan whipped topping; it's available in coconut, soy, and rice varieties. Serve with fruit salad or sliced berries.

serves 4

6 cups (1.5 L) water
1½ cups (375 mL) coarsely ground yellow cornmeal
2 tbsp (30 mL) organic vegan sugar
1 tsp (5 mL) ground cinnamon
¼ cup (60 mL) sunflower oil

4 bananas, sliced
½ cup (125 mL) pure dark maple syrup
1 cup (250 mL) chopped walnuts, toasted (page 274)
1 batch Tofu Whip or Coconut Whip

1. Bring water to a boil in a large saucepan.

2. Combine cornmeal, sugar, and cinnamon in a bowl.

3. While stirring, pour cornmeal mixture into the boiling water in a slow, steady stream.

4. Bring mixture to a boil, stirring constantly, then reduce heat to low. Cook for 40 minutes, stirring occasionally.

5. Using a spatula, spread polenta into a ½-inch (1 cm) thick rectangle on an oiled baking sheet, smoothing the top as much as you can.

6. Cover with plastic wrap and refrigerate for about 30 minutes, until polenta firms up.

7. Cut polenta into 8 squares, and then cut those squares in half on the diagonal to form triangles.

8. Bake, grill, or sauté polenta until heated through, then keep warm in a 250°F (120°C) oven (see Tip).

9. Heat oil in a frying pan over medium heat. Add bananas and cook, stirring occasionally, until browned, about 2 minutes.

10. Add maple syrup and walnuts, and cook until heated through, about 1 minute.

11. Divide polenta among plates, pour banana mixture over top, and garnish with coconut cream or tofu whip.

Tip: To bake polenta, brush with 1 tbsp (15 mL) oil. Arrange in a single layer on a baking sheet and bake in a 400°F (200°C) oven for 10 to 15 minutes or until heated through. To grill polenta, brush polenta with 1 tbsp (15 mL) oil, then grill for about 5 minutes per side or until heated through. To sauté polenta, heat 1 tbsp (15 mL) of oil in a skillet over medium heat. Add polenta and cook for about 5 minutes per side or until heated through.

coconut whip

Coconut whip is simple to make, but it is totally dependent upon whether your can of coconut milk separates or not—it is the thick cream that settles in the can that you need to make this recipe. The contents of some cans just don't separate, even when you buy brands that have no emulsifiers like guar gum. So if you are lucky enough to get a can that does separate, make this coconut whip! If not, have another kind of vegan whipped topping standing by!

1 can (14 oz/414 mL) coconut milk, refrigerated overnight

1 tsp (5 mL) pure vanilla extract

1 tbsp (15 mL) sweetener of your choice (raw agave nectar, pure dark maple syrup, coconut sugar)

1. Turn the can upside down, open, and pour off the liquid. (You can save this liquid to add to smoothies, soups, or anywhere that you could use a little coconut flavour.)

2. Place solids in a large bowl and add vanilla and sweetener.

3. Whip with a whisk or electric mixer until light, fluffy, and mixture resembles whipped cream. (You could also use a stand mixer with the wire whisk attachment.) Coconut whip is best if used immediately, but will keep in the fridge in an airtight container for up to 1 week. You may need to re-whip it after it sits in the fridge to fluff it back up.

tofu whip

To get a perfectly smooth consistency from the tofu, a high-speed blender is your best friend. If you don't have one, you can use a food processor, but it will take quite a while for it to get through the gritty stage and enter the creamy stage. Just be patient and scrape down the sides of the work bowl periodically, and it will eventually get there.

2 cups (500 mL) chopped extra firm tofu

½ tsp (2 mL) pure vanilla extract

3 tbsp (45 mL) raw agave nectar

¼ tsp (1 mL) sea salt

½ cup (125 mL) vanilla non-dairy milk

1. Combine all of the ingredients in a blender.

2. Blend on high speed until smooth. Use immediately or transfer to an airtight container and refrigerate for up to 3 days.

overnight oats

My trainer, Jessica Manning, turned me on to the concept of overnight oats. They are the perfect thing to eat before a morning workout if you're not really a breakfast person but need something to give you energy. There's no excuse for skipping breakfast if you've already made this the night before! These are even good as a treat at night.

I've provided 7 variations, and most don't include any sweeteners, since I've found that the sweetness seems to dissipate overnight. Add the sweetener of your choice right before eating, if you like. Each variation includes 1 tbsp (15 mL) steel-cut oats. The steel-cut oats stay quite firm and add a chewiness that I like, but feel free to omit them if you prefer a softer texture.

Overnight oats will keep for up to 3 days in the fridge, so make up to 3 servings at a time so you can enjoy them several times during the week.

serves 1

peach melba
⅓ cup (75 mL) large flake (old-fashioned) rolled oats

1 tsp (5 mL) chia seeds

1 tbsp (15 mL) steel-cut oats

¾ cup (175 mL) vanilla almond milk

½ cup (125 mL) sliced fresh peaches

¼ cup (60 mL) raspberries (fresh or frozen)

2 tsp (10 mL) sliced almonds

bananas foster
⅓ cup (75 mL) large flake (old-fashioned) rolled oats

1 tsp (5 mL) chia seeds

1 tbsp (15 mL) steel-cut oats

⅛ tsp (0.5 mL) ground allspice

⅛ tsp (0.5 mL) ground nutmeg

⅛ tsp (0.5 mL) ground cinnamon

¾ cup (175 mL) vanilla almond milk

½ cup (125 mL) sliced bananas

very berry
⅓ cup (75 mL) large flake (old-fashioned) rolled oats

1 tsp (5 mL) chia seeds

1 tbsp (15 mL) steel-cut oats

¾ cup (175 mL) vanilla almond milk

½ cup (125 mL) frozen berries (mixed or just one kind)

1 tbsp (15 mL) dried golden berries (optional)

1 tsp (5 mL) raw hemp hearts

1 tsp (5 mL) raw flaxseeds

1 tsp (5 mL) raw pumpkin seeds

pineapple upside down cake
⅓ cup (75 mL) large flake (old-fashioned) rolled oats

1 tsp (5 mL) chia seeds

1 tbsp (15 mL) steel-cut oats

½ cup (125 mL) vanilla almond milk

¼ cup (60 mL) pineapple juice

½ cup (125 mL) crushed pineapple

1 tbsp (15 mL) dried unsweetened cherries, chopped

almond joy

⅓ cup (75 mL) large flake (old-fashioned) rolled oats

1 tsp (5 mL) chia seeds

1 tbsp (15 mL) steel-cut oats

¾ cup (175 mL) chocolate almond milk

2 tsp (10 mL) sliced almonds

2 tbsp (30 mL) dried coconut chips

cranachan

⅓ cup (75 mL) large flake (old-fashioned) rolled oats

1 tsp (5 mL) chia seeds

1 tbsp (15 mL) steel-cut oats

1 tsp (5 mL) ground flaxseeds

½ cup (125 mL) raspberries (fresh or frozen)

¾ cup (175 mL) vanilla almond milk

peanut butter cup

1 tbsp (15 mL) natural peanut butter

¾ cup (175 mL) chocolate almond milk

⅓ cup (75 mL) large flake (old-fashioned) rolled oats

1 tsp (5 mL) chia seeds

1 tbsp (15 mL) steel-cut oats

1. Combine all of the ingredients in a 16-oz (448 mL) resealable glass jar and shake to combine.

2. Refrigerate overnight.

3. In the morning, either eat as is or heat up for a warming start to your day.

Tip: Peanut Butter Cup Overnight Oats: Combine peanut butter and almond milk in a small bowl and stir until smooth before adding to jar with other ingredients.

Almond Joy Overnight Oats: Dried coconut chips are relatively new to the marketplace. These large flakes of dried coconut are much thinner and wider than traditional desiccated coconut. If you can't find them, feel free to use whatever dried unsweetened coconut you have on hand.

basic pancake mix

Our pancakes sell like hotcakes! Every weekend, our flat-top is chock full of pancakes from the moment we open at 10:30 a.m. (well, even before that, because the staff has to get theirs first!) until brunch is over at 3:00 p.m., so much so that we have to take some items off the menu during brunch to make room for the pancakes.

Our pancake mix is made with Bob's Red Mill Gluten Free All Purpose Flour, and it gets its rising power from the baking powder and baking soda. The batter keeps fine overnight, but it will only really puff up if you make it and use it right away. This batter can be used as is, topped with your favourite fruits, berries, nuts, and seeds, or changed up with the addition of spices, supplements, grains, or anything your heart desires. Here is the basic pancake batter recipe and a few of my favourite variations.

serves 4 to 6 (makes about 10 5- to 6-inch pancakes)

2 cups (500 mL) gluten-free all-purpose flour (we prefer Bob's Red Mill)

¼ cup (60 mL) ground flaxseeds

1¼ tsp (6 mL) baking powder

1 tsp (5 mL) baking soda

¼ tsp (1 mL) sea salt

1½ cups (375 mL) non-dairy milk of your choice

¼ cup (60 mL) raw agave nectar

Oil, for frying (sunflower, canola, neutral-flavoured coconut oil)

Pure dark maple syrup

Non-dairy buttery spread (we prefer Earth Balance)

1. Combine flour, ground flaxseeds, baking powder, baking soda, and salt in a large bowl.

2. Combine non-dairy milk and agave nectar in a small bowl or measuring cup. (It's okay if the agave nectar doesn't mix well with the milk.)

3. Make a well in the centre of the dry ingredients. Pour a little of the liquid into the well and, using a wooden spoon, stir to combine. Gradually add more liquid, stirring after each addition and incorporating more and more of the dry ingredients from the sides of the well, until all of the liquid is incorporated and a batter is formed. (It's okay if there are a few lumps.)

4. Heat oil in a frying pan over medium heat.

5. Using a small ladle or spoon, drop batter into pan, using about ¼ cup (60 mL) batter per pancake.

6. Cook pancakes until browned on bottom and bubbling on top, 2 to 3 minutes. Flip and cook other sides until browned and pancakes are cooked through.

7. Repeat Steps 4 to 6 with remaining batter, lightly oiling pan again if needed.

8. Serve immediately with maple syrup and pats of non-dairy butter.

banana nut

Banana and banana nut pancakes have been on our brunch menu for years, and we still sell tons of them every weekend.

1 batch Pancake Mix [page 128]

2 bananas, sliced

⅔ to 1 cup [150 to 250 mL] Toasted Mixed Nuts [page 274]

1. Make pancake mix.

2. Follow cooking instructions [Steps 4 to 6, page 128], but as soon as you drop the batter in the pan, place 5 slices of banana on top of each pancake and sprinkle with about 1 tbsp [15 mL] mixed nuts. Serve banana side up.

apple fritter

Apple fritters are my all-time favourite doughnut, and these pancakes give you the same feeling with much better ingredients. The cinnamon and sugar on the apple slices caramelize in the pan to add a really delicious element.

1 batch Basic Pancake Mix (page 128)

¼ cup (60 mL) organic vegan sugar

1 tbsp (15 mL) ground cinnamon

1 to 2 green apples, peeled, cored, and cut into ¼-inch (0.5 cm) slices

1. Make pancake mix.

2. Combine sugar and cinnamon in a small jar. Seal and shake to combine. (This quantity will make more than you need for this recipe, but leftovers will last for up to 1 year in a tightly sealed jar.)

3. Follow cooking instructions (Steps 4 to 6, page 128), but as soon as you drop the batter in the pan, place a few apple slices on each pancake and sprinkle the cinnamon sugar directly onto the apple slices, using about ¼ tsp (1 mL) per pancake. Serve apple side up.

mandarin five-spice

Chinese five-spice powder is normally used in savoury applications, but it's great in sweet things, too. When combined with the sweet tartness of the mandarin oranges, it's a match made in heaven.

1 batch Basic Pancake Mix (page 128)

1 tsp (5 mL) Chinese five-spice powder

2 to 3 cups (500 to 750 mL) canned mandarin oranges, drained

1. Add five-spice powder to the dry ingredients when you make pancake mix (page 128).

2. Follow cooking instructions (Steps 4 to 6, page 128), but as soon as you drop the batter in the pan, place about ¼ cup (60 mL) mandarin segments on each pancake. Serve mandarin side up.

blueberry almond

These are a bestseller for us, every season of the year.

1 batch Basic Pancake Mix [page 128]
⅔ cup [150 mL] sliced almonds

1 to 1½ cups [250 to 375 mL] fresh blueberries

1. Make pancake mix.

2. Follow cooking instructions [Steps 4 to 6, page 128], but as soon as you drop the batter in the pan, add about 1 tbsp [15 mL] almonds and 2 tbsp [30 mL] blueberries on top of each pancake. Serve blueberry side up.

pumpkin spice

I don't like pumpkin pie, but I love these pancakes. (I think it's just the texture of pumpkin pie I don't like.) These pancakes deliver the scrumptious flavour of the pie in a much better format (in my humble opinion!). The spicing in these is subtle, so if you prefer a stronger flavour, increase the amounts a little.

1 batch Basic Pancake Mix [page 128]
½ tsp [2 mL] ground cinnamon
¼ tsp [1 mL] ground ginger

¼ tsp [1 mL] ground allspice
¼ tsp [1 mL] ground nutmeg
¼ cup [60 mL] canned pure pumpkin purée

1. Add cinnamon, ginger, allspice, and nutmeg to the dry ingredients in Step 1 when you make pancake mix [page 128].

2. Add pumpkin purée to the wet ingredients in Step 2 and continue with Step 3 of recipe.

3. Follow cooking instructions [Steps 4 to 6, page 128]. Serve.

blueberry almond

purple puff

The combination of a purple-tinged batter and the puffed quinoa coating the top of these pancakes makes for an unusual and fun appearance that kids love! Açai is a superfood native to South America, and is now available in powder form. It is a good source of antioxidants, omega fats, protein, and fibre. Puffed quinoa is good for you as well. High in protein, fibre, and non-saturated fats, it is also a great source of calcium, iron, and vitamins. You'll find both açai and puffed quinoa at health-food stores and some well-stocked grocery stores. Look for puffed quinoa in the breakfast cereal section.

1 batch Basic Pancake Mix (page 128)
4 tsp (20 mL) açai powder

⅔ to 1 cup (150 to 250 mL) puffed quinoa or millet

1. Add açai powder to the dry ingredients when you make pancake mix (page 128).

2. Follow cooking instructions (Steps 4 to 6, page 128), but as soon as you drop the batter in the pan, scatter 1 tbsp (15 mL) puffed quinoa on top of each pancake. Serve quinoa side up.

power pancakes

These pancakes get their own recipe because the ingredients are a bit different. This is a great way to use up any cooked grains you have in the fridge. If you don't have any on hand, just use extra oats.

Feel free to add some sliced bananas or fresh blueberries to these pancakes in the pan. Just put them on while the first side cooks, and then turn them fruit side up when you serve them.

If you have a little jar of lemon flavouring, go ahead and add that in. If not, use lemon zest. The heartiness of the grains tends to make these pancakes feel dense, but the lemon adds a freshness that lightens them up and pairs really well with maple syrup.

serves 4 to 6

2 cups (500 mL) gluten-free all-purpose flour (we prefer Bob's Red Mill)

¼ cup (60 mL) cooked quinoa

¼ cup (60 mL) cooked millet

¼ cup (60 mL) quick-cooking oats

1½ tsp (7 mL) raw hemp hearts

1½ tsp (7 mL) ground flaxseeds

1¼ tsp (6 mL) baking powder

1 tsp (5 mL) baking soda

¼ tsp (1 mL) sea salt

1¼ cups (300 mL) non-dairy milk

¼ cup (60 mL) raw agave nectar

1 tsp (5 mL) freshly grated lemon zest or lemon flavouring

Oil, for frying (sunflower, canola, neutral-flavoured coconut oil)

Pure dark maple syrup, to taste

Non-dairy buttery spread (we prefer Earth Balance)

1. Combine flour, quinoa, millet, oats, hemp hearts, flaxseeds, baking powder, baking soda, and salt in a large bowl.

2. Combine non-dairy milk and agave nectar in a small bowl or measuring cup. (It's okay if the agave nectar doesn't mix well with the milk.)

3. Make a well in the centre of the dry ingredients. Pour a little of the liquid into the well and, using a wooden spoon, stir to combine. Gradually add more liquid, stirring after each addition and incorporating more and more of the dry ingredients from the sides of the well until all of the liquid is incorporated and a batter is formed. Add lemon zest or flavouring and stir to incorporate.

4. Heat oil in a frying pan over medium heat.

5. Using a small ladle or spoon, drop batter into pan, using about ¼ cup (60 mL) batter per pancake.

6. Cook pancakes until browned on bottoms and bubbling on top, 2 to 3 minutes. Flip and cook until other sides are browned and pancakes are cooked through.

7. Repeat Steps 4 to 6 with remaining batter, lightly oiling pan again if needed.

8. Serve immediately with maple syrup and pats of non-dairy butter.

TASTERS

The perfect appetizer whets your appetite but doesn't fill you up too much.
It sets the tone for the meal and gets you excited about what is to come.
But there is nothing stopping you from having a meal made entirely of
appetizers. Often, when Ruth and I have lunches and dinners at Fresh,
our meals are drawn entirely from the appetizer section. Part of this is a
function of naturally smaller appetizer portions and a chance to taste more
delicious things.

When entertaining at home, try serving your guests dinner from dishes
in this chapter—it's fun, more informal, and social.

green herb chickpea fries

Also called *panisses*, these fries—crispy on the outside and smooth and custardy on the inside—have been around for over a century. Very popular in Marseille, France, in the 1930s, they are now enjoying a resurgence.

3 cups [750 mL] water

1 tsp [5 mL] sea salt

½ tsp [2 mL] freshly ground black pepper

1¼ cups [300 mL] chickpea flour

⅓ cup [75 mL] chopped fresh herbs [basil, mint, chives, tarragon, savory; optional]

Canola oil, for frying

Garlic Mayo or Chipotle Mayo [page 268]

1. **Make chickpea batter** Bring water, salt, and pepper to a boil in a medium pot. Reduce heat to low.

2. Gradually add chickpea flour, whisking constantly to prevent large lumps. Reduce heat to low and cook for 7 to 10 minutes, stirring often, until very thick. [You will have small lumps in the batter, but don't worry; you won't notice them in the finished product.]

3. Add herbs [if using] and whisk well.

4. Remove pan from heat and pour mixture into a non-stick 8-inch [20 cm] square cake pan. Let cool on counter until no longer steaming.

5. Cover with plastic wrap, pressing it right down onto the surface of the batter, and refrigerate until completely firm, for at least 1 hour, or overnight.

6. **Cook chickpea fries** Turn mixture out onto a cutting board and cut into long fries, about ½ inch [1 cm] thick. [An easy way to do this is to cut the mixture into 4 equal squares, and then cut each of those squares into 5 equal french-fry shapes.]

7. Heat oil in a large frying pan over medium-high heat. [You need just enough oil to come halfway up the thickness of your fries.]

8. Working in batches so as not to crowd the pan, fry fries until golden brown and crispy on both sides, about 2 minutes per side. Transfer to paper towel to drain. Repeat with remaining fries. Keep cooked fries warm in a 250°F [120°C] oven while you cook the others, if you like.

9. Serve with garlic or chipotle mayo on the side.

Tip: For another tasty version of this recipe, omit the fresh herbs in Step 3. Serve chickpea fries with Red Chimichurri Sauce [page 204] for dipping.

super bowl

Our bookkeeper and all-around superwoman Nancy DeCaria described this dish perfectly when she said it was like eating a hot home-cooked meal. It gives all the satisfaction of a roast dinner, but in a healthy, green, plant-based way.

serves 2

8 cups (2 L) mixed greens (kale, bok choy, Swiss chard)
1 cup (250 mL) Roasted Mushroom Gravy, heated (page 259)
2 tsp (10 mL) Toasted Mixed Seeds (page 274)
4 slices Herb-Marinated Tempeh, grilled (page 271)

1. Steam the greens and divide between 2 large bowls.

2. Top each bowl with gravy, seed mix, and tempeh.

Tip: *To steam greens:* If you have a steamer insert, bring 1 to 2 inches (2.5 to 5 cm) of water to a boil in your saucepan. Add greens to the steamer insert, place over the boiling water, cover with lid, and steam for 3 to 5 minutes or until greens are tender and vibrant green. If you don't have an insert, place 2 to 3 tbsp (30 to 45 mL) of water in the bottom of a large wok or pan, top with mixed greens, cover with a lid, and cook over high heat until greens are tender. Use tongs or a slotted spoon to remove steamed greens so you don't add water to your dish.

collard green spring rolls

To make these cute little green rolls, you can either use the collards raw or blanch them. I like them both ways, but the leaves are a bit more pliable, are easier to roll, and stick together really well after being blanched.

I've provided my favourite combination for the filling, but the amount you use will totally depend on the size of your collard leaves and the number of leaves in the bunch (this recipe assumes you will get 8 good-sized leaves out of your bunch). As a general rule, use ¼ to ½ cup (60 to 125 mL) of filling in every roll—just enough so that you can fold the edges in and roll it up easily.

I like avocado in these rolls, but if you don't have any ripe avocados, use Grilled Marinated Tofu Steaks (page 272) instead.

serves 4 (2 rolls each)

1 bunch collard greens

½ red bell pepper, sliced

¼ English cucumber, julienned

½ avocado, sliced

2 fresh red chilies, sliced

¼ red onion, thinly sliced

1 batch Vietnamese All-Purpose Sauce (page 261)

1. **Prepare collard greens** Separate each leaf from bunch. Working with 1 leaf at a time, lay leaf flat on a cutting board, smooth side down, and cut out the middle raised rib, starting at the point where the rib sticks up from the surface of the leaf. (You will probably end up cutting a V-shaped wedge out of one side of the leaf to remove the rib, and that's okay.) Repeat with remaining leaves.

2. If you're going to eat them raw, wash and dry the prepared leaves. If you're going to blanch them, bring a pot of water to a boil. Create an ice bath by placing some ice cubes and cold water in a large mixing bowl.

3. To blanch greens, add prepared leaves to the boiling water and cook, stirring, for just a few seconds, until the leaves are bright green and softened. Immediately transfer leaves to the ice bath.

4. When ready to use, dry each leaf with a clean kitchen towel.

5. **Assemble spring rolls** Lay one leaf flat on a clean work surface, round end farthest from you. Place the red pepper, cucumber, avocado, chilies, and onion horizontally across the middle of the leaf, leaving ½ to ¾ inch (1 to 2 cm) border on each side. Fold in the edges slightly, and then roll into a tight cylinder.

6. To serve, cut in half on the diagonal and serve with Vietnamese All-Purpose Sauce on the side.

avocado dosas with two chutneys

Inspired by the huge dosas at the Hampton Chutney Company in New York, these are miniature versions that you can easily make at home.

Traditional dosa batter is made of rice and lentils that have been soaked and fermented overnight. Ours is made of spelt flour and only takes a minute to make.

These dosas are stuffed with avocado, cilantro, and tomato, but the possibilities for fillings are endless. Some of my favourite things to add to the avocado filling are sautéed napa cabbage, mushrooms, green onions, grilled spinach, and baby arugula.

serves 4 as an appetizer (2 dosas each)

red chili and coconut chutney
makes 1 cup (250 mL)

1 tsp (5 mL) sunflower oil or neutral-flavoured coconut oil

⅔ cup (150 mL) chopped tomato

⅓ cup (75 mL) chopped fresh red chilies

⅓ cup (75 mL) chopped onion

2 tsp (10 mL) chopped peeled ginger

2 cloves garlic, minced

1 tsp (5 mL) sea salt

1⅓ cups (325 mL) unsweetened desiccated coconut

⅓ cup (75 mL) water

4 tsp (20 mL) freshly squeezed lemon juice

green pistachio chutney
makes 1 cup (250 mL)

1½ cups (375 mL) chopped fresh cilantro

½ cup (125 mL) fresh mint

2 cloves garlic, roughly chopped

2 tbsp (30 mL) peeled and roughly chopped fresh ginger

½ cup (125 mL) chopped onion

2 tbsp (30 mL) raw pistachios

¼ cup (60 mL) freshly squeezed lemon juice

Sea salt, to taste

¼ cup (60 mL) water

dosas

1 batch Dosa Batter (page 266)

Oil, for frying

1 cup (250 mL) shredded vegan cheddar cheese (optional)

24 grape tomatoes, halved

16 slices avocado

½ cup (125 mL) chopped fresh cilantro

1. **Prepare red chili and coconut chutney** Heat oil in a frying pan over medium heat. Add tomato, chilies, onion, ginger, garlic, and salt. Cook, stirring occasionally, for 3 to 4 minutes, until softened. Stir in coconut, water, and lemon juice. Remove from heat and set aside to cool.

2. Transfer tomato mixture to a food processor and purée, scraping down the sides of the work bowl as needed. Transfer to a bowl and set aside.

3. **Prepare green pistachio chutney** Combine all of the ingredients in a food processor, and process until smooth, scraping down the sides of the work bowl as needed. Transfer to a bowl and set aside.

4. **Prepare dosas** Make dosa batter.

5. Coat the bottom of a large non-stick frying pan with oil. Heat over medium heat.

6. Ladle about 2 tbsp (30 mL) of dosa batter into the pan and swirl around in a circular motion until you have a thin, round pancake. (If using cheese, sprinkle it on now, while the batter is still wet.)

7. Cook for 1 to 2 minutes or until bubbles appear on top and surface no longer looks wet. Transfer to a plate and keep warm in a 250°F (120°C) oven. Repeat with remaining dosa batter, adding more oil to pan as needed (you should end up with 8 pancakes).

8. **Assemble dosas** Lay 1 dosa flat on a clean work surface. Place 6 grape tomato halves, 2 slices avocado, and 1 tbsp (15 mL) cilantro across the centre. Roll into a cylinder. Repeat with remaining dosas and fillings.

9. Place 2 dosas on each plate and serve with chutneys on the side.

crispy cauliflower bites with sriracha salt and miso mayo

We get our Sriracha salt from Toronto's Stiff Salt (owned by Nadia Alam and Steve Thomas, two ex-Fresh cooks who met and married while working at Fresh!). If you don't have access to flavoured salts, just top with regular sea salt and serve a little Sriracha on the side for dipping.

serves 4 as an appetizer

1 batch Dosa Batter (page 266)

4 cups (1 L) chopped cauliflower (cut into small florets)

1½ cups (375 mL) panko crumbs

Oil, for frying

garnishes

Sriracha salt, to taste

2 cups (500 mL) finely sliced napa cabbage

¼ cup (60 mL) sliced green onions

4 tsp (20 mL) raw sesame seeds

Lemon wedges, to taste

1 batch Miso Mayo (page 267)

1. Combine dosa batter and cauliflower in a large bowl. Toss until cauliflower is completely coated. Set aside.

2. Place about one-quarter of the panko in a shallow bowl. Working in batches, use a slotted spoon to add battered cauliflower to panko and toss until thoroughly coated. (Discard panko that has become saturated with dosa batter, and add fresh panko to the bowl as needed.) Set aside coated florets.

3. In a large frying pan or wok, heat about ¼ inch (0.5 cm) of oil over medium-high heat.

4. When oil is hot (see Tip), carefully add prepared cauliflower to pan, working in batches if necessary so as not to crowd the pan.

5. Cook for 2 to 4 minutes, turning cauliflower as needed to brown on all sides.

6. Transfer cooked cauliflower to paper towel to drain. Immediately sprinkle with Sriracha salt. Repeat with remaining battered cauliflower.

7. Arrange cabbage on the bottom of either a large platter or individual serving bowls. Top with cooked cauliflower. Scatter green onions and sesame seeds over top.

8. Serve with lemon wedges and miso mayo on the side.

Tip: The cauliflower can be coated up to a day ahead and refrigerated in an airtight container.

You want your oil to be 350°F (180°C) for frying. If you don't have a thermometer, use one of the following methods to determine if your oil is hot enough: Stick a wooden spoon into the oil; if the wood starts to bubble, the oil is hot enough. Alternatively, drop a piece of popcorn into the oil; when it pops, the oil is hot enough. Or, simply put a drop of water into the oil; if it sizzles, you are good to go.

mighty greens

This simple appetizer is a great way to eat more greens. Enjoy it as a light lunch with some Marinated Tofu Steaks (page 272) or Marinated Tofu Cubes (page 272) and a cup of soup.

serves 1

4 cups (1 L) mixed greens (kale, bok choy, Swiss chard)

2 tbsp (30 mL) 3-6-9 Dressing (page 173) or Miso Tahini Sauce (page 257)

1 tsp (5 mL) raw hemp hearts

1. Steam the greens and put into a large bowl.

2. Top with dressing and hemp hearts.

Tip: *To steam greens:* If you have a steamer insert, bring 1 to 2 inches (2.5 to 5 cm) of water to a boil in your saucepan. Add greens to the steamer insert, place over boiling water, cover with lid, and steam for 3 to 5 minutes or until greens are tender and vibrant green. If you don't have an insert, place 2 to 3 tbsp (30 to 45 mL) of water in the bottom of a large wok or pan, top with mixed greens, cover with a lid, and cook over high heat until greens are tender. Use tongs or a slotted spoon to remove steamed greens so you don't add water to your dish.

green poutine-style sweet potato

At the restaurants we make vegan poutine with sweet potato fries. At home, when I'm craving our Green Poutine, I find it much easier to just roast a whole sweet potato and not bother with the whole process of making fries. The measurements for the "cheese" sauce and gravy are not exact because it totally depends on how big your sweet potato is and how much sauce you like!

Another quick and easy sweet potato idea comes from my right-hand woman at Fresh, Gillian Mountney, who tops a baked sweet potato with a drizzle of olive oil, some finely chopped walnuts, and some salt and pepper.

serves 2

2 sweet potatoes

½ tsp (2 mL) sunflower oil (optional)

4 cups (1 L) mixed greens (bok choy, Swiss chard, kale), steamed (see Tip)

½ to 1 cup (125 to 250 mL) Fresh "Cheese" Sauce (page 251)

½ to 1 cup (125 to 250 mL) Roasted Mushroom Gravy (page 259), warmed

4 tsp (20 mL) raw sunflower seeds

1. Preheat oven to 400°F (200°C).

2. Using a fork, poke a bunch of holes in each sweet potato. Rub potatoes all over with oil (if using). Place on a baking sheet and bake in preheated oven until tender, 45 to 60 minutes. (Alternatively, you can cook the potatoes in a microwave on High for 5 to 10 minutes or until tender.)

3. Cut cooked potatoes in half lengthwise, and place two halves on each serving plate. Mash potatoes slightly with a fork to make some nooks and crannies for the sauces.

4. Place steamed greens on top, then pour over "cheese" sauce and mushroom gravy.

5. Sprinkle with sunflower seeds.

Tip: *To steam greens:* If you have a steamer insert, bring 1 to 2 inches (2.5 to 5 cm) of water to a boil in your saucepan. Add greens to the steamer insert, place over the boiling water, cover with lid, and steam for 3 to 5 minutes, until greens are tender and vibrant green. If you don't have an insert, place 2 to 3 tbsp (30 to 45 mL) of water in the bottom of a large wok or pan, top with mixed greens, cover with a lid, and cook over high heat until greens are tender. Use tongs or a slotted spoon to remove steamed greens so you don't add water to your dish.

quinoa and hemp tabouleh

This recipe was created by Chef Ricardo Morales, our favourite Mexican vegan chef. Ruth met Rich when he was surfing and running his own beach-side restaurant in Puerto Escondido, Oaxaca. After a hurricane blew out his restaurant, we persuaded him to fly to Moscow on our behalf to launch the first Fresh in Moscow. Hugely successful, there are now two locations running in Moscow, along with a new Fresh Mexico City location in the works. We are so proud of this guy!

This tabouleh tastes better at room temperature, so if you have made it ahead of time, just take it out of the fridge an hour before you want to serve it.

serves 6

2 cups (500 mL) water or vegetable stock

1 cup (250 mL) red or white quinoa, rinsed and drained

½ cup (125 mL) olive oil

6 cloves garlic, minced or halved

2 cups (500 mL) finely chopped English cucumber

½ cup (125 mL) finely chopped celery

¼ cup (60 mL) freshly squeezed lemon juice

½ cup (125 mL) tightly packed fresh mint, finely chopped

1 tsp (5 mL) freshly ground Szechuan peppercorns or black pepper to taste

½ tsp (2 mL) sea salt

1 avocado, sliced

2 tbsp (30 mL) raw hemp hearts

30 grape tomatoes, halved

1. **Cook quinoa** Combine water and quinoa in a rice cooker or pot. Cook until quinoa is tender and all of the liquid has been absorbed. Set aside and let cool.

2. **Make garlic oil** While quinoa is cooking, make garlic oil. Combine oil and garlic in a small saucepan over medium heat. Cook just until garlic starts to brown, and then remove pan from heat and immediately pour oil into a heat-proof container (a resealable jar or glass measuring cup works well). Let cool. (This recipe makes more than you will need for this dish. Store leftover garlic oil in an airtight container in the fridge and be sure to use up within 1 week.)

3. **Assemble tabouleh** Combine cooked quinoa, cucumber, celery, lemon juice, mint, ¼ cup (60 mL) of the garlic oil, pepper, and salt in a large mixing bowl. Stir well.

4. To serve, divide tabouleh among plates and top with avocado, hemp hearts, and tomatoes. Drizzle with ½ to 1 tsp (2 to 5 mL) garlic oil.

Tip: If you prefer a mild garlic flavour, slice garlic cloves in half. If you prefer a stronger flavour, mince the garlic.

fresh platter

Looking for a vegan alternative to a cheese platter? This combination of dips and olives is great as an appetizer or as a buffet item.

At the restaurants we serve this platter with crusty whole-grain bread and a little bowl of olive oil for dipping with the dukkah. We also add sliced cucumber and heirloom grape tomatoes for some fresh crunch. It's a great plate for sharing, and the flavours work together to really wake up your taste buds. Serve with your favourite bread, crackers, vegetables, or all three. I love using Belgian endive with these dips—just pull the leaves apart and you have perfect canoe-shaped vessels great for dipping.

serves 6

green pea and tarragon dip

This bright green dip is so tasty it will keep you coming back for more. Joyce Leung, head bartender at our Spadina location, loved it so much when we had it as a special that she used to order multiple sides of it and eat it for her lunch, straight out of the bowl with a spoon!

makes 1¼ cups (300 mL)

1 tbsp (15 mL) canola oil
1 cup (250 mL) chopped onions
1 cup (250 mL) green peas, thawed, rinsed, and drained
¼ cup (60 mL) soaked raw cashews
1½ tsp (7 mL) fresh tarragon leaves

1½ tsp (7 mL) white wine vinegar
½ tsp (2 mL) sea salt
¼ tsp (1 mL) freshly ground black pepper
1 tbsp (15 mL) olive oil

1. Heat canola oil in a frying pan over medium heat. Add onions and cook for 3 to 4 minutes, until softened. Set aside to cool.

2. Combine cooled onions, peas, cashews, tarragon, vinegar, salt, pepper, and olive oil in a food processor. Process until as smooth as possible. Serve immediately or transfer to an airtight container and refrigerate for up to 4 days.

Tip: To soak the cashews for this recipe, place in a small bowl and cover with water. Cover and let soak for at least 1 hour. Drain, and then rinse under cool running water until water runs clear. Drain.

sikil pak

This is our version of the ancient Mayan pumpkin seed dip. It may not be a traditional interpretation, but it certainly is yummy!

makes 1½ cups (375 mL)

1 cup (250 mL) raw pumpkin seeds
2 tbsp (30 mL) canola oil
½ cup (125 mL) finely chopped onion
1 jalapeño pepper, seeded and chopped
3 cloves garlic, chopped
½ tsp (2 mL) sea salt, divided

¼ cup (60 mL) fresh parsley
¼ cup (60 mL) cilantro
2 tbsp (30 mL) freshly squeezed lime juice
¼ cup (60 mL) water
1 tbsp (15 mL) olive oil

1. In a dry frying pan over medium heat, toast pumpkin seeds, stirring, for 3 to 5 minutes, until browned and starting to pop.

2. Transfer pumpkin seeds to a bowl and set aside to cool.

3. In same pan, heat canola oil over medium-high heat. Add onion, jalapeño, garlic, and ¼ tsp (1 mL) salt. Cook for 3 to 4 minutes, until softened. Remove from heat and let cool.

4. Combine onion mixture, toasted pumpkin seeds, parsley, cilantro, lime juice, water, olive oil, and remaining ¼ tsp (1 mL) salt in a food processor and process until smooth.

5. Serve immediately or transfer to an airtight container and refrigerate for up to 3 days.

dukkah

The word *dukkah* means "to pound" in Arabic, and it is a traditional Egyptian blend of nuts, herbs, and spices. There are countless versions of dukkah, but this is the one we like to use on our Fresh Platter (page 150). To eat it, you just take a piece of bread, dip it in olive oil, then in the dukkah, and enjoy!

Don't skip the toasting of the seeds—it's a really important part in getting the right flavour profile. Traditionally the nuts are roasted, too, but we like to leave those raw.

makes 1 cup (250 mL)

1 tbsp (15 mL) coriander seeds

1 tbsp (15 mL) cumin seeds

1 tbsp (15 mL) fennel seeds

¼ cup (60 mL) finely chopped hazelnuts

¼ cup (60 mL) finely chopped pistachios

2 tbsp (30 mL) raw sesame seeds

2 tbsp (30 mL) ground flaxseeds

1 tsp (5 mL) sea salt

1 tsp (5 mL) freshly ground black pepper

1. Combine coriander, cumin, and fennel seeds in a small, dry frying pan over medium-high heat and cook, shaking or stirring often, until very fragrant and starting to darken a little.

2. Remove spice mixture from heat and transfer to a spice grinder or blender and process until finely ground.

3. Combine ground spices, hazelnuts, pistachios, sesame seeds, ground flaxseeds, salt, and pepper in a small bowl. Stir to combine. Serve immediately or transfer to an airtight container and refrigerate for up to 1 month.

marinated olives

These olives are deliciously herby and lemony.

makes 3 cups (750 mL)

1½ cups (375 mL) green olives, with pits

1½ cups (375 mL) kalamata olives, with pits

2 cups (500 mL) olive oil

2 tbsp (30 mL) chopped red chilies

4 tsp (20 mL) freshly grated lemon zest

2 tsp (10 mL) whole fennel seeds

2 sprigs fresh rosemary

2 cloves garlic, roughly chopped

1. Combine olives in a bowl and set aside.

2. In a saucepan, heat oil over medium heat.

3. Remove pan from heat and stir in chilies, lemon zest, fennel seeds, rosemary, and garlic. Let cool.

4. Pour seasoned oil over olives and stir until well coated. Cover and refrigerate overnight to allow seasonings to penetrate the olives. These will keep for up to 2 weeks in the fridge.

flax hummus

Our hummus has ground flaxseeds added for an extra nutritional *oomph*. You can also customize it to your taste by adding some spices, herbs, extra lemon, hot sauce, or whatever your palate is craving.

makes 2½ cups (625 mL)

2 cloves garlic

½ to ¾ cup (125 to 175 mL) water

1 can (19 oz/540 mL) chickpeas, drained and rinsed

2 tbsp (30 mL) extra virgin olive oil

2 tbsp (30 mL) freshly squeezed lemon juice

2 tbsp (30 mL) ground flaxseeds

1 tbsp (15 mL) raw tahini

1 tsp (5 mL) sea salt

1. Pulse garlic in a food processor until minced.

2. Add ½ cup (125 mL) water and remaining ingredients. Process until smooth (add another ¼ cup/60 mL water if needed to achieve a smooth consistency). Serve immediately or transfer to an airtight container and refrigerate for up to 2 days.

scallion cashew spread

The creaminess of the puréed seeds and cashews, juxtaposed with the tartness of the lemon and the depth of the miso and nutritional yeast, give this raw paté an interesting flavour. We use it in the Transformer Salad (page 167), and it also works well spread inside the Collard Green Spring Rolls (page 140).

makes 1 cup (250 mL)

⅓ cup (75 mL) soaked shelled unsalted raw sunflower seeds

⅔ cup (150 mL) soaked raw cashews

¼ cup (60 mL) freshly squeezed lemon juice

¼ cup (60 mL) chopped green onions

1 garlic clove, minced

½ tsp (2 mL) white miso

1½ tbsp (22 mL) flaked nutritional yeast

¼ tsp (1 mL) sea salt

1. Soak seeds and nuts Place sunflower seeds and cashews in a bowl and cover with water. Let soak for at least 1 hour.

2. Drain and rinse soaked seeds and nuts under cool running water until water runs clear. Drain.

3. Prepare spread Combine soaked seeds and nuts and lemon juice in a food processor. Process until smooth.

4. Add green onions, garlic, miso, nutritional yeast, and sea salt and pulse to combine. (Add a little water, 1 tbsp/15 mL at a time if needed, to get things moving.) Serve immediately or transfer to an airtight container and refrigerate for up to 2 days.

SALADS AND DRESSINGS

Think salads are healthy, but boring? We think these recipes will change your mind. Fresh has become very well known in Toronto for our salads, and I really believe that good salads can win over even the most carnivorous of eaters. Our salads range from simple vegetable combinations to complex layered bowls of greens, sprouts, veggies, grains, patés, nuts, and seeds.

A salad at Fresh showcases the beauty and abundance that a plant-based diet can hold. For us, salads are a focus, and we treat them as a whole meal, not a side dish. Our distinctive house-made dressings make our salads tempting and gratifying, and are designed to keep you coming back for bite after bite. After all, getting your daily intake of veggies should be a pleasure, not a chore!

SALADS

gem salad

This refreshing combination was invented by our area kitchen manager, Gillian Mountney. The combination of peppery arugula, cooling mint, and sweet apple is divine.

serves 2

8 cups (2 L) lightly packed baby arugula

1 cup (250 mL) cooked or canned chickpeas (drained and rinsed if canned)

1 cup (250 mL) chopped apple of your choice (unpeeled)

½ cup (125 mL) frozen green peas, thawed and rinsed

½ cup (125 mL) julienned jicama

¼ cup (60 mL) toasted unsalted sunflower seeds (see page 274)

1 cup (250 mL) chopped avocado

2 tbsp (30 mL) chopped fresh mint

¼ cup (60 mL) diced red onion

¼ cup (60 mL) House Dressing (page 169)

4 lemon wedges

1. Combine all of the ingredients, except the lemon wedges, in a large mixing bowl and toss to combine. Divide between 2 bowls. Serve with lemon wedges on the side for squeezing over just before eating.

superfood salad

This simple combination of greens, herbs, and sprouts is the kind of salad you can eat every day. We recently took it off the menu, but so many people asked for us to bring it back that within 3 months, we did! Marinated Tofu Steaks (page 272), Marinated Tofu Cubes (page 272), or vegan cheddar cheese all go nicely on this salad, and it goes particularly well with our House Dressing (page 169).

serves 2

8 cups (2 L) spring mix lettuce

½ to 1 cup (125 to 250 mL) House Dressing (page 169)

½ cup (125 mL) shredded napa cabbage

½ cup (125 mL) frozen shelled edamame, thawed, rinsed, and drained

½ cup (125 mL) diced English cucumber

2 tbsp (30 mL) chopped fresh parsley

2 tbsp (30 mL) chopped fresh cilantro

1 cup (250 mL) assorted microgreens

¼ cup (60 mL) Fresh Salad Topper (page 275)

1. Divide lettuce between 2 large bowls.

2. Drizzle with dressing of your choice.

3. Top each salad with half each of the cabbage, edamame, cucumber, parsley, and cilantro, finishing with microgreens, salad topper, and another drizzle of dressing.

big salad

Seinfeld has been off the air for over a decade, but Elaine's favourite Big Salad lives on at Fresh! We created the Big Salad for customers who crave a straightforward salad that is delicious and satisfying. Still, we couldn't resist Freshifying it by throwing in at least one unusual ingredient: raw hemp hearts. When we first started using these seeds, they were hard to find, but now you'll have no trouble locating them. Keep them in the freezer to add to salads, soups, smoothies, and more. They work anywhere!

This salad lends itself to any dressing, and works well with the addition of Marinated Tofu Cubes (page 272) or Marinated Tofu Steaks (page 272).

serves 2

8 cups (2 L) mixed lettuce greens

½ to 1 cup (125 to 250 mL) dressing of your choice (pages 168 to 175)

1 red bell pepper, chopped

½ English cucumber, chopped

1 carrot, grated or finely chopped

1 avocado, chopped

1 tomato, chopped

¼ cup (60 mL) raw hemp hearts

1. Divide lettuce between 2 large bowls. Drizzle with dressing.

2. Top each salad with half each of the red pepper, cucumber, carrot, avocado, and tomato.

3. Garnish with hemp hearts. Serve.

big easy

Named after my all-time favourite *Amazing Race* participant, Big Easy (half of the Harlem Globetrotter duo), this salad is so quick and easy to make that it couldn't be named anything else! Get into the habit of keeping a can of lentils in your pantry so you can whip up a bowl of this salad with whatever you have on hand. Our Poppy Seed Dressing (page 168) also works really well here.

serves 2 as a meal or 4 as an appetizer

1 can (19 oz/540 mL) brown lentils, drained and rinsed

½ avocado, diced

1 cup (250 mL) diced English cucumber

¼ cup (60 mL) diced red onion

½ cup (125 mL) diced red bell pepper

1 cup (250 mL) halved grape tomatoes

2 cups (500 mL) mixed microgreens (arugula, sunflower sprouts, micro basil)

6 tbsp (90 mL) House Dressing (page 169)

Cayenne pepper, to taste

Lemon wedges

1. Combine lentils, avocado, cucumber, onion, red pepper, tomatoes, microgreens, and dressing in a large bowl and toss to combine.

2. Serve with cayenne and lemon wedges on the side.

all star

This is the bestselling salad on our Fresh menu every season of the year. The combination of kale and quinoa, with the warm sweet potato and tofu steaks, is simply delicious.

You can customize the flavour by the dressing you choose. Our bestselling combinations are the All Star with our House Dressing (page 169) or with Peanut Lime Dressing (page 172), but this salad works with any dressing you can dream up.

serves 2

grilled sweet potato

½ sweet potato, cut into 4 pieces (each about ½ inch/1 cm thick)

2 tbsp (30 mL) sunflower oil (approx.)

salad

2 cups (500 mL) finely shredded kale, large stems and ribs removed

2 cups (500 mL) cooked quinoa

½ batch Marinated Adzuki Beans (page 263)

10 grape tomatoes

½ cup (125 mL) chopped English cucumber

¼ cup (60 mL) chopped fresh cilantro

¼ cup (60 mL) chopped fresh parsley

4 Marinated Tofu Steaks, cooked (page 272)

1½ cups (375 mL) sunflower sprouts

2 tsp (10 mL) dried goji berries

2 tbsp (30 mL) Toasted Mixed Nuts (page 274)

½ to 1 cup (125 to 250 mL) House Dressing (page 169) or Peanut Lime Dressing (page 172)

1. Preheat panini grill to high or preheat oven to 350°F (180°C).

2. **Prepare grilled sweet potato** Coat sweet potato slices in oil. If using a panini grill, grill until tender, 7 to 10 minutes. If using oven method, place on a baking sheet and bake in preheated oven for about 20 minutes, turning once, until tender.

3. **Assemble salads** Divide kale among 4 large bowls.

4. Top each bowl with equal amounts of quinoa, marinated adzuki beans, tomatoes, cucumber, cilantro, parsley, tofu steaks, grilled sweet potato, sunflower sprouts, goji berries, and toasted nuts.

5. Serve with dressing of your choice.

phytosalad

Phyto is the Latin word for "plant," and seems perfect to describe this salad, which contains plants in all forms. The soba noodles ground the salad and make it satisfying enough to be a meal on its own.

serves 2

2 cups (500 mL) cooked soba noodles

2 cups (500 mL) lightly packed shredded napa cabbage

6 tbsp (90 mL) frozen shelled edamame, thawed, rinsed, and drained

¼ cup (60 mL) thinly sliced sun-dried tomatoes

4 cups (1 L) mixed long-stemmed sprouts and microgreens

¼ cup (60 mL) thinly sliced fresh mint

4 Marinated Tofu Steaks (page 272), cooked

2 lime wedges

2 lemon wedges

¼ cup (60 mL) Toasted Mixed Nuts (page 274)

¼ cup (60 mL) Crispy Onions (page 264)

2 tbsp (30 mL) mixed edible flowers

1 cup (250 mL) 3-6-9 Dressing (page 173)

1. Divide soba noodles between 2 large plates.

2. Top each with equal amounts of napa cabbage.

3. Scatter edamame and sun-dried tomatoes over top.

4. Fluff up sprouts and microgreens and place an even amount on top of each plate, in a high pile. Scatter mint over top.

5. Arrange 2 tofu steaks on one side of each plate, and the lime and lemon wedges on the other side.

6. Top salads with mixed nuts, crispy onions, and edible flowers.

7. Serve with dressing in a small bowl or ramekin on the side.

green destiny

The name for this salad was inspired by the magical and all-powerful sword in the movie *Crouching Tiger, Hidden Dragon*. The Wild Ginger Dressing (page 174) is a good match for the flavours in this salad.

serves 2

marinated arame

½ cup (125 mL) dried arame

1 tbsp (15 mL) tamari

1½ tsp (7 mL) freshly squeezed lemon juice

1 tsp (5 mL) sesame oil

½ tsp (2 mL) freshly grated peeled ginger

salad

8 cups (2 L) mixed lettuce greens

1 cup (250 mL) bean sprouts

½ cup (125 mL) chopped English cucumber

½ cup (125 mL) sliced roasted red bell peppers

½ to 1 cup (125 to 250 mL) Wild Ginger Dressing (page 174)

4 Marinated Tofu Steaks (page 272), cooked

6 tbsp (90 mL) sliced almonds, toasted (page 274)

2 tbsp (30 mL) thinly sliced green onions

1. **Make marinated arame** Place arame in a bowl and cover with room-temperature water; let soak for about 15 minutes or until softened and pliable. Drain.

2. Combine tamari, lemon juice, sesame oil, and ginger in a small bowl. Add drained arame and toss until each strand is well coated. Cover and set aside for 15 minutes to 1 hour to marinate.

3. **Assemble salad** In a large mixing bowl, toss together lettuce greens, bean sprouts, cucumber, red peppers, and dressing.

4. Divide salad evenly between 2 large bowls. Top each salad with equal amounts of marinated arame and arrange 2 cooked tofu steaks on either side. Garnish with toasted almonds and green onions.

Tip: Roasting brings out the sweetness in red, yellow, and orange bell peppers and creates a velvety texture. To roast peppers, place on an open flame or on a hot burner. Turn the pepper as it cooks, until the skin is black. Place in a bowl and tightly cover with plastic wrap or a lid to trap the steam. Wait until the pepper is cool enough to handle, then remove the skin and seeds. Proceed with the recipe or slice and eat.

ironman

The combination of tahini, chili oil, and date syrup on this salad is one that took me a while to get to, but as soon as I did, I knew it was a keeper. Look for date syrup in well-stocked health-food stores. If you can't find date syrup, substitute molasses, maple syrup, or dark agave nectar.

serves 2

8 cups (2 L) lightly packed spring mix lettuce
½ to 1 cup (125 to 250 mL) Tahini Dressing (page 174)
2 tsp (10 mL) Chili Oil (page 264)
2 tbsp (30 mL) chopped fresh cilantro
2 tbsp (30 mL) chopped fresh mint
2 tbsp (30 mL) chopped fresh parsley
8 Herb Falafel Balls (page 270)

6 tbsp (90 mL) Flax Hummus (page 153)
½ cup (125 mL) chopped English cucumber
10 grape tomatoes, halved
4 dried figs, chopped
¼ cup (60 mL) Crispy Onions (page 264)
4 tsp (20 mL) date syrup (we prefer Date Lady)

1. Divide lettuce between two large bowls. Top with tahini dressing and chili oil. Scatter cilantro, mint, and parsley over top.

2. Top with falafel balls, hummus, cucumber, tomatoes, figs, and crispy onions.

3. Drizzle date syrup over top. Serve.

ace of kales

The name of this salad was inspired by *Ace of Cakes*, the TV show about Charm City Cakes, Duff Goldman's bakery in Baltimore, Maryland. It's one of our most popular salads year-round. If you like, you can marinate the kale a few hours ahead and just add the other ingredients right before serving.

serves 2

12 cups (3 L) lightly packed chopped green kale, large stems and ribs removed (cut into bite-size pieces)
½ cup (125 mL) House Dressing (page 169)
4 slices Tempeh Bacon (page 273), cooked and cut into bite-size pieces

½ cup (125 mL) julienned jicama
10 grape tomatoes
¼ cup (60 mL) Toasted Mixed Nuts (page 274)
2 tbsp (30 mL) sliced green onions
½ avocado, chopped

1. Combine kale and dressing in a large bowl, using your hands to massage the dressing into each piece of kale and making sure the dressing gets into every nook and cranny. Cover and set aside in the fridge for at least 1 hour.

2. Divide marinated kale between 2 large bowls. Top with tempeh bacon, jicama, tomatoes, nuts, green onions, and avocado.

ten veg salad

You may not have tried kohlrabi, but you've probably seen this knobby purple or green vegetable in the grocery store or market. It wasn't long ago that I first tried it. I was visiting my parents when family friend Tim Turner (aka Chewy) and I got to talking about vegetables. He couldn't believe I'd never had kohlrabi. He went right out and got me one, and I've been a fan of it ever since. If you can't find kohlrabi, just substitute broccoli stems, jicama, or even chopped cucumber—you just want something light and crunchy.

Having some warm elements on a salad always makes it feel more special, and the grilled asparagus and oyster mushrooms on this salad really elevate it.

Nuts, seeds, tofu, or tempeh are great additions and round out this medley of cold and warm veggies.

serves 2

8 stalks asparagus

8 large oyster mushrooms

½ tsp (2 mL) tamari

½ to 1 tsp (2 to 5 mL) sunflower oil

4 cups (1 L) shredded napa cabbage

½ cup (125 mL) shredded carrot

½ cup (125 mL) shelled edamame

½ cup (125 mL) frozen corn, thawed, rinsed, and drained

8 grape tomatoes, halved

½ cup (125 mL) shredded kohlrabi

½ cup (125 mL) chopped red bell pepper

8 slices avocado

½ to 1 cup (125 to 250 mL) dressing of your choice (pages 168 to 175)

1. Combine the asparagus, mushrooms, tamari, and oil in a large bowl and toss to combine.

2. Cook asparagus and mushrooms until asparagus is crisp-tender and mushrooms are browned and tender. (You can either grill them on a panini grill set on high, or spread them over a baking sheet and roast in a preheated 350°F (180°C) oven for 3 to 5 minutes.) Set aside.

3. Place cabbage in a large bowl. Around the edge, arrange carrot, edamame, corn, tomatoes, kohlrabi, red pepper, and avocado.

4. On top, in the middle, place the cooked asparagus and mushrooms. Serve with dressing.

flora

Flora was the Roman goddess of plants, flowers, and fertility, and the word *flora* now means "plant life." This salad explores many different kinds of flora—leaves, sprouts, beans, fungi, nuts, and seeds—so this name seemed fitting.

Lots of new and interesting salad greens combinations are popping up in grocery stores with names like "power greens." They usually contain greens like baby kale and baby spinach, among others. Find one that appeals to you and try it in this salad.

serves 2

¼ cup (60 mL) olive, sunflower, or neutral-flavoured coconut oil
4 cups (1 L) shiitake mushroom caps
2 tbsp (30 mL) tamari
8 cups (2 L) lightly packed mixed salad greens
2 cups (500 mL) canned or cooked chickpeas (drained and rinsed if canned)
2 green onions, chopped
½ batch Poppy Seed Dressing (page 168)
2 cups (500 mL) lightly packed assorted microgreens
6 tbsp (90 mL) toasted pecans (page 274)

1. Heat oil in a large frying pan over medium-high heat.

2. Add mushrooms and tamari. Sauté for 3 to 4 minutes or until mushrooms are tender and browned. Remove from heat and set aside.

3. Combine salad greens, chickpeas, green onions, and dressing in a mixing bowl and toss until well coated.

4. Divide salad between 2 salad bowls.

5. Top each salad with equal amounts of sautéed mushrooms, microgreens, and toasted pecans.

6. Drizzle with a little more dressing.

transformer

This salad is one of our most popular new menu items. We serve it with a raw green tortilla, and it was named for its ability to transform from a salad to a wrap. If you can't find the raw green wraps, don't worry. This salad is also amazing without them.

serves 2

8 cups (2 L) lightly packed chopped romaine lettuce leaves
2 raw green wraps (optional)
1 cup (250 mL) cooked quinoa
¼ cup (60 mL) Scallion Cashew Spread (page 153)
¼ cup (60 mL) Sikil Pak (page 151)
½ avocado, diced
12 Marinated Tofu Cubes (page 272)
¼ cup (60 mL) Marinated Adzuki Beans (page 263)
¼ cup (60 mL) canned or cooked chickpeas (drained and rinsed if canned)
¼ cup (60 mL) shelled edamame
¼ cup (60 mL) chopped English cucumber
10 grape tomatoes
½ to 1 cup (125 to 250 mL) Carrot Miso Dressing (page 171)

1. Divide lettuce between 2 large salad bowls.

2. Place raw wrap (if using) on the side of each bowl, sticking up over the edge. (The lettuce should hold the wraps in place.)

3. Top each bowl of lettuce with equal amounts of cooked quinoa.

4. In the middle of the quinoa, place half each of the spread and sikil pak.

5. Around the edges of each bowl, place equal amounts of avocado, tofu cubes, adzuki beans, chickpeas, edamame, cucumber, and tomatoes.

6. Serve with carrot miso dressing on the side.

DRESSINGS

poppy seed dressing

This sweet dressing works really well on salads that have savoury and tart components, like nuts and citrus fruits. It was on our menu for years, and although it had to go recently to make room for some new items, it's one of those dressings that may be resurrected one day!

Either follow the method below or just put all the ingredients in a resealable jar and shake really well before serving. It will separate, but you just have to give it a good shake whenever you want to use it.

makes 1 cup (250 mL)

6 tbsp (90 mL) raw agave nectar

3 tbsp (45 mL) apple cider vinegar

1 tbsp (15 mL) finely chopped onion

½ tsp (2 mL) mustard powder

½ tsp (2 mL) sea salt

½ cup (125 mL) sunflower oil

2 tsp (10 mL) poppy seeds

1. Combine agave nectar, vinegar, onion, mustard powder, and salt in a blender. Blend on high speed until smooth. (Alternatively, use a large measuring cup and an immersion blender.)

2. With the motor running, slowly add the oil—start with just drops, then gradually increase to a thin stream—and blend until quite thick.

3. Transfer to an airtight container. Add poppy seeds and stir well (alternatively, seal and shake well). Use immediately or refrigerate for up to 2 weeks.

caesar dressing

We've had a few different versions of Caesar dressing over the years, but this latest one is my new favourite.

makes 2 cups (500 mL)

½ cup (125 mL) freshly squeezed lemon juice

3 cloves garlic, minced

¼ cup (60 mL) capers, drained

¼ tsp (1 mL) caper brine

¼ cup (60 mL) Dijon mustard

2 tsp (10 mL) gluten-free vegan Worcestershire sauce

2 tbsp (30 mL) red wine vinegar

2 tbsp (30 mL) flaked nutritional yeast

1 tbsp (15 mL) freshly ground black pepper

½ cup (125 mL) unsweetened plain soy milk

⅓ cup (75 mL) extra virgin olive oil

1 cup (250 mL) sunflower oil

½ tsp (2 mL) raw agave nectar

1 tsp (5 mL) sea salt

1. Combine all of the ingredients in a container. Using an immersion blender, blend until thickened. (Alternatively, you can use a standard blender.) Use immediately or transfer to an airtight container and refrigerate for up to 4 days.

house dressing

This is by far our most popular dressing. It works well on any salad, and is also amazing on rice or noodle bowls, especially when paired with our Miso Gravy (page 256). Make sure you like the taste of your flaxseed oil before making this. If you don't, you won't like the finished dressing. Some flaxseed oils have a very strong, bitter taste, and you definitely don't want to use those. (We prefer Maison Orphée brand, as it has a nice mild flavour.)

makes 1¾ cups (425 mL)

¼ cup (60 mL) water

¼ cup (60 mL) apple cider vinegar

1 tsp (5 mL) freshly squeezed lemon juice

½ tsp (2 mL) raw agave nectar

2 tsp (10 mL) sea salt

¾ tsp (3 mL) freshly ground black pepper

¾ tsp (3 mL) tamari

¼ tsp (1 mL) dry mustard powder

1 clove garlic

¼ cup (60 mL) flaxseed oil

¾ cup (175 mL) sunflower oil

1. Combine all of the ingredients, except the oils, in a blender. Blend on high speed until smooth. (Alternatively, use a large measuring cup and an immersion blender.)

2. With the motor running, add oils in a thin, steady stream and blend until dressing is emulsified. Use immediately or transfer to an airtight container and refrigerate for up to 2 weeks.

carrot miso dressing

This dressing gets its depth of flavour in part from the mirin, which is a sweet Japanese rice wine, similar to sake. You will see versions of mirin in the grocery store, but most of them won't be real mirin. If you see corn syrup in the ingredient list, put the bottle back and look for one that contains only water, rice, and rice koji. You might need to go to a health-food store to find the real deal.

You'll need to start thinking about making this dressing at least an hour in advance, so you have time to soak the cashews.

This recipe makes plenty of dressing, enough for about 10 servings. If you don't need that much, or don't want leftovers, just make a half batch. But this dressing is so luscious, you'll want to have extra on hand just for dipping veggies in.

makes 2½ cups (625 mL)

¼ cup (60 mL) raw cashews

2 cups (500 mL) chopped carrot

½ cup (125 mL) sunflower oil

2 tbsp (30 mL) chopped onion

¼ cup (60 mL) rice vinegar

2 tbsp (30 mL) tamari

1 tbsp (15 mL) date syrup or raw agave nectar

2 tbsp (30 mL) light miso

2 cloves garlic

¼ tsp (1 mL) sea salt

2 tbsp (30 mL) mirin

2 tsp (10 mL) peeled and chopped fresh ginger

1. Place cashews in a bowl and cover with water. Set aside for at least 1 hour to soak. Drain, then rinse under cool running water until water runs clear. Drain.

2. Combine the soaked cashews and remaining ingredients in a high-speed blender. Blend on high speed until smooth. Use immediately or transfer to an airtight container and refrigerate for up to 1 week.

peanut lime dressing

Sweet and nutty, with a little bit of spice from the sambal oelek, this dressing is one of our top sellers.

makes 1 cup (250 mL)

1 tbsp (15 mL) peeled and chopped fresh ginger

3 cloves garlic, minced (about 1 tbsp/15 mL)

¾ tsp (3 mL) sambal oelek

2 tbsp (30 mL) tightly packed fresh cilantro

2 tbsp (30 mL) natural peanut butter

2 tbsp + 2 tsp (30 mL + 10 mL) freshly squeezed lime juice

1 tbsp (15 mL) rice vinegar

5 tsp (25 mL) tamari

1½ tsp (7 mL) raw agave nectar

2 tsp (10 mL) coconut milk

¾ tsp (3 mL) sesame oil

½ cup (125 mL) sunflower oil

1. Combine all of the ingredients, except the sunflower oil, in a blender. Blend on high speed until smooth.

2. With the motor running, add sunflower oil in a thin, steady stream and blend until dressing is emulsified. Use immediately or transfer to an airtight container and refrigerate for up to 1 week.

raw sunflower dressing

If you can't find raw unsalted sunflower seeds, you can use roasted and salted ones—just omit the salt from the recipe. Note that if roasted seeds are used the end result will not be a pure white dressing—it will be more of a tan colour—but it will still taste great!

For a change, try making this dressing with orange or pineapple juice instead of grapefruit juice. You can also switch out the sunflower seeds for any other nut or seed. Use this recipe as a template for any number of flavour combinations.

makes 2 cups (500 mL)

1 cup (250 mL) water

⅓ cup (75 mL) grapefruit juice

3 tbsp (45 mL) freshly squeezed lemon juice

⅔ cup (150 mL) raw unsalted sunflower seeds

½ tsp (2 mL) sea salt

3 cloves garlic, minced

1. Combine all of the ingredients in a high-speed blender. Blend on high speed until smooth and frothy. (Alternatively, use a large measuring cup and an immersion blender.) This dressing is best when used right away, but you can transfer it to an airtight container and refrigerate for up to 2 days, if needed.

3-6-9 dressing

Named after the 3-6-9 oil it contains, this dressing is hard to describe. It's savoury and sweet all at the same time. It is very versatile, working equally well on salads as on rice or noodle bowls. We use it in the Phytosalad (page 160) and the Tiger Bowl (page 245).

A blend of different oils, 3-6-9 oil is designed to contain the ideal balance of omega-3 and omega-6 essential fatty acids. It provides all of the good fats you need, without any of the bad fats you should avoid. If you can't find it at health-food stores, you can substitute flaxseed oil, hemp oil, or even olive oil.

makes 2 cups (500 mL)

1 tsp (5 mL) sunflower oil
2 cups (500 mL) chopped onions
2 cloves garlic, minced
⅓ cup (75 mL) raw tahini
¼ cup (60 mL) extra virgin olive oil
¼ cup (60 mL) 3-6-9 oil

¼ cup (60 mL) freshly squeezed lemon juice
3 tbsp (45 mL) tamari
2 tbsp (30 mL) vegetable stock
1 tbsp (15 mL) sesame oil
1 tbsp (15 mL) pure dark maple syrup

1. Heat sunflower oil in a frying pan over medium heat.

2. Add onions and garlic, and cook for 5 to 7 minutes, until softened and starting to brown. Remove from heat and set aside to cool.

3. Combine cooked onions and garlic, tahini, olive oil, 3-6-9 oil, lemon juice, tamari, stock, sesame oil, and maple syrup in a blender. Blend on high speed until smooth. Use immediately or transfer to an airtight container and refrigerate for up to 5 days.

tahini dressing

Tahini, or sesame butter, is made from ground sesame seeds and is high in protein and a good source of essential fatty acids. Tahini is the traditional accompaniment for falafel, but it can also be used as a salad dressing or as a sauce for rice bowls or noodles.

This is our most versatile dressing; it tastes great on everything. It pairs particularly well with tamari and hot sauce, as you'll see in our Powerhouse Bowl (page 239), and with date syrup and chili oil in our Ironman Salad (page 163) and Falafel Tacos (page 209).

makes 1½ cups (375 mL)

½ cup (125 mL) chopped fresh parsley

2 tbsp (30 mL) freshly squeezed lemon juice

2 cloves garlic, minced

½ tsp (2 mL) sea salt

⅔ cup (150 mL) water (see Tip)

½ cup (125 mL) raw tahini

1. Combine parsley, lemon juice, garlic, and salt in a blender. Blend on high speed until smooth.

2. Add water and tahini. Blend until smooth. Use immediately or transfer to an airtight container and refrigerate for up to 4 days.

Tip: If your tahini is especially thick, you may need to add more water, 1 tbsp (15 mL) at a time, until you achieve a pourable consistency.

wild ginger dressing

Inspired by the dressing served at many sushi restaurants, this version is really light and fresh, with just a little bite from the ginger. It goes especially well with the Green Destiny Salad (page 162). You will need a blender to get the proper smooth consistency.

makes 1½ cups (375 mL)

½ cup (125 mL) chopped sweet onion (such as Vidalia)

½ cup (125 mL) sunflower oil

⅓ cup (75 mL) rice vinegar

2 tbsp (30 mL) water

2 tbsp (30 mL) minced peeled fresh ginger

¼ stalk celery, chopped

1 tbsp (15 mL) tamari

1½ tsp (7 mL) raw agave nectar

1½ tsp (7 mL) freshly squeezed lemon juice

½ tsp (2 mL) sea salt

¼ tsp (1 mL) freshly ground black pepper

1. Combine all of the ingredients in a blender. Blend on high speed until smooth. (Alternatively, use a large measuring cup and an immersion blender.) Use immediately or transfer to an airtight container and refrigerate for up to 2 weeks.

sriracha maple dressing

Spicy, zesty, and sweet! This dressing livens up even the most basic salads. The addition of yellow mustard was inspired by Carmel Oren, a Fresh manager who likes it on everything and really got me back into it after years of only using Dijon!

makes ¾ cup (175 mL)

¼ cup (60 mL) pure dark maple syrup

¼ cup (60 mL) Sriracha sauce

2 tbsp (30 mL) sunflower oil

1 tsp (5 mL) prepared yellow mustard

¼ tsp (1 mL) freshly grated lime zest

2 tsp (10 mL) freshly squeezed lime juice

¼ tsp (1 mL) tamari

1 garlic clove, minced

1. Combine all of the ingredients in a blender. Blend on high speed until smooth. (Alternatively, use a large measuring cup and an immersion blender.) Use immediately or transfer to an airtight container and refrigerate for up to 2 weeks.

wasabi dill dressing

This dressing was developed for the Ninja Bowl (page 241). The heat of the wasabi and the coolness of the dill make a great combination, and the sautéed onion and garlic give a depth of flavour that counteracts the blandness of tofu.

Be sure to follow the method below, because mixing the water and wasabi first, before adding any other ingredients, really seems to wake up the wasabi. Otherwise, the wasabi flavour never seems to develop and will just get lost.

makes 2 cups (500 mL)

⅓ cup (75 mL) olive oil, divided

1 cup (250 mL) diced onion

3 cloves garlic, minced

1 tbsp (15 mL) wasabi powder

¼ cup (60 mL) water, divided

2 cups (500 mL) chopped extra firm tofu

1 tsp (5 mL) Dijon mustard

1 tbsp (15 mL) dried dill

¼ cup (60 mL) rice vinegar

¼ tsp (1 mL) sea salt

1. Heat 1 tbsp (15 mL) of oil in a frying pan over medium heat.

2. Add onion and garlic and cook, stirring occasionally, for 3 to 5 minutes, until softened. Remove from heat and set aside to cool.

3. Combine wasabi and 2 tbsp (30 mL) water in a blender. Pulse to combine.

4. Add onion mixture, remaining ¼ cup (60 mL) oil, tofu, mustard, dill, rice vinegar, salt, and remaining 2 tbsp (30 mL) water. Blend on high speed until smooth. (If dressing seems too thick, add water, 1 tbsp/15 mL at a time, until you achieve a pourable consistency.) Use immediately or transfer to an airtight container and refrigerate for up to 3 days.

SOUPS

Winter or summer, spring or fall—it's always time for soup! At Fresh, soup is the item ordered more often than anything else on our entire menu. We serve thousands of cups and bowls of it every week.

Every day at the restaurants we offer two different soups: one with beans or grains, and the other with only vegetables. We have lots of different soup recipes, so we don't repeat ourselves too often. The recipes in this book include some that we've loved for 15 years, and others that are brand-new favourites.

We take the inspiration for our soups from all over the world, and they range from thin broths to thick, hearty stews and chilis. There are traditional combos like vegetable barley and vegan chicken noodle, as well as combinations that I don't think anyone has ever done before, like the African Black Bean with Berbere and Hominy (page 188).

The nice thing about soups is that they make great leftovers and taste even better the next day. Most of these soups last from a few days to up to a week in the fridge and also freeze well.

Choose a really big pot with a heavy bottom so you can sauté right in the pot and stir easily without the soup overflowing. I like using my big Le Creuset enamelled cast iron soup pots because they are great to work with and hold the heat forever, but most of all it's because they are bright yellow and they make me feel happy while I'm cooking!

roasted vegetable stock

When making soup, good ingredients are essential, none more so than a good vegetable stock. Though it is fine to use ready-made stocks, none can parallel a homemade stock. Also, many store-bought stocks contain MSG (monosodium glutamate), so read the label carefully. Even if it doesn't say MSG, look for words like "hydrolyzed" and "autolyzed." If you see either of them, steer clear. There are a few good stock powders and pastes out there, but you have to really scrutinize the ingredient list to make sure they don't contain MSG.

This Roasted Vegetable Stock is simple to prepare. Roasting the vegetables first gives a much richer flavour to the finished stock. This recipe is for a totally fat-free stock, but if you wanted, you could add some oil to the vegetables while they are roasting, as this helps them caramelize a bit better.

makes 8 cups (2 L)

3 celery stalks, roughly chopped

2 carrots, roughly chopped

2 tomatoes, roughly chopped

1 onion, roughly chopped

4 cloves garlic

2 cups (500 mL) halved button mushrooms

16 cups (4 L) water, divided

½ cup (125 mL) roughly chopped fresh parsley

½ tsp (2 mL) whole black peppercorns

1. Preheat oven to 400°F (200°C).

2. Arrange celery, carrots, tomato, onion, garlic, and mushrooms in a single layer on a rimmed baking sheet and pour about ¼ cup (60 mL) water over top.

3. Roast in preheated oven for about 20 minutes or until vegetables start to brown at the edges.

4. Remove from oven and transfer roasted vegetables to a large pot. Add the remaining water, parsley, and black peppercorns. Stir.

5. Bring to a boil over high heat, then reduce heat and simmer for about 2 hours.

6. Strain through a fine-mesh sieve; discard solids. Use immediately or let cool, transfer to an airtight container, and refrigerate for up to 1 week.

spring vegetable and barley soup

Usually you only see barley in winter soups, but I love it any time of year. With asparagus and other spring vegetables, it makes a hearty yet light combination.

When making this soup, start with just 6 cups (1.5 L) of stock and only add the extra 2 cups (500 mL) if needed to get the barley tender.

You want to serve this soup as soon as it's ready to maintain the bright green colour of the vegetables, so if you are making it for just two or three people, make a half batch.

serves 4 to 6

2 tbsp (30 mL) sunflower oil or neutral-flavoured coconut oil

1 cup (250 mL) chopped onion

1 cup (250 mL) sliced leeks (see Tip, page 181)

1 cup (250 mL) chopped celery

¼ cup (60 mL) chopped carrots

1 cup (250 mL) pearl barley, rinsed and drained

6 to 8 cups (1.5 to 2 L) vegetable stock

2 cups (500 mL) lightly packed chopped kale, large stems and ribs removed, or dandelion greens

2 cups (500 mL) chopped asparagus (cut into bite-size pieces)

1 cup (250 mL) frozen green peas, rinsed and drained

½ tsp (2 mL) sea salt

1. Heat oil in a large pot over medium-high heat.

2. Add onion, leeks, celery, and carrots and cook for 3 to 4 minutes, until softened.

3. Stir in barley and stock. Bring to a boil, then reduce heat to medium-low and simmer until barley is tender.

4. Add kale, asparagus, and peas. Return to a boil, reduce heat, and cook for 3 to 4 minutes, until asparagus is tender.

5. Stir in salt. Serve immediately.

hampton green pea soup with fresh herbs

This bright green purée would be perfect for an outdoor summer party. You can use whatever combination of fresh herbs you like. The first time I made it I went and grabbed a handful of all the herbs I had growing on my front steps, and I happened to have sorrel and lemon thyme, so that's why they are listed. But I know you don't often see those in the stores, so just use whatever you can find. Just be sure not to use too much mint or it will overpower the rest—2 tbsp (30 mL) of mint out of the ½ cup (125 mL) total herbs should be about right. Try this soup garnished with some raw hemp hearts or ground flaxseeds.

serves 4 to 6

2 tbsp (30 mL) olive oil

2 cups (500 mL) sliced leeks

1 cup (250 mL) diced onion

2 cups (500 mL) peeled and diced potatoes

6 cups (1.5 L) vegetable stock

4 cups (1 L) frozen green peas, rinsed and drained

½ cup (125 mL) tightly packed fresh mixed herbs (basil, sorrel, lemon thyme, mint, chives, tarragon)

Sea salt, to taste

1. Heat oil in a pot over medium-high heat.

2. Add leeks and onion and cook, stirring occasionally, for 2 to 4 minutes, until soft.

3. Add potatoes and stock. Bring to a boil, reduce heat, and simmer until potatoes are tender.

4. Stir in peas and herbs. Return to a boil.

5. Remove from heat. Using an immersion blender, blend soup until creamy smooth. (Soup will go through a grainy stage, but continue blending until mixture is super smooth.)

6. Stir in salt. Serve immediately to retain the soup's bright green colour.

Tip: Be sure to clean the leeks carefully, as there's generally dirt hidden in their layers. To clean leeks, cut off the top and tail (bulb end) and remove the outer leaves. Cut in half lengthwise and then chop into pieces. Transfer chopped leek to a large bowl and place in the sink. Fill bowl with cold water and swoosh the leeks around with your hands to release the dirt from in between the layers. Lift the leeks out with your hands and transfer them to another container. Rinse the bowl, then return the leeks to the bowl. Cover with cold water, swoosh around, and repeat this process until no dirt is left behind in the bowl.

kashmir vegetable soup

This soup is based on a dish I used to make at Henderson's in Edinburgh, Scotland. It was inspired by the Broccoli and Cauliflower Harlequin, a delicious casserole that I still miss, even though it's been 20 years since I worked there! This soup gets better with every delicious spoonful. It has a creamy texture and a pungent exotic spiciness that keeps you going back for more.

serves 4 to 6

¼ cup (60 mL) olive oil

2 cups (500 mL) diced onions

6 cloves garlic, minced

1 stalk celery, finely diced

1 carrot, finely diced

1 tsp (5 mL) ground cinnamon

1 tbsp (15 mL) ground coriander

1 tsp (5 mL) cayenne pepper

1 tbsp (15 mL) curry powder

1 cup (250 mL) dried red lentils

¼ cup (60 mL) tomato paste

1 cup (250 mL) light spelt flour

8 cups (2 L) vegetable stock

1 cup (250 mL) canned tomatoes, puréed (see Tip, page 189)

1 cup (250 mL) broccoli florets

1 cup (250 mL) cauliflower florets

Sea salt, to taste

1. Heat oil in a pot over medium heat.

2. Add onions, garlic, celery, and carrot. Cook, stirring occasionally, for 3 to 4 minutes, until softened.

3. Stir in cinnamon, coriander, cayenne, and curry powder. Cook for a few seconds.

4. Add lentils, tomato paste, and flour. Cook, stirring, for 1 to 2 minutes, until the raw taste of the flour cooks out.

5. Gradually add stock, stirring constantly to avoid lumps. Add tomatoes and cook for about 15 minutes, until lentils are soft and nearly cooked.

6. Stir in broccoli and cauliflower, and cook for another 15 minutes or until vegetables are tender.

7. Stir in salt. Serve immediately or let cool, transfer to an airtight container, and refrigerate for up to 4 days.

jamaican spinach soup

This soup has been a favourite at Fresh for over 15 years. The velvety texture and brilliant green colour are both very appealing. Grated vegan cheddar cheese sprinkled on top is a great addition. And if you like your food very spicy, increase the cayenne pepper to taste. The spinach is added after the soup comes off the heat. Spinach needs barely any time to cook, so the residual heat in the soup will be sufficient to soften it.

Spinach is high in antioxidants such as beta-carotene and lutein, which helps lower blood cholesterol. It also has carbohydrates, protein, fibre, vitamins A and C, calcium, iron, and folic acid. Zucchini is high in folic acid and potassium.

serves 4 to 6

2 tbsp (30 mL) sunflower oil or neutral-flavoured coconut oil

1 cup (250 mL) chopped onion

2 stalks celery, chopped

4 cloves garlic, minced

2 tbsp (30 mL) minced peeled ginger

1 tbsp (15 mL) raw agave nectar

2 tsp (10 mL) sea salt

¼ tsp (1 mL) ground turmeric

¼ tsp (1 mL) ground allspice

¼ tsp (1 mL) ground nutmeg

2 potatoes, peeled and diced

4 cups (1 L) chopped zucchini

6 cups (1.5 L) vegetable stock

1 cup (250 mL) tightly packed chopped spinach

Pinch cayenne pepper

1. Heat oil in a pot over medium heat.

2. Add onion, celery, garlic, ginger, and agave nectar. Cook, stirring occasionally, for 3 to 4 minutes, until onion is softened.

3. Stir in salt, turmeric, allspice, and nutmeg and cook for a few seconds.

4. Add potatoes, zucchini, and stock. Bring to a boil, reduce heat, and simmer until potatoes are soft.

5. Remove from heat. Stir in spinach and cayenne.

6. Using an immersion blender, blend until smooth. (If you are using a regular blender, let the soup cool before blending, then reheat; see page 98.)

supergrain soup

Have you tried freekeh yet? It has been around for centuries but is only now enjoying increased popularity in North America. It consists of green wheat that goes through a roasting and rubbing process. Because the grains are young when harvested, it contains more protein, vitamins, and minerals than mature grains. Freekeh has three times the fibre and protein of brown rice and twice as much as quinoa!

serves 4 to 6

2 tbsp (30 mL) sunflower oil or neutral-flavoured coconut oil

1 cup (250 mL) diced onion

1 cup (250 mL) sliced leeks (see Tip, page 181)

1 cup (250 mL) diced carrots

1 cup (250 mL) chopped celery

½ tsp (2 mL) dried thyme

3 bay leaves

3 cloves garlic

¼ cup (60 mL) red or white quinoa, rinsed and drained

¼ cup (60 mL) freekeh, rinsed and drained

¼ cup (60 mL) wild rice, rinsed and drained

¼ cup (60 mL) millet, rinsed and drained

2 cups (500 mL) cauliflower florets (small)

6 to 8 cups (1.5 to 2 L) vegetable stock

4 cups (1 L) lightly packed shredded kale, large stems and ribs removed

1. Heat oil in a large pot over medium-high heat.

2. Add onion, leeks, carrots, and celery and cook, stirring occasionally, for 3 to 4 minutes, until softened.

3. Add thyme, bay leaves, and garlic. Cook, stirring, for about 1 minute, until fragrant.

4. Add quinoa, freekeh, wild rice, millet, cauliflower, and 6 cups (1.5 mL) of stock and stir to combine. Bring to a boil, reduce heat, and simmer until all grains are tender, about 1 hour (add remaining 2 cups/500 mL stock, if needed to help cook the grains).

5. Stir in kale. Return to a boil, reduce heat, and simmer for 2 or 3 minutes, until kale is tender. Serve immediately or let cool, transfer to an airtight container, and refrigerate for up to 4 days.

vegan chicken noodle soup

This soup will transport you back to your childhood with its familiar flavours and textures!

serves 4 to 6

soy curl marinade

1 cup (250 mL) water

1 cup (250 mL) Butler Soy Curls (see Tip) or TVP chunks (reconstituted according to package directions)

1 tsp (5 mL) sea salt

½ tsp (2 mL) garlic powder

¼ tsp (1 mL) poultry seasoning

soup

¼ cup (60 mL) sunflower oil

1 cup (250 mL) chopped celery

2 carrots, chopped

1 onion, diced

1 leek, sliced (see Tip, page 181)

5 cloves garlic, minced

½ tsp (2 mL) dried thyme

2 bay leaves

¼ cup (60 mL) all-purpose flour

6 cups (1.5 mL) vegetable stock

½ cup (125 mL) dried filini pasta (or any other small dried pasta)

½ cup (125 mL) frozen green peas, rinsed and drained

¼ cup (60 mL) chopped fresh parsley

Sea salt, to taste

Freshly ground black pepper, to taste

1. **Make soy curl marinade** Combine water, reconstituted soy curls, salt, garlic powder, and poultry seasoning in a bowl. Cover and set aside for 1 hour to marinate. Drain, discarding liquid. Set aside.

2. **Make soup** Heat oil in a large pot over medium heat.

3. Add celery, carrots, onion, leek, and garlic. Cook, stirring occasionally, for 3 to 4 minutes, until softened.

4. Stir in thyme and bay leaves.

5. Add flour and stir until all of the vegetables are coated.

6. Gradually add stock, a little at a time, stirring to prevent lumps.

7. Add marinated soy curls and noodles. Return to a boil over high heat, then reduce heat to medium and simmer, stirring often, until noodles are al dente, 10 to 15 minutes.

8. Stir in green peas and parsley. Return to a boil.

9. Remove from heat. Add salt and pepper. Discard bay leaves. Serve immediately or let cool, transfer to an airtight container, and refrigerate for up to 4 days.

Tip: Poultry seasoning, which doesn't actually contain any poultry, can be found in grocery stores, but if you want to make your own, simply combine equal quantities of ground sage, thyme, rosemary, marjoram, nutmeg, onion powder, and black pepper.

This soup is best made with Butler Soy Curls, but if you can't find them, use textured vegetable protein (TVP) slices or even some Gardein Chick'n Strips. If using Gardein or any other brand of faux chicken strips that are not dried, add them to the soup a few minutes before it finishes cooking, just long enough to heat them through.

curried lentil soup with sage

This is another soup based on a casserole I used to make when I worked at Henderson's Vegetarian Restaurant in Edinburgh, Scotland. I can't recall ever seeing curry and sage together in a dish anywhere else, but it's a combination that works surprisingly well.

The amount of stock needed in this soup totally depends on how dry your lentils are and how much liquid they will need to absorb to become soft. Just keep adding more liquid until the lentils are totally soft. If you're not sure if they're soft enough, they probably aren't, so just keep adding. This soup is quite thick, so you can add more stock or water if you prefer a thinner soup.

serves 4 to 6

2 tbsp (30 mL) sunflower oil or neutral-flavoured coconut oil

1 cup (250 mL) diced onion

1 clove garlic, minced

2 cups (500 mL) diced zucchini

1 tbsp (15 mL) curry powder

1 tsp (5 mL) dried sage

1 can (19 oz/540 mL) white kidney beans, drained and rinsed

1 potato, peeled and diced

2 cups (500 mL) dried red lentils

4 to 6 cups (1 to 1.5 L) vegetable stock

2 tsp (10 mL) tomato paste

3 cups (750 mL) canned whole tomatoes, puréed (about one 28 oz/794 g can)

¾ tsp (3 mL) sea salt

1. Heat oil in a large pot over medium heat.

2. Add onion and cook, stirring occasionally, for 1 to 2 minutes, until softened.

3. Stir in garlic, zucchini, curry powder, and sage and cook for 30 seconds to 1 minute, until fragrant.

4. Stir in beans, potato, lentils, stock, tomato paste, and puréed tomatoes. Bring to a boil, reduce heat, and simmer for at least 30 minutes or until lentils are soft. (Add more stock if needed to allow lentils to fully cook.)

5. Remove from heat and stir in salt. Serve immediately or let cool, transfer to an airtight container, and refrigerate for up to 4 days.

african black bean soup with berbere and hominy

This spicy soup is great on a cold winter night. It warms you up from the inside out!

Berbere is a traditional Ethiopian spice mix. There are many different versions out there, but this one is my favourite. The spice mix here makes more than you'll need for this soup, but it keeps well in a tightly sealed glass jar, and then you'll have it already the next time you want to use it.

Hominy has been around forever, but I only tried it recently. It's made from corn that has been soaked in an alkali solution that removes the hull and germ of the corn and makes it puff up to about twice its normal size. It's made from white or yellow corn, not sweet corn, which is the kind that you eat on the cob. It's so cute looking and adds a really interesting texture and flavour, kind of like little mini dumplings. Look for it in the Mexican section of your supermarket.

serves 4 to 6

berbere spice mix

6 cardamom pods or ⅛ tsp (0.5 mL) ground cardamom

1 tsp (5 mL) cumin seeds

1 tsp (5 mL) fenugreek seeds

1 tsp (5 mL) allspice berries or ½ tsp (2 mL) ground allspice

2 whole cloves

1 tsp (5 mL) whole black peppercorns

½ tsp (2 mL) coriander seeds

1 tsp (5 mL) crushed red chilies

1 tsp (5 mL) dried thyme

½ tsp (2 mL) ground ginger

½ tsp (2 mL) ground nutmeg

¼ tsp (1 mL) cayenne pepper

1 tsp (5 mL) ground cinnamon

1 tsp (5 mL) onion powder or dried onion flakes

1 tsp (5 mL) garlic powder

3 tbsp (45 mL) sweet paprika

1 tbsp (15 mL) sea salt

soup

2 tbsp (30 mL) sunflower oil or neutral-flavoured coconut oil

2 cups (500 mL) diced onions

2 tbsp (30 mL) minced garlic

¼ cup (60 mL) diced carrot

½ cup (125 mL) diced celery

3 tbsp (45 mL) Berbere Spice Mix

1 can (28 oz/794 g) whole tomatoes, puréed

4 cups (1 L) vegetable stock

3 cups (750 mL) chopped green or napa cabbage

1 can (14 oz/398 mL) black beans, drained and rinsed

1 can (15 oz/425 g) hominy, drained and rinsed

1. **Make berbere spice mix** Combine cardamom, cumin, fenugreek, allspice (only if using whole), cloves, black peppercorns, and coriander in a frying pan over medium heat. Cook, stirring, for 1 to 2 minutes, until fragrant and just starting to smoke. Remove from heat, pour into a bowl, and set aside to cool.

2. Remove cardamom pods from pan, crack open, and remove inner seeds from outer hull; discard outer hull.

3. Transfer toasted cardamom seeds and other whole spices to a spice grinder and process until finely ground. (If using onion flakes, add them to the grinder.)

4. Combine ground spices, crushed red chilies, thyme, ginger, nutmeg, cayenne, cinnamon, onion powder (if using), garlic powder, paprika, and salt in a bowl. Set aside.

5. **Make soup** Heat oil in a large pot.

6. Add onions, garlic, carrot, and celery. Cook, stirring occasionally, for 5 to 10 minutes or until softened.

7. Stir in berbere spice mix.

8. Add tomatoes, stock, cabbage, black beans, and hominy. Bring to a boil, reduce heat to low, and cook until cabbage is soft, 15 to 20 minutes. Serve immediately or let cool, transfer to an airtight container, and refrigerate for up to 4 days.

Tip: For the puréed tomatoes, I like to use whole canned tomatoes and purée them myself. It just seems to taste better than canned crushed tomatoes. Pour them into a large measuring cup and blend with an immersion blender, or purée in a food processor or stand blender.

golden curried dal

We've been making this soup for over a decade now, and it's still one of our most popular. At home, you can just eat it straight, like a soup, or make it a complete meal in a bowl by pouring it over some brown rice, adding some sautéed spinach, kale, or mushrooms, and scattering some hemp seeds, flaxseeds, or pumpkin seeds over top. Hot sauce, green onions, and cilantro are also great additions.

serves 4 to 6

2 tbsp (30 mL) sunflower oil or neutral-flavoured coconut oil

2 cups (500 mL) diced onions

1 carrot, diced

4 cloves garlic, minced

3 tbsp (45 mL) minced peeled ginger

2 tsp (10 mL) curry powder

1 tsp (5 mL) ground cumin

½ tsp (2 mL) ground turmeric

2½ cups (625 mL) dried red lentils

8 cups (2 L) vegetable stock

1 can (14 oz/414 mL) coconut milk

2 green onions, finely sliced (optional)

¼ cup (60 mL) chopped fresh cilantro (optional)

1. Heat oil in a large pot over medium heat.

2. Add onions, carrot, garlic, and ginger and cook for 3 to 5 minutes, until onions are softened.

3. Stir in curry powder, cumin, and turmeric and cook for a few seconds.

4. Add lentils, stock, and coconut milk. Stir to combine. Bring to a boil, stirring often with a wooden spoon to prevent lentils from sticking to the bottom of the pot.

5. Reduce heat and simmer until lentils are soft, about 20 minutes.

6. Remove from heat and garnish with green onions and cilantro (if using). Serve immediately or transfer to an airtight container and refrigerate for up to 2 days. (Once refrigerated, dal tends to solidify, so just add a little bit of water or stock when you reheat it.)

Tip: The taste of this soup depends largely on the curry powder that you use. At the restaurant, we like to use an Indian curry powder called Lalah's. It has lots of flavour and the perfect amount of heat. You can find it at Indian grocers.

montego bay corn soup with red lentils and spinach

The balance of the pungent garlic, sweet corn, creamy coconut, and Jamaican spices works really well in this soup. The Jamaican curry powder recipe will make more than you need for one batch of soup, but it keeps well in a tightly closed jar. And the eight cloves of garlic may seem like a lot, but don't worry—it's not overwhelming.

serves 4 to 6

jamaican curry powder

2 tbsp (30 mL) coriander seeds

1 tbsp (15 mL) cumin seeds

1 tbsp (15 mL) mustard seeds

1 tbsp (15 mL) anise seeds

2 tsp (10 mL) fenugreek seeds

1½ tsp (7 mL) allspice berries or 1 tsp (5 mL) ground allspice

2 tbsp (30 mL) ground turmeric

1 tsp (5 mL) ground ginger

½ tsp (2 mL) cayenne pepper

soup

2 tbsp (30 mL) sunflower oil or neutral-flavoured coconut oil

2½ cups (625 mL) chopped onion

8 cloves garlic, minced

¼ cup (60 mL) Jamaican Curry Powder

3 cups (750 mL) frozen corn, rinsed and drained

1 can (14 oz/414 mL) coconut milk

1 cup (250 mL) dried red lentils

7 cups (1.75 L) vegetable stock

4 cups (1 L) lightly packed chopped spinach

1. **Make Jamaican Curry Powder** Combine coriander, cumin, mustard seeds, anise seeds, fenugreek, and allspice (only if using whole) in a dry frying pan over medium heat and cook, stirring, for 1 to 2 minutes, until fragrant and just starting to smoke. Remove from heat, pour into a bowl, and let cool.

2. Transfer toasted spices to a spice grinder and process until finely ground.

3. Combine ground spices, turmeric, ginger, and cayenne in a bowl. Set aside.

4. **Make soup** Heat oil in large pot over medium heat.

5. Add onion and garlic and cook for 3 to 4 minutes, stirring occasionally, until softened.

6. Add curry powder and stir.

7. Stir in corn, coconut milk, lentils, and stock and bring to a boil.

8. Reduce heat and simmer until lentils are soft, about 20 minutes.

9. Add spinach and stir to combine. Return to a boil.

10. Remove from heat. Serve immediately or let cool, transfer to an airtight container, and refrigerate for up to 4 days.

east african pea soup

This soup has been a favourite of staff and customers for almost 15 years. The flavour here is savoury, with a little bit of sweetness from the sweet potato. The 10 cups (2.5 L) of vegetable stock for only 1 cup (250 mL) of split peas may seem like a lot, but it usually takes this much stock to cook the peas until they are nice and soft.

serves 4 to 6

2 tbsp (30 mL) sunflower oil or neutral-flavoured coconut oil

2 cups (500 mL) diced onions

4 cloves garlic, minced

¼ cup (60 mL) minced peeled fresh ginger

½ tsp (2 mL) Mexican chili powder

2 tbsp (30 mL) curry powder

2 tomatoes, chopped

½ sweet potato, peeled and chopped

1 cup (250 mL) dried yellow split peas

10 to 16 cups (2.5 to 4 L) vegetable stock

Sea salt, to taste

garnishes

Sliced green onions (optional)

Chopped fresh cilantro (optional)

1. Heat oil in a pot over medium heat.

2. Add onions, garlic, and ginger. Cook, stirring occasionally, for 3 to 4 minutes, until onions are softened.

3. Stir in chili powder and curry powder.

4. Add tomatoes, sweet potato, split peas, and stock (see Tip).

5. Bring to a boil, reduce heat, and simmer until split peas are soft, about 1 hour.

6. Remove from heat. Stir in salt.

7. Serve immediately, garnished with green onions and cilantro (if using), or let cool, transfer to an airtight container, and refrigerate for up to 4 days.

Tip: We make this soup all the time, and the amount of vegetable stock needed seems to change with every batch of split peas that we get. So if 10 cups (2.5 L) isn't enough, add more stock by the cupful while cooking until the peas are soft.

white lentil soup with ras el hanout

Ras el hanout is a complex Moroccan spice mix. Its literal translation from Arabic is "head of the shop," implying that it's a mixture of the best spices the seller has to offer. There are as many different versions as there are spice merchants, and it can contain up to 30 different ingredients. It pairs beautifully in this soup, with the sweetness from the apricots and raisins, and the earthiness from the broccoli stems and lentils.

If you can't find the dried white lentils, substitute dried red lentils. You will need much less stock in that case, so start with 4 cups (1 L) and add more only if needed to cook the lentils until tender.

serves 4 to 6

2 tbsp (30 mL) sunflower oil or neutral-flavoured coconut oil

1 cup (250 mL) chopped red bell pepper (about ½ large pepper)

1 cup (250 mL) chopped carrots

1 cup (250 mL) diced onion

3 cloves garlic, minced

1 tbsp (15 mL) ras el hanout

6 to 8 cups (1.5 to 2 L) vegetable stock

1½ cups (375 mL) puréed canned tomatoes (see Tip, page 189; about one 14 oz/397 g can)

1 cup (250 mL) chopped broccoli stems or zucchini (see Tip)

1 cup (250 mL) dried white lentils (urad dal)

2 tbsp (30 mL) sliced dried apricots

2 tbsp (30 mL) raisins

4 cups (1 L) lightly packed baby spinach leaves

Sea salt, to taste

1. Heat oil in a large pot.

2. Add red pepper, carrots, onion, and garlic. Cook, stirring occasionally, for 3 to 4 minutes, until softened.

3. Add ras el hanout and stir.

4. Add 6 cups (1.5 L) stock, tomatoes, broccoli, lentils, apricots, and raisins. Bring to a boil, reduce heat to low, and simmer for 30 to 40 minutes, until lentils are soft (add remaining 2 cups/500 mL stock if needed to cook lentils).

5. Transfer 2 cups (500 mL) of soup to a heat-proof container. Using an immersion blender, blend until smooth. (Alternatively, let cool and then use a regular blender; see page 98). Pour back into pot.

6. Stir in spinach. Cook for a minute or less, until spinach is wilted.

7. Add salt. Serve immediately or let cool, transfer to an airtight container, and refrigerate for up to 4 days.

Tip: If you can't find ras el hanout, make your own by combining 2 tsp (10 mL) each ground ginger, ground cardamom, ground mace; 1 tsp (5 mL) each ground cinnamon, ground allspice, ground coriander seeds, ground nutmeg, ground turmeric; ½ tsp (2 mL) each freshly ground black pepper, freshly ground white pepper, cayenne pepper, ground anise seeds; and ¼ tsp (1 mL) ground cloves. Stored in an airtight container in a cool, dry place, ras el hanout will keep for up to 1 year.

One of my favourite vegetables is broccoli, but the tops and stems are such different textures and flavours that they don't usually go together that well in the same dish. So once I've used the tops, rather than wasting the stem part, I like to peel off the outer layer and chop them up to use in any number of ways, like in this soup. If you don't have broccoli stems around, just use zucchini instead.

roasted cauliflower soup with sumac and lemon

Once you've had cauliflower roasted, you'll never want it any other way. Roasting takes this most mundane of veggies and makes it so delicious, you'll be tempted to eat the whole tray of it when it comes out of the oven. Just be sure to let it roast long enough that the edges get browned—that's what gives it the most amazing flavour. Garnish with some toasted pumpkin seeds or a sprinkle of raw hemp hearts, or mix some olive oil and sumac together in a small bowl and drizzle that on right before digging in.

serves 4 to 6

6 cups (1.5 L) chopped cauliflower

⅓ cup (75 mL) olive oil, divided

½ tsp (2 mL) sea salt

1 tsp (5 mL) ground sumac

1 cup (250 mL) chopped onion

2 cups (500 mL) sliced leeks (see Tip, page 181)

2 cups (500 mL) chopped celery

¼ tsp (1 mL) dried thyme or 1 tbsp (15 mL) chopped fresh thyme leaves

2 cups (500 mL) peeled and diced potato

4 cups (1 L) vegetable stock

1 cup (250 mL) unsweetened plain soy milk (optional; see Tip)

1 tsp (5 mL) freshly grated lemon zest

1 tsp (5 mL) sea salt

1. Preheat oven to 450°F (230°C).

2. In a large bowl, combine cauliflower, 3 tbsp (45 mL) olive oil, salt, and sumac and toss until each piece of cauliflower is well coated.

3. Spread coated cauliflower over a baking sheet and roast in pre-heated oven until soft and browned, 20 to 30 minutes, turning halfway through cooking time.

4. Just before cauliflower is ready, heat 1 tbsp (15 mL) of oil in a large pot over medium-high heat.

5. Add onion, leeks, celery, and thyme. Cook, stirring occasionally, for 3 to 4 minutes, until softened.

6. Add potato, stock, and roasted cauliflower. Bring to a boil, reduce heat, and cook until potato is tender, 15 to 20 minutes.

7. Stir in soy milk. Return to a boil.

8. Remove from heat. Add lemon zest and salt.

9. Using an immersion blender, blend until totally smooth. (If you are using a regular blender, let the soup cool before blending, then reheat.) Serve immediately or let cool, transfer to an airtight container, and refrigerate for up to 4 days.

Tip: You can substitute 1 cup (250 mL) of additional vegetable stock for the soy milk, if desired.

moroccan chickpea and stars soup

This soup is one of my all-time favourites. It was inspired by the "chicken and stars" soup that my mum used to give me when I was a kid, home from school with a cold. I still love the look and feel of the little star-shaped pasta! If you can't find them, just substitute any other small dried pasta.

There is something so satisfying and hearty about this soup, yet it is still light enough to enjoy in the middle of summer. And it's good for you, too! Chickpeas and white kidney beans are high in fibre and a good source of vitamins and minerals.

serves 4 to 6

2 tbsp (30 mL) olive oil

2 onions, diced

3 tbsp (45 mL) minced peeled ginger

2 cloves garlic, minced

Pinch ground cinnamon

Pinch ground allspice

Pinch ground coriander

Pinch ground cardamom (optional)

Pinch ground turmeric

Pinch cayenne pepper

1 tomato, chopped

½ cup (125 mL) dried red lentils

8 cups (2 L) vegetable stock

1 cup (250 mL) canned chickpeas, drained and rinsed

1 cup (250 mL) canned white kidney beans, drained and rinsed

½ cup (125 mL) small dried pasta (stars, alphabets, or orzo)

1 tsp (5 mL) sea salt

¼ tsp (1 mL) freshly ground black pepper

1 tbsp (15 mL) freshly squeezed lemon juice

1. Heat oil in a pot over medium heat.

2. Add onions, ginger, and garlic and cook for 3 to 4 minutes, stirring occasionally, until onions are softened.

3. Add cinnamon, allspice, coriander, cardamom (if using), turmeric, and cayenne and cook, stirring, for a few seconds.

4. Stir in tomato, lentils, and stock. Cook until lentils are softened, about 20 minutes.

5. Add chickpeas, beans, and pasta and stir to combine. Cook for 3 to 4 minutes or until pasta is al dente.

6. Remove from heat. Stir in salt, pepper, and lemon juice. Serve immediately or let cool, transfer to an airtight container, and refrigerate for up to 4 days.

winter vegetable stew with butternut squash and kale

We took this soup to Soupstock, an event in 2012 where tons of restaurants from Toronto and the surrounding area gathered together to raise money to protest a planned mega-quarry in Melancthon Township, 100 kilometres north of Toronto, Ontario. Forty thousand people showed up to support the cause, and it worked! The mega-quarry proposal was withdrawn.

This soup was a big hit, with lots of people coming back for seconds and thirds, and also requesting the recipe.

serves 4

first pot

2 cups (500 mL) chopped cauliflower

1 cup (250 mL) peeled and diced potato

1½ cups (375 mL) vegetable stock

½ cup (125 mL) unsweetened rice milk

1 clove garlic, minced

¼ tsp (1 mL) sea salt

¼ tsp (1 mL) freshly ground black pepper

second pot

1 tbsp (15 mL) sunflower oil or neutral-flavoured coconut oil

1 cup (250 mL) chopped leeks (see Tip, page 181)

1 small onion, diced

3 cloves garlic, minced

½ cup (125 mL) diced celery

1 cup (250 mL) peeled and diced potato

1 cup (250 mL) peeled and diced butternut squash

½ cup (125 mL) diced carrot

¼ tsp (1 mL) dried thyme

¼ tsp (1 mL) dried rosemary

2 cups (500 mL) vegetable stock

½ cup (125 mL) chopped kale, large stems and ribs removed

1. **Cook first pot** Combine cauliflower, potato, stock, rice milk, garlic, salt, and pepper in a large pot and bring to a boil.

2. Reduce heat and simmer until all vegetables are soft, 15 to 20 minutes.

3. Using an immersion blender, purée soup. (Alternatively, let cool and then use a regular blender; see page 98.)

4. Taste and season with additional salt and pepper, if needed. Set aside.

5. **Cook second pot** Heat oil in a large pot. Add leeks, onion, garlic, and celery and cook, stirring occasionally, for 3 to 4 minutes, until softened.

6. Add potato, squash, carrot, thyme, rosemary, and stock and cook, stirring occasionally, until all vegetables are soft, 15 to 20 minutes.

7. **Assemble soup** Add kale and then cauliflower and potato purée from first pot. Stir well.

8. Return to a boil and cook for 1 to 2 minutes, until kale is tender.

9. Add salt and pepper to taste. Serve immediately or let cool, transfer to an airtight container, and refrigerate for up to 4 days.

double black chili

Black lentils and black beans make for a super-dark and satisfying chili. The flavour and texture of hominy make a great addition here, but if you can't find it, just use extra sweet corn instead.

serves 4 to 6

2 tbsp (30 mL) sunflower oil or neutral-flavoured coconut oil

2 cups (500 mL) chopped onion

8 cloves garlic, minced

1 jalapeño pepper, seeded and chopped

1 tbsp (15 mL) unsweetened cocoa powder

¼ tsp (1 mL) ground cinnamon

¼ cup (60 mL) Mexican chili powder

½ cup (125 mL) dry white wine

4 cups (1 L) quartered button mushrooms

1 cup (250 mL) chopped zucchini

3 cups (750 mL) canned whole tomatoes, puréed (one 28 oz/794 g can)

½ cup (125 mL) black beluga lentils

1 can (14 oz/398 mL) black beans, drained and rinsed

4 cups (1 L) vegetable stock

1 cup (250 mL) canned hominy, drained and rinsed

1 cup (250 mL) frozen corn, rinsed and drained

4 cups (1 L) lightly packed baby spinach leaves

garnishes

Chopped fresh cilantro

Sliced green onions

Chopped avocado

Tofu Sour Cream (page 275)

1. Heat oil in a pot over medium heat.

2. Add onion, garlic, and jalapeño and cook for 1 to 2 minutes, stirring occasionally, until softened.

3. Add cocoa, cinnamon, and chili powder and cook, stirring, for 30 seconds.

4. Add white wine and cook for 1 minute.

5. Add mushrooms, zucchini, tomatoes, lentils, black beans, and stock. Bring to a boil, reduce heat to low, and simmer, stirring occasionally, until lentils are soft, 30 to 45 minutes.

6. Stir in hominy, corn, and spinach. Return to a boil and cook for 1 minute, until heated through.

7. Serve garnished with cilantro, green onions, avocado, and sour cream.

Tip: Black beluga lentils glisten when they're cooked, like beluga caviar, hence the name. If you can't find them, substitute French green lentils.

spicy detox noodle soup

The first time I made this soup I had a cold, with a sore throat and stuffed nose. This soup made me feel so much better, I just had to share it with you. It's light but so satisfying because of the noodles and the heat from the sambal oelek. This recipe makes just one serving, because it's not the kind of thing you want for leftovers. Just double the batch if you're making it for more than just you.

serves 1

2 cups (500 mL) Roasted Vegetable Stock (page 178)

1 clove garlic, minced

1 tbsp (15 mL) tamari

½ tsp (2 mL) sambal oelek or more to taste

¼ tsp (1 mL) umami paste (optional; see Tip)

1 package (7 oz/198 g) shirataki noodles, drained and rinsed

1 cup (250 mL) lightly packed baby spinach

½ cup (125 mL) Marinated Tofu Cubes (page 272)

1 tbsp (15 mL) chopped fresh cilantro

1 tbsp (15 mL) chopped green onions

1 tbsp (15 mL) sliced red chilies

2 lime wedges

1. Heat about ¼ cup (60 mL) of the stock in a pot over medium-high heat.

2. Add garlic and cook for 1 minute.

3. Add remaining stock, tamari, sambal oelek, and umami paste (if using). Bring to a boil.

4. Add drained noodles. Return to a boil.

5. Place spinach and marinated tofu cubes in a large bowl.

6. Pour broth and noodle mixture over top.

7. Garnish with cilantro, green onions, chilies, and lime wedges.

Tip: The shirataki noodles used here—also called miracle noodles—are available with or without tofu, and contain either 0 calories or about 20 calories with tofu. At first you might think their texture is a bit weird, but you'll soon get used to it. You can find them in the refrigerated case at most supermarkets. Usually they'll be near the tofu and tempeh. They smell a bit "ocean-y" when you open the package. That's normal, so don't worry—they don't taste that way at all.

Umami paste is packaged in a tube, kind of like toothpaste. Just be sure to purchase the vegetarian kind (there is also a version that contains fish).

SANDWICHES, WRAPS, AND TACOS

What is it about food wrapped in other food that's so appealing? Sandwiches, wraps, and tacos are such a beautiful and comforting choice for lunch or any time of day. Our most popular handheld food items always seem to follow the same formula: they have a crispy element, a creamy element, and a crunchy element. And sometimes a spicy element to give it some kick. From that basic premise there is a world of options to explore and countless accents to try, from the familiar to the exotic—and usually both in the same bite.

Whether it's the crunchy broccoli slaw in the Oyster Mushroom Po'boy (page 206), the crispy squash in the Squash Tacos (page 210), or the garlic mayo in the Clubhouse Wrap (page 205), you need a balance of all the textures and flavours to really make a sandwich, wrap, or taco sing. With these recipes I've tried to give you that balance every time.

Sam Houston

chimichurri tofu steak sandwich

According to Fresh staff member Linda Weinz, this sandwich is the love of her life, and she had a month-long love affair with it while it was our monthly special. I always know a special is a winner if Linda likes it!

serves 4

crispy tofu steaks

16 Marinated Tofu Steaks (page 272)

1 batch Crispy Tofu Coating (page 266)

Oil, for frying (sunflower, canola, or neutral-flavoured coconut oil)

sandwiches

4 whole-grain submarine buns

½ cup (125 mL) Lemon Aioli (page 268)

4 cups (1 L) lightly packed greens of your choice (spring mix, baby kale, baby arugula)

24 thin slices English cucumber

¾ cup (175 mL) Red Chimichurri Sauce

12 slices tomato

1. **Make crispy tofu steaks** Dredge tofu steaks in crispy tofu coating until totally coated.

2. In a large frying pan or wok, heat about ¼ inch (0.5 cm) of oil over medium-high heat. Cook tofu steaks for 1 or 2 minutes per side, until browned. Set aside.

3. **Assemble sandwiches** Toast the buns and spread each side with 1 tbsp (15 mL) of lemon aioli.

4. Top the bottom half of each bun with 1 cup (250 mL) of greens. Then add, in this order: 6 slices of cucumber, 4 crispy tofu steaks, 3 tbsp (45 mL) of chimichurri, and 3 slices of tomato. Sandwich with top of bun. Cut in half on a slight diagonal.

red chimichurri sauce

makes 2 cups (500 mL)

4 cups (1 L) roughly chopped fresh cilantro

4 cups (1 L) roughly chopped fresh parsley

1 small onion, roughly chopped

1 tsp (5 mL) sea salt

⅔ cup (150 mL) chipotles in adobo sauce

1 cup (250 mL) ready-to-eat sun-dried tomatoes

½ cup (125 mL) olive oil

¼ cup (60 mL) freshly squeezed lime juice

1. Pulse cilantro, parsley, onion, salt, chipotles, and sun-dried tomatoes in food processor until finely chopped. Put into a bowl and stir in olive oil and lime juice. Mix well and refrigerate.

clubhouse wrap

With flavours reminiscent of a traditional club sandwich, this wrap seems to appeal to meat eaters and those who are skeptical about having a vegan meal. This is also delicious with the addition of some Fresh "Cheese" Sauce (page 251).

At the restaurants we use 12-inch (30 cm) tortillas, but if you can't find them, just use 10-inch (25 cm) tortillas and use a little less lettuce so you can still wrap it up.

serves 4

crispy tofu steaks

12 Marinated Tofu Steaks (page 272)

1 batch Crispy Tofu Coating (page 266)

Oil, for frying (sunflower, canola, neutral-flavoured coconut oil)

tortillas

4 12-inch (30 cm) whole-wheat flour tortillas

¾ cup (175 mL) Garlic Mayo (page 268)

8 slices Tempeh Bacon (page 273), cooked

1 cup (250 mL) chopped tomato

8 cups (2 L) shredded romaine lettuce

1. **Make crispy tofu steaks** Dredge tofu steaks in crispy tofu coating until totally coated.

2. In a large frying pan or wok, heat about ¼ inch (0.5 cm) of oil over medium-high heat. Cook tofu steaks for 1 or 2 minutes per side, until browned. Set aside.

3. **Assemble tortillas** Heat tortillas on a grill, on a baking sheet in a preheated 350°F (180°C) oven, or in a microwave on High, just until warmed.

4. Spread each warmed tortilla with 3 tbsp (45 mL) garlic mayo. Top each with equal amounts of crispy tofu steaks, tempeh bacon, tomato, and lettuce. Fold edges of tortilla in, and then roll into a cylinder. Using a sharp knife, cut in half on the diagonal.

oyster mushroom po'boy

This is our version of the Louisiana classic. Crunchy, creamy, and spicy, it's great on an airy whole-wheat bun, but is also really good in a wrap. You can also skip the bread altogether and serve it as a salad. Note that you can coat the mushrooms up to 2 days ahead.

serves 2

spicy slaw

2 cups (500 mL) broccoli coleslaw mix

¼ cup (60 mL) Sriracha Maple Dressing (page 175)

crispy oyster mushrooms

2 cups (500 mL) oyster mushrooms

1 cup (250 mL) Dosa Batter (page 266)

1 cup (250 mL) panko crumbs

¼ to ½ cup (60 to 125 mL) sunflower oil or neutral-flavoured coconut oil

Sea salt, to taste

sandwiches

2 whole-wheat submarine buns

¼ to ½ cup (60 to 125 mL) Garlic Mayo (page 268)

2 cups (500 mL) shredded napa cabbage

2 cups (500 mL) spring mix lettuce

20 slices English cucumber

1 tsp (5 mL) raw sesame seeds

2 lemon wedges

1. **Make spicy slaw** Combine broccoli coleslaw and dressing in a bowl and toss until well coated. Set aside.

2. **Make crispy oyster mushrooms** Separate mushrooms and cut off large stems.

3. Place dosa batter in a shallow bowl. Place panko in another bowl. Dredge mushrooms in batter until well coated. Transfer to panko and toss to coat thoroughly.

4. Heat ¼ cup (60 mL) sunflower oil in a large frying pan over medium-high heat. Add mushrooms, being careful not to crowd the pan. Cook, turning and pressing mushrooms into the oil with a fork (if necessary—it depends on the shape of your mushrooms), until all surfaces are browned, 3 to 5 minutes.

5. Transfer cooked mushrooms to paper towel to drain. Immediately sprinkle with salt.

6. Repeat with remaining mushrooms, adding more oil to the pan if needed.

7. **Assemble sandwiches** Cut buns in half, toast lightly, and spread each side with 1 tbsp (15 mL) garlic mayo (or more if desired).

8. Top bottom halves with napa cabbage, spicy slaw, and crispy oyster mushrooms.

9. On top halves, add spring mix and cucumber slices, and sprinkle with sesame seeds. Serve open-faced, with lemon wedges to squeeze on right before eating.

grilled tofu tacos

This is our simplest and quick-to-make taco. If you have some tofu steaks marinating in your fridge already, and use a purchased mayo to make the jalapeño lime sauce, you can have these ready to go in a few minutes. I sometimes order these at the restaurants without the tortillas, as a simple tofu taco salad.

makes 8 tacos

8 6-inch [15 cm] whole-wheat tortillas

2 cups [500 mL] shredded trimmed kale, large stems and ribs removed

16 Marinated Tofu Steaks [page 272], grilled

2 to 3 tomatoes, diced

3 tbsp [45 mL] diced red onion

1 batch Jalapeño Lime Sauce [page 254]

Lime wedges, to taste

1. Heat tortillas on a grill, on a baking sheet in a preheated 350°F [180°C] oven, or in a microwave on High, just until warmed.

2. Fill each warmed tortilla with equal amounts of kale, tofu steaks, tomato, onion, and jalapeño lime sauce. Serve with lime wedges on the side.

adzuki wrap

This hot wrap is very filling and highly nutritious. Combining adzuki beans and whole-wheat tortilla makes this a good protein option. If you can't find 12-inch (30 cm) tortillas, use smaller ones and serve two per person.

Use a slotted spoon to drain off some of the liquid from the adzuki bean stew before you put it into the wrap, otherwise it'll be a bit of a mess—a delicious mess, but a mess all the same.

serves 4

4 12-inch [30 cm] whole-wheat tortillas

8 cups [2 L] lightly packed spring mix lettuce

2 cups [500 mL] lightly packed alfalfa sprouts

4 cups [1 L] grated carrots

1 avocado, sliced

4 cups [1 L] Adzuki Bean Stew [page 263]

½ batch Raw Sunflower Dressing [page 172]

1. Heat tortillas on a grill, on a baking sheet in a preheated 350°F [180°C] oven, or in a microwave on High, just until warmed.

2. Arrange equal amounts of lettuce, sprouts, carrots, and avocado in the middle of each tortilla.

3. Top with adzuki bean stew and a drizzle of raw sunflower dressing.

4. Fold edges of tortilla in, and then roll into a cylinder. Using a sharp knife, cut in half on the diagonal.

falafel tacos

The combination of our herby falafel balls with creamy tahini, spicy chili oil, sweet date syrup, and crispy onions is unusual and scrumptious. You could also stuff these ingredients inside a pita, which is the more traditional vessel for falafel.

makes 8 tacos

8 6-inch [15 cm] whole-wheat tortillas

2 cups [500 mL] shredded romaine lettuce

1 cup [250 mL] diced tomatoes

16 Herb Falafel Balls, cooked [page 270]

½ cup [125 mL] Crispy Onions [page 264]

½ cup [125 mL] Tahini Dressing [page 174]

8 tsp [40 mL] date syrup

Chili Oil [page 264], to taste

1. Heat tortillas on a grill, on a baking sheet in a preheated 350°F [180°C] oven, or in a microwave on High, just until warmed.

2. Fill each warmed tortilla with equal amounts of lettuce, tomato, falafel balls, crispy onions, and tahini dressing. Drizzle with date syrup and chili oil.

voodoo sandwich

This combo of mushrooms, tofu, and hot sauce with our creamy garlic mayo is amazing. If you haven't made a batch of our hot sauce, just use Sriracha, sambal oelek, or any favourite hot sauce.

serves 4

¼ cup [60 mL] olive oil

4 cups [1 L] sliced button mushrooms

1 thinly sliced red onion

2 tbsp [30 mL] tamari

¼ cup [60 mL] Hot Sauce [page 253]

1 block [9 oz/250 g] extra firm tofu, cut into 4 pieces

4 whole-grain kaiser buns, halved

¾ to 1 cup [175 to 250 mL] Garlic Mayo [page 268]

4 cups [1 L] lightly packed alfalfa sprouts

1. Heat oil in a large frying pan over medium-high heat.

2. Add mushrooms and onion and cook, stirring occasionally, for 7 to 10 minutes or until mushrooms are browned.

3. Stir in tamari, hot sauce, and tofu. Cook, stirring occasionally, for 1 to 2 minutes per side, until tofu is browned and hot.

4. Meanwhile, toast buns and spread both halves with garlic mayo.

5. Place alfalfa sprouts on bottom half of buns.

6. Top with tofu mixture and sandwich with other half of buns.

squash tacos

These tacos took the Fresh world by storm in 2013, becoming the fastest-selling special since the All Star (page 159)! We're not sure if it's the squash or the sauce that keeps people coming back, but we do know that the combination of the two is irresistible.

There are some options for how to make the squash: you either steam it first until it's just tender and then bread it, or you can double-fry it. At the restaurants we steam it first. You also have to decide whether you will finish cooking it in a frying pan or in the oven. If you want to do it in the oven, it's handy to have an oil sprayer so that you can get a thin coating of oil on the panko. (These are available at most kitchen supply stores—you fill it with oil, pump it, and then spray a fine mist of oil on your food.) The squash can be prepared up to 3 days in advance.

makes 8 tacos

squash

24 pinky finger–size sticks peeled and sliced butternut squash (about 2 cups/500 mL)

1 batch Dosa Batter (page 266)

1 to 1½ cups (250 to 375 mL) panko crumbs

Oil, for frying (sunflower, canola, or neutral-flavoured coconut oil)

Sea salt, to taste

tacos

8 6-inch (15 cm) whole-wheat tortillas

4 cups (1 L) shredded kale, large stems and ribs removed

2 to 3 tomatoes, diced (about 1 cup/250 mL)

3 tbsp (45 mL) diced red onion

½ cup (125 mL) chopped fresh cilantro

1 batch Jalapeño Lime Sauce (page 254)

Lime wedges

1. **Prepare squash**
   Steaming method: Using a steamer, microwave, or pot of boiling water with a colander on top, steam squash sticks until just tender. Remove from heat and let cool. Place dosa batter in one shallow bowl, and panko in another. Dip steamed squash sticks in dosa batter and then into panko, turning to coat well.
   Frying method: Place dosa batter in one shallow bowl, and panko in another. Dip raw squash sticks in dosa batter and then into panko, turning to coat well. Heat ½ inch (1 cm) oil in a large frying pan over medium-low heat. Cook squash sticks, a few at a time, until barely browned and just tender, 3 to 5 minutes, turning as needed to cook all surfaces. Remove from heat and transfer to paper towels to drain. Set aside. (At this point you can cool the sticks and then transfer to an airtight container and refrigerate for up to 3 days.)

2. **Finish cooking squash**
   Oven method: Preheat oven to 400°F (200°C). Arrange prepared squash sticks in a single layer on a baking sheet and spray with oil. Bake in preheated oven for 10 to 20 minutes, turning halfway through, or until browned and crispy on the outside and tender on the inside. Remove from oven and sprinkle with a little sea salt.
   Frying method: Heat oil in a large frying pan over medium-high heat. Add prepared squash sticks, being careful not to crowd the pan, and cook until browned and crispy on the outside and tender on the inside, about 5 minutes, turning as needed to brown all surfaces. Transfer to paper towels to drain. Immediately sprinkle with salt. Repeat with remaining squash. Set aside.

3. **Assemble tacos** Heat tortillas on a grill, on a baking sheet in a preheated 350°F (180°C) oven, or in a microwave on High, just until warmed.

4. Fill each warmed tortilla with equal amounts of kale, cooked squash sticks, tomato, onion, cilantro, and jalapeño lime sauce. Serve with lime wedges on the side.

sam houston burrito

The original Sam Houston was a Texan statesman who the city of Houston is named after. My dad's friends all called my dad Sam, since our last name is Houston. I loved that nickname so much that I named my bulldog Sam Houston. And this burrito, with its spicy Tex Mex–style flavours, just begged for the name, too. This is the newest incarnation of this dish, with sprouted lentils instead of TVP as the filling.

The Sprouted Lentil Filling recipe makes a little more than you'll need for four wraps. A good way to use up the leftovers is to serve them on some rice with a little of the glaze and some chopped veggies on top. If you have any leftover Jalapeño Lime Sauce (page 254), pour some of that on top as well.

We use sprouted lentils, but if you can't find those, just use regular brown or green lentils.

serves 4

sprouted lentil filling

makes 3 cups (750 mL)

2 tsp (10 mL) canola oil

½ cup (125 mL) chopped onion

1 clove garlic, minced

½ cup (125 mL) peeled and chopped sweet potato

1 tbsp (15 mL) Mexican chili powder

½ tsp (2 mL) onion powder

½ tsp (2 mL) garlic powder

½ cup (125 mL) diced tomatoes

1 cup (250 mL) sprouted lentils, soaked

3 to 5 cups (750 mL to 1.25 L) vegetable stock

2 tbsp (30 mL) freshly squeezed lime juice

½ tsp (2 mL) dried oregano

1 tsp (5 mL) ground cinnamon

Sea salt, to taste

burritos

4 12-inch (30 cm) whole-wheat tortillas

¼ cup (60 mL) Chipotle Mayo (page 268)

1⅓ cups (325 mL) shredded napa cabbage

1 cup (250 mL) cooked brown basmati rice

¼ cup (60 mL) Lemon Garlic Glaze (page 255)

¾ cup (175 mL) diced tomato

¼ cup (60 mL) chopped fresh cilantro

8 cups (2 L) spring mix lettuce

1. **Make sprouted lentil filling** Heat oil in a saucepan. Add onion and garlic and cook, stirring occasionally, for 3 to 5 minutes, until softened.

2. Add sweet potatoes, chili powder, onion powder, garlic powder, tomatoes, lentils, 3 cups (750 mL) stock, lime juice, oregano, cinnamon, and salt and bring to a boil. Reduce heat and simmer until lentils are soft and mixture is thick, 30 to 60 minutes. (If needed, add remaining 2 cups/500 mL stock to cook the lentils until totally soft. If in doubt about whether they're soft enough, they probably aren't.) Keep warm over low heat.

3. Heat tortillas on a grill, on a baking sheet in a preheated 350°F (180°C) oven, or in a microwave on High, just until warmed.

4. **Assemble burritos** Spread each warmed tortilla with 1 tbsp (15 mL) chipotle mayo. Top each with equal amounts of napa cabbage, rice, lemon garlic glaze, lentil filling, tomato, cilantro, and lettuce, in that order.

5. Fold edges of tortilla in, and then roll into a cylinder. Using a sharp knife, cut in half on the diagonal.

Tip: To soak sprouted lentils, place in a bowl and cover with lots of water. Set aside for at least 30 minutes to soak. Drain well.

FRESH BURGERS

Chock full of barley, millet, tofu, nuts, seeds, veggies, and herbs, our burgers incorporate all the fundamentals of a plant-based diet. We serve them with unique sauces and toppings, but they work equally well with traditional burger toppings like mayo, mustard, ketchup, tomato, pickles, and onions. Serve on a crusty whole-wheat bun, in a grilled tortilla, or even on a bed of lettuce.

FRESH BURGER MIX

There are so many elements in this burger mix that—depending on the water content in the tofu and veggies on any given day—it can turn out a little differently every time. If you're having a hard time getting your burger mix firm enough to make nice, stable, easy-to-manage patties, just add a little more spelt flour, stir, and refrigerate until it firms up. If that doesn't work, whiz up 1 cup (250 mL) of tofu in a food processor to make a paste and incorporate that into the mix.

makes 8 burger patties

12 cups (3 L) water, divided

½ cup (125 mL) pearl barley, rinsed and drained

½ cup (125 mL) hulled millet

1 clove garlic

3 tbsp (45 mL) raw sunflower seeds

2 tbsp (30 mL) raw almonds

2 green onions, roughly chopped

2 tbsp (30 mL) roughly chopped fresh parsley

½ cup (125 mL) roughly chopped red onion

1 cup (250 mL) chopped extra firm tofu

¼ cup (60 mL) grated carrot

¼ cup (60 mL) grated beet

1½ tbsp (22 mL) tamari

¼ tsp (1 mL) cayenne pepper

¼ tsp (1 mL) Mexican chili powder

1 tsp (5 mL) curry powder

1 tsp (5 mL) sea salt

1 tsp (5 mL) cornstarch

3 tbsp (45 mL) Mixed Herb Blend (page 271) or 1 tbsp (15 mL) each of 3 of your favourite dried herbs (basil, oregano, marjoram, etc.)

¼ cup (60 mL) spelt flour

2 tbsp (30 mL) powdered nutritional yeast

Oil, for frying (sunflower, canola, neutral-flavoured coconut)

1. In a pot, combine 6 cups (1.5 L) water and barley and bring to a boil. Reduce heat and simmer until barley is tender, 30 to 60 minutes. Drain and set aside.

2. Rinse pot, add millet and remaining 6 cups (1.5 L) water, and bring to a boil. Reduce heat and simmer until millet is tender (it will take about half the time of the barley). Drain and set aside.

3. In a food processor, pulse garlic until finely chopped. Add sunflower seeds, almonds, green onions, parsley, and red onion. Process until finely chopped. Transfer to a large mixing bowl.

4. Place tofu into food processor (no need to clean food processor in between items) and process until just turning creamy and paste-like. Transfer tofu to mixing bowl.

5. Add remaining ingredients to mixing bowl, along with cooled barley and millet. Stir well. (The easiest way to make sure it is thoroughly combined is to do it with your hands.) You can use the mix right away, but it will be easier to handle if you refrigerate it for at least 1 hour, or overnight.

6. Using your hands, divide mixture into 8 equal portions and form patties.

7. Heat a thin layer of oil in a frying pan over medium heat. Cook patties until browned on both sides and heated through, 3 to 5 minutes per side, adding more oil as needed.

8. Serve right away or, if you want to cook them later on a grill or barbecue, let cool, transfer to an airtight container, and refrigerate. (At the restaurants we store them this way and then heat them up on the grill when they are ordered.)

BURGER VARIATIONS

To make any of the following variations, start with a cooked Fresh burger patty and a toasted whole-wheat bun.

1. Arrange the first set of ingredients on the bottom half of the bun, following the order listed, and the second set of ingredients on the top half of the bun.

2. Serve open-faced and put together at the table.

banquet burger

Did you know that the term "banquet burger" is a Canadianism, and maybe even a Toronto-ism? I just assumed it was a worldwide thing, but apparently not. We always had Banquet Burgers in my high-school cafeteria, along with something called a "Big Eric," which was a battered fish sandwich with cheese and tartar sauce. I Googled it and it came up on some local menus, so I guess that's another Ontario-ism!

serves 1

on bottom half of bun

¼ cup (60 mL) alfalfa sprouts

2 to 4 tbsp (30 to 60 mL) Fresh "Cheese" Sauce (page 251)

2 slices Tempeh Bacon, cooked (page 273)

1 Fresh Burger Patty (page 215)

1 tbsp (15 mL) Garlic Mayo (page 268)

on top half of bun

½ cup (125 mL) spring mix lettuce or chopped romaine

2 slices tomato

2 to 3 rings red onion

chipotle bacon burger

The spice from the Chipotle Mayo (page 268) works really well with the smoky
Tempeh Bacon (page 273) in this popular burger.

on bottom half of bun

¼ cup (60 mL) julienned jicama

2 slices Tempeh Bacon, cooked (page 273)

1 Fresh Burger Patty (page 215)

2 tbsp (30 mL) Chipotle Mayo (page 268)

on top half of bun

½ cup (125 mL) spring mix lettuce or chopped romaine

2 slices tomato

walk on the wild side burger

This spicy burger was named by our partner Barry, a big Lou Reed fan.

on bottom half of bun

½ cup (125 mL) alfalfa sprouts

4 slices English cucumber

2 tbsp (30 mL) Chipotle Mayo (page 268)

1 Fresh Burger Patty (page 215)

1 tbsp (15 mL) Sriracha ketchup

on top half of bun

½ cup (125 mL) spring mix lettuce or chopped romaine

2 slices tomato

6 to 8 slices hot banana chilies

Tip: To make the Sriracha ketchup, combine equal parts ketchup and
Sriracha sauce.

works burger

All I can say about this one is YUM! Rich Miso Gravy (page 256) with hot chilies
and dill pickle is an unusual but amazingly delicious combination.

on bottom half of bun

¼ cup (60 mL) shredded napa cabbage

¼ cup (60 mL) grated carrot

1 Fresh Burger Patty (page 215)

¼ cup (60 mL) Miso Gravy, hot (page 256)

6 to 8 slices hot banana chilies

on top half of bun

½ cup (125 mL) spring mix lettuce

2 slices tomato

2 slices kosher dill pickle

bbq burger

This is our most popular burger. There's just something about the crunchy onion rings when combined with the BBQ Sauce, Garlic Mayo, and hot chilies that is crave-worthy.

The recipe for the Fresh Onion Rings (page 221) makes about 20 onion rings, enough for 8 burgers and some extra rings to snack on while you're cooking!

on bottom half of bun

¼ cup (60 mL) napa cabbage

1 tbsp (15 mL) Garlic Mayo (page 268)

1 Fresh Burger Patty (page 215)

2 tsp (10 mL) BBQ Sauce (page 249)

2 Fresh Onion Rings (page 221)

on top half of bun

⅓ cup (75 mL) spring mix lettuce or chopped romaine

2 slices tomato

6 to 8 slices hot banana chilies

picnic burger

The combo of curry and avocado may seem a little weird, but I promise it's a winner. This is my friend Melissa's favourite. For two years in a row she requested these burgers as her birthday dinner!

on bottom half of bun

½ cup (125 mL) alfalfa sprouts

1 Fresh Burger Patty (page 215)

2 tbsp (30 mL) Curry Mayo (page 268)

3 slices avocado

Pinch sea salt

on top half of bun

½ cup (125 mL) spring mix lettuce or chopped romaine

2 slices tomato

1 tbsp (15 mL) sliced green onions

bbq burger

fresh onion rings

These onion rings are featured on our BBQ Burger (page 218), but make the perfect side to any Fresh burger!

makes 20 large onion rings

quinoa coating

1½ cups (375 mL) puffed quinoa, millet, or amaranth

1½ cups (375 mL) fresh breadcrumbs

1 tsp (5 mL) sea salt

1 tsp (5 mL) garlic powder

onion rings

1 large Spanish onion, sliced thickly and separated into 20 rings

1 cup (250 mL) all-purpose flour

½ batch Dosa Batter (page 266)

4 cups (1 L) canola or sunflower oil, for frying

Sea salt, to taste

1. **Make quinoa coating** Combine puffed quinoa, breadcrumbs, salt, and garlic powder in a large bowl. Set aside.

2. **Prepare onion rings** In a plastic bag or bowl, toss onion rings with flour.

3. Place dosa batter in a shallow bowl. Dip 1 or 2 onion rings in batter, making sure they are totally coated.

4. Dredge battered rings in quinoa coating, making sure all surfaces are coated. Repeat with remaining rings.

5. Arrange coated rings on a baking sheet, cover with plastic wrap, and refrigerate for at least 30 minutes, or overnight, to firm up.

6. Heat oil in a large saucepan to 350°F (180°C).

7. Working in small batches so as not to crowd the pan, carefully drop onion rings into the hot oil and cook for 2 or 3 minutes, until browned and crispy.

8. Transfer cooked rings to paper towel to drain. Immediately sprinkle with sea salt.

FRESH BOWLS

Bowls have been the cornerstone of our menu since day one. Fresh bowls follow a basic formula: a grain, a noodle, or greens as the base, with a sauce or two, a plant-based protein, loads of vegetables, and accents like herbs, lemon, nuts and seeds, or chili oil.

There are millions of potential combinations, and you can make it as easy or as complicated as you want. From the simplest of bowls made from stuff you have in your fridge to a complex bowl that requires a few different recipes to execute, these all have one thing in common—they're delicious!

Whether you follow these recipes exactly, or read through them, get some ideas, and then make up your own combinations, I hope this will inspire you to start making vegan meals-in-a-bowl at home.

broccoli and mushroom noodles with cashews

This combination of vegetables, cashews, and noodles is a simple, light, and delicious meal.

serves 2

2 tbsp (30 mL) olive oil

1½ cups (375 mL) shiitake mushrooms (stems removed and halved if large)

1½ cups (375 mL) halved button mushrooms

6 cups (1.5 L) broccoli florets

½ cup (125 mL) water

1 batch Lemongrass Sauce (page 261)

4 cups (1 L) cooked soba noodles

½ cup (125 mL) roasted unsalted cashews

¼ cup (60 mL) finely diced red bell pepper

2 tbsp (30 mL) raw sesame seeds

1. Heat oil in a frying pan over high heat. Add mushrooms and cook, stirring occasionally, until browned, 3 to 4 minutes.

2. Add broccoli and water, and cook, stirring occasionally, until water evaporates.

3. Add lemongrass sauce and bring to a boil. When broccoli is almost tender, add noodles and cashews. Cook, stirring, for 1 to 2 minutes or until heated through.

4. Divide mixture between two large bowls. Garnish with red pepper and sesame seeds.

emerald city

This dish was named after the city in *The Wizard of Oz* by Ryan Kelly, a multitalented former staff member. It uses gochujang, a Korean fermented chili paste with a unique flavour and bright red colour, which is available at some supermarkets and at most Asian groceries. If you can't find it, substitute a bit of hot sauce—it won't give you the same flavour as gochujang, but it'll still be delicious. Feel free to substitute our Raw Sunflower Dressing (page 172) for the Pineapple Cashew Sauce (page 258).

serves 2

2 tbsp (30 mL) sunflower oil or neutral-flavoured coconut oil

2 cups (500 mL) sliced button mushrooms

2 tsp (10 mL) balsamic vinegar

4 cloves garlic, minced

1 tsp (5 mL) gochujang

¼ cup (60 mL) tamari

½ cup (125 mL) water

4 cups (1 L) cooked kamut udon or soba noodles

4 cups (1 L) lightly packed spinach

6 tbsp (90 mL) Pineapple Cashew Sauce (page 258)

¼ cup (60 mL) raw cashews, toasted (page 274)

1 cup (250 mL) sunflower sprouts

1. Heat oil in a frying pan over low heat. Add mushrooms and balsamic vinegar and cook until mushrooms are browned, 3 to 4 minutes.

2. In a separate large frying pan or wok over high heat, combine garlic, gochujang, tamari, water, noodles, and spinach. Cook for 1 to 2 minutes or until heated through, liquid is reduced, and spinach is tender.

3. Divide noodle mixture between 2 large bowls.

4. Top with mushrooms and drizzle with pineapple cashew sauce.

5. Garnish with toasted cashews and sunflower sprouts.

buddha

This bowl has been on our menu since the very beginnings of Fresh and remains one of the most popular even after all these years. There's something about peanut sauce on rice or noodles that just keeps people coming back.

serves 2

4 cups (1 L) cooked brown basmati rice or soba noodles

16 Marinated Tofu Cubes (page 272)

1½ cups (375 mL) Buddha Sauce, heated (page 250)

2 cups (500 mL) bean sprouts

8 slices tomato, halved

8 slices English cucumber, halved

¼ tsp (1 mL) Mexican chili powder

2 tbsp (30 mL) chopped unsalted peanuts

¼ cup (60 mL) fresh cilantro

2 lemon wedges

1. Divide cooked rice or soba between 2 large bowls.

2. Top with tofu cubes.

3. Pour an even amount of Buddha sauce over cubes in each bowl.

4. Arrange equal amounts of bean sprouts, tomato, and cucumber on top, then sprinkle with chili powder and chopped peanuts.

5. Garnish with cilantro and lemon wedges. Serve.

samurai soba

This simple noodle and greens bowl was a popular special back in the first days of Fresh and it still feels current today. Add some hot sauce if you want to spice it up a bit.

serves 2

1 cup (250 mL) water

¼ cup (60 mL) tamari

4 cups (1 L) mixed greens (bok choy, kale, Swiss chard)

4 cloves garlic, minced

4 cups (1 L) cooked soba noodles

6 Marinated Tofu Steaks (page 272)

6 tbsp (90 mL) Raw Sunflower Dressing (page 172)

1 cup (250 mL) sunflower sprouts

1 tbsp (15 mL) raw sunflower seeds, toasted (page 274)

1 tbsp (15 mL) raw sesame seeds

1. Combine water, tamari, mixed greens, and garlic in a large frying pan or wok over high heat and cook until greens are tender.

2. Add soba noodles and cook for a couple of minutes, until most of the cooking liquid has evaporated and noodles are heated through.

3. Divide cooked noodles and greens between 2 large bowls.

4. Top each with 3 tofu steaks and drizzle with raw sunflower dressing.

5. Garnish with sunflower sprouts, sunflower seeds, and sesame seeds.

shinto rice bowl

This stir-fried rice bowl was inspired by an amazing dish I once had at Wagamama restaurant in London, England. It's chock full of tofu, snow peas, and corn, which may seem like an odd combo, but it works, I promise! Topped with slices of vegan omelette and served with a side of miso broth that can be poured over top or sipped separately, this bowl is somehow perfect for both a cold winter night and for a hot summer afternoon. The seasonings are quite subtle, so if you prefer spice, just drizzle with some of our Chili Oil (page 264).

serves 2

½ cup (125 mL) water

1 tsp (5 mL) + 2 tbsp (30 mL) tamari, divided

2 tsp (10 mL) light soy miso

2 tbsp (30 mL) olive oil, divided

¼ batch Tofu Omelette (page 112)

1 block (9 oz/250 g) extra firm tofu, cut into 1-inch (2.5 cm) cubes

2 cups (500 mL) button mushrooms, halved

2 cups (500 mL) snow peas, trimmed and cut in half on the diagonal

1 cup (250 mL) frozen sweet corn, thawed and rinsed

3 cups (750 mL) cooked jasmine rice

2 tbsp (30 mL) thinly sliced green onions

2 tsp (10 mL) Chili Oil (optional; page 264)

1. Heat water in a small saucepan over high heat. Add 1 tsp (5 mL) of tamari and bring to a boil. Reduce heat and whisk in miso. Keep warm over low heat.

2. Heat 1 tbsp (15 mL) of oil in a frying pan over medium heat.

3. Press the tofu omelette mixture into a thin pancake and cook for 2 minutes per side, until browned. Remove from heat and let cool slightly. Cut into thin strips. Set aside.

4. Heat remaining 1 tbsp (15 mL) of oil in a large frying pan or wok over medium-high heat. Add tofu and cook for a minute or two per side, until browned on all sides.

5. Add mushrooms and snow peas, and cook until mushrooms release their liquid and start to brown, 5 to 7 minutes.

6. Add corn and cook for 1 minute, until corn is heated through.

7. Add rice and remaining 2 tbsp (30 mL) of tamari. Stir well and cook for 1 to 2 minutes, until heated through.

8. Divide mixture into 2 bowls.

9. Garnish with green onions and tofu omelette strips. Drizzle with chili oil (if using). Serve with miso broth on the side.

jerusalem

This has been on our Fresh menu for years and years. The last time we changed the menu we took it off, but little did we know how passionate fans were about the Jerusalem! Needless to say, it's back on the menu and here to stay.

Hummus on rice with veggies and herbs is a really simple but satisfying combination. Our Tahini Dressing (page 174) or 3-6-9 Dressing (page 173) also go really well here if you want a change from the Beach Sauce. Our Herb Falafel Balls (page 270) are also a great addition to this bowl.

serves 2

1 tsp [5 mL] sunflower oil

6 cups [1.5 L] lightly packed spinach

1 tsp [5 mL] tamari

4 cups [1 L] cooked brown basmati rice or soba noodles

2 to 4 tbsp [30 to 60 mL] Beach Sauce [page 249]

6 tbsp [90 mL] Flax Hummus [page 153]

Pinch Mexican chili powder

2 tbsp [30 mL] diced red onion

½ cup [125 mL] diced tomato

½ cup [125 mL] diced English cucumber

¼ cup [60 mL] chopped fresh parsley

1 cup [250 mL] sunflower sprouts

2 lemon wedges

1. **Cook the spinach** Use either a panini grill like we do at Fresh, or sauté in a pan.
   Panini grill: Coat the grill with half of the oil, top with the spinach, and then drizzle with the remaining oil and tamari. Close lid and cook for a few seconds, until spinach is softened.
   Pan: Heat oil in a pan over medium-high heat. Add spinach and tamari and cook, tossing occasionally, for less than a minute, until spinach is softened.

2. **Assemble the bowl** Divide rice or soba between 2 large bowls and drizzle with beach sauce.

3. Place an even amount of hummus in the middle of each bowl and sprinkle with chili powder.

4. Around the edge of each bowl, arrange red onion, tomato, cucumber, parsley, and spinach.

5. Top with sunflower sprouts and garnish with lemon wedges.

rice, beans, and greens

This is one of my all-time favourite taste combinations. There's something about the Adzuki Bean Stew (page 263), Tahini Dressing (page 174), and cucumber that really hits every note—creamy, spicy, crunchy, hot, and cool all at the same time.

If you have leftovers, you can make a great little snack by combining some rice, Adzuki Bean Stew, Tahini Dressing, and chopped cucumber or avocado. That combo was a favourite of all the cooks when this stew was on our menu.

serves 4

2 tbsp (30 mL) extra virgin olive oil

2¼ tsp (11 mL) Bragg Liquid Aminos or tamari

¼ tsp (1 mL) Mixed Herb Blend (page 271)

12 cups (3 L) mixed greens (kale, bok choy, Swiss chard)

4 cups (1 L) cooked brown basmati rice

¾ cup (175 mL) Tahini Dressing (page 174)

1 batch Adzuki Bean Stew (page 263)

2 cups (500 mL) chopped English cucumber

4 tsp (20 mL) raw sesame seeds

1 cup (250 mL) mixed microgreens or sunflower sprouts

1. Combine oil, liquid aminos, and mixed herbs in a small bowl. Set aside.

2. If you have a steamer insert, steam the greens over boiling water. If not, place 2 to 3 tbsp (30 to 45 mL) of water in the bottom of a large wok or pan, top with mixed greens, cover with a lid, and cook over high heat for 3 to 5 minutes, until greens are tender.

3. Divide rice evenly among 4 large bowls.

4. Top each bowl with 1 tbsp (15 mL) of tahini dressing and equal amounts of adzuki bean stew, steamed greens, cucumber, and an additional 2 tbsp (30 mL) of tahini dressing. Drizzle with prepared sauce.

5. Garnish each bowl with 1 tsp (5 mL) of sesame seeds and ¼ cup (60 mL) of microgreens.

beach

The Beach is our bestselling Fresh bowl, and has been for years. It's simple but interesting at the same time, and I think that's why it's so popular. This version features Grilled Marinated Tofu Steaks (page 272). We use zucchini, red pepper, and sweet potato, but grilled eggplant, asparagus, spinach, or any other favourites of yours will work equally well.

serves 2

6 slices sweet potato

6 slices red bell pepper

6 slices zucchini

1 tbsp (15 mL) olive oil

4 cups (1 L) cooked brown basmati rice or soba noodles

¼ to ½ cup (60 to 125 mL) Beach Sauce (page 249)

6 ready-to-eat sun-dried tomatoes, sliced

6 slices avocado

2 cups (500 mL) sunflower sprouts

2 wedges lemon

4 Grilled Marinated Tofu Steaks (page 272)

1. Brush sweet potato, red pepper, and zucchini with olive oil. Grill or broil for 5 to 10 minutes, until tender, turning vegetables midway through. (Start the sweet potato before the other ingredients, since they take longer to cook.) Transfer to a plate as they are done.

2. Divide cooked rice or noodles between 2 large bowls and drizzle each with 2 tbsp (30 mL) of beach sauce.

3. Arrange grilled vegetables, sun-dried tomatoes, and avocado on top.

4. Finish with sunflower sprouts and another drizzle of beach sauce, to taste.

5. Garnish with lemon wedges and grilled tofu steaks.

Tip: There are many different types of sun-dried tomatoes available. The type we use at the restaurants comes to us nice and soft, and ready to eat. But if you can only find the dried ones, you will have to reconstitute them. Just bring some water to a boil in a small saucepan, remove from the heat, and add the dried tomatoes. Let sit for 10 minutes or until softened, then drain and use right away. If you want to keep some in the fridge, place them in an airtight container and cover with olive oil; they will keep for up to 2 weeks.

naked sushi

There's something about the Miso Mayo (page 267) in this dish that when combined with the nori really makes you think you're eating sushi! We offer this bowl with rice, soba noodles, or just veggies. You can also use shirataki noodles as the base. Marinated Tofu Steaks (page 272) are also a great addition if you want to increase the protein. And if you don't feel like making the squash, just double up on the sweet potato.

Shichimi togarashi is a Japanese spice mixture containing chili peppers, ginger, sesame seeds, and orange peel. You can find it at Asian grocers, but it is also starting to show up at major grocery stores.

serves 4

2 tbsp (30 mL) rice vinegar

1 tsp (5 mL) raw agave nectar

2 tsp (10 mL) tamari

1 sweet potato, cut into 8 slices
(each about ½ inch/1 cm thick)

¼ cup (60 mL) sunflower oil (approx.)

4 cups (1 L) rice or soba noodles, cooked (optional)

8 cups (2 L) lightly packed sliced napa cabbage

24 pieces panko-coated squash, cooked (page 211)

2 cups (500 mL) chopped English cucumber

1 cup (250 mL) chopped red bell pepper

1 large avocado, cut into 12 slices

¾ cup (175 mL) Miso Mayo (page 267)

¼ cup (60 mL) shredded nori

1 cup (250 mL) assorted microgreens

2 tsp (10 mL) shichimi togarashi

4 tsp (20 mL) raw sesame seeds

4 lemon wedges

1. In a small bowl, combine rice vinegar, agave nectar, and tamari.

2. Coat sweet potato slices with oil. Cook using a panini grill or oven.
   Panini grill: Grill until tender, 7 to 10 minutes.
   Oven: Preheat oven to 350°F (180°C). Arrange sweet potato slices in an even layer on a baking sheet and bake for about 20 minutes, turning once, until tender.

3. In each of 4 large bowls, place 1 cup (250 mL) of rice or soba noodles (if using) and drizzle with vinegar mixture. Top with napa cabbage (if not using rice or soba, drizzle vinegar mixture on top of napa). Arrange squash, sweet potato, cucumber, red pepper, and avocado around the edges.

4. Drizzle each bowl with about 3 tbsp (45 mL) of miso mayo and top with 1 tbsp (15 mL) of nori, microgreens, shichimi togarashi, and sesame seeds. Garnish with a lemon wedge.

Tip: To shred nori, just cut the sheets into strips with scissors, and then cut the strips into little matchsticks.

naked burrito

This bowl has all of your favourite burrito fillings on a bed of rice instead of in a tortilla. The version here includes quite a few different recipes, but you can easily make a simplified version—just use store-bought salsa and guacamole, and plain canned black beans (drained and rinsed) instead of the Spicy Black Beans. Really, it's the sautéed vegetables and Cilantro Lime Glaze that make this so crave-worthy. You could also just use chopped fresh avocado instead of guacamole.

serves 4

spicy black beans

2 tbsp (30 mL) sunflower oil or neutral-flavoured coconut oil

1 cup (250 mL) diced onions

2 tsp (10 mL) coriander seeds, toasted and ground (see page 274)

1¼ tsp (6 mL) Mexican chili powder

1¼ tsp (6 mL) garlic powder

1¼ tsp (6 mL) dried oregano

1 tsp (5 mL) sea salt

¼ tsp (1 mL) cayenne pepper

3 cloves garlic, minced

1 cup (250 mL) chopped tomatoes

½ cup (125 mL) water

½ cup (125 mL) chopped fresh cilantro

3 tbsp (45 mL) tomato paste

1 tsp (5 mL) diced canned chipotle pepper with adobo sauce or ¼ tsp (1 mL) chipotle powder

1 can (14 oz/398 mL) black beans, drained and rinsed, or 2 cups (500 mL) cooked black beans

cilantro lime glaze

2 tbsp (30 mL) freshly squeezed lime juice

1 cup (250 mL) chopped fresh cilantro

½ tsp (2 mL) sea salt

2 tbsp (30 mL) sunflower oil

¼ cup (60 mL) non-dairy buttery spread (we prefer Earth Balance)

avocado chipotle sauce

¼ cup (60 mL) water

¼ cup (60 mL) chopped fresh cilantro

1 tbsp (15 mL) freshly squeezed lemon juice

2 tsp (10 mL) freshly squeezed lime juice

2 tsp (10 mL) diced canned chipotle pepper with adobo sauce or ½ tsp (2 mL) chipotle powder

¼ tsp (1 mL) sea salt

½ tsp (2 mL) garlic powder

¾ cup (175 mL) avocado, chopped (1 medium avocado)

salsa

¼ cup (60 mL) tightly packed fresh cilantro

2 tbsp (30 mL) chopped onion

2 tbsp (30 mL) pickled jalapeño peppers

¾ cup (175 mL) canned tomatoes

Pinch sea salt

⅛ tsp (0.5 mL) raw agave nectar

vegetable mix

Oil, for frying (sunflower, canola, neutral-flavoured coconut)

2 cups (500 mL) sliced green bell peppers

1 cup (250 mL) sliced onions

1 cup (250 mL) frozen corn, rinsed and thawed

assembly

6 cups (1.5 L) cooked brown basmati rice

1 batch Cilantro Lime Glaze

1 batch Spicy Black Beans

1 batch Avocado Chipotle Sauce

1 batch Salsa

2 cups (500 mL) thinly sliced napa cabbage

¼ cup (60 mL) sliced green onions

¼ cup (60 mL) chopped fresh cilantro

4 tsp (20 mL) raw hemp hearts

Vegan cheddar cheese, shredded (optional)

1. **Prepare spicy black beans** Heat oil in a pot over medium heat. Add onions and cook for 2 to 4 minutes, until softened. Add coriander, chili powder, garlic powder, oregano, salt, and cayenne. Cook, stirring, for a few seconds. Add garlic, tomatoes, water, cilantro, tomato paste, and chipotle. Stir to combine, then bring to a boil. Stir in black beans. Return to a boil, reduce heat, and simmer for 5 minutes. Remove from heat and set aside until ready to use.

2. **Make cilantro lime glaze** Combine lime juice, cilantro, and sea salt in a blender. Blend on high speed until smooth. Add a little of the oil if needed to keep blender moving. Transfer purée to saucepan. Add non-dairy butter and remaining oil. Cook over low heat until non-dairy butter is melted. Remove from heat and set aside until ready to use.

3. **Make avocado chipotle sauce** Combine water, cilantro, lemon and lime juice, chipotle, salt, and garlic powder in a blender. Add avocado and blend on high speed until smooth. Taste and add more sea salt if needed. Set aside until ready to use.

4. **Make salsa** Combine cilantro, onion, and pickled jalapeños in a food processor and pulse for 2 or 3 seconds, just long enough to chop them up. Add tomatoes, salt, and agave nectar. Process until combined but still chunky. Set aside until ready to use.

5. **Cook vegetable mix** Coat bottom of a large frying pan with a thin layer of oil and heat over high heat. Add green peppers and onions. Cook, stirring or tossing occasionally, until charred in spots and just starting to soften, 3 to 5 minutes. Add corn and continue to cook for a few minutes until vegetables are crisp-tender and browned in spots.

6. **Assemble bowls** For each bowl, start with 1½ cups (375 mL) of cooked brown basmati rice. Drizzle with 1 tbsp (15 mL) of cilantro lime glaze and top with ¾ cup (175 mL) of spicy black beans. On top of the beans, place cooked vegetables, avocado chipotle sauce, salsa, and napa cabbage. Drizzle each bowl with another 1 tbsp (15 mL) of cilantro lime glaze.

7. Garnish with green onions, cilantro, hemp hearts, and vegan cheese of your choice. Serve.

powerhouse

Packed with nutrition, this excellent meal in a bowl is guaranteed to fuel your body for whatever your day brings. It's a staple on our menu and has been for over a decade.

serves 2

½ cup (125 mL) Miso Tahini Sauce (page 257)

2 tbsp (30 mL) tamari

1 tsp (5 mL) Hot Sauce (page 253)

4 cups (1 L) cooked brown basmati rice or soba noodles

6 Marinated Tofu Steaks, cooked (page 272)

1 cup (250 mL) cooked or canned chickpeas (drained and rinsed if canned)

6 slices avocado

3 cups (750 mL) sunflower sprouts or microgreens

¼ cup (60 mL) Toasted Mixed Nuts (page 274)

1 tomato, chopped

¼ cup (60 mL) chopped red onion

1. In a small bowl, combine miso tahini sauce, tamari, and hot sauce.

2. Divide cooked rice or noodles between 2 large bowls. Drizzle each with about a third of the tahini mixture.

3. Place 3 tofu steaks in each bowl and top with equal amounts of chickpeas, avocado, sprouts, toasted nuts, tomato, and red onion.

4. Drizzle with remaining sauce.

curried sri lankan rice noodles

This was taught to me by Prapa, a former Fresh staff member, and was the dinner of choice for lots of our staff. I took it as a great compliment the day that one of our brigade of Sri Lankan kitchen staff exclaimed, "Jennifer understands Sri Lankan noodles!"

These noodles are great as is, but they are also fantastic with Raw Sunflower Dressing (page 172) drizzled on top. We always use our house-made hot sauce, but if you don't have that, substitute some sambal oelek.

Rice noodles come in various thicknesses, from thread-like vermicelli to about ½ inch (1 cm) wide. For this dish, look for ones about ¼ inch (0.5 cm) thick. The brown rice version of these noodles is becoming more widely available, but if you can't find them, go ahead and use regular rice noodles. Once soaked, these noodles can stay in the fridge for up to 2 days.

serves 2

¼ cup (60 mL) sunflower oil or neutral-flavoured coconut oil

1 cup (250 mL) diced zucchini

½ cup (125 mL) diced red bell pepper

½ cup (125 mL) diced green bell pepper

1 cup (250 mL) small florets broccoli

½ cup (125 mL) chopped tomato

1 cup (250 mL) sliced button mushrooms

4 cloves garlic, minced

½ cup (125 mL) chopped red onion

¼ cup (60 mL) tamari

2 tbsp (30 mL) curry powder

2 tsp (10 mL) Hot Sauce (page 253)

1 cup (250 mL) water

4 cups (1 L) brown rice noodles, soaked and drained (see Tip)

2 cups (500 mL) bean sprouts

2 tbsp (30 mL) chopped fresh cilantro

2 lemon wedges

Raw Sunflower Dressing (page 172); optional

1. Heat oil in a large frying pan or wok over medium-low heat. Add zucchini, red pepper, green pepper, broccoli, tomato, mushrooms, garlic, red onion, and tamari. Sauté for 3 to 5 minutes, until softened.

2. Add curry powder and hot sauce and cook, stirring, for a few seconds, until vegetables are well coated.

3. Add water and soaked rice noodles. Increase heat to high and cook, stirring often, for 3 to 4 minutes, until noodles are tender and most of the liquid has evaporated.

4. Divide noodle mixture between 2 bowls. Garnish with bean sprouts, cilantro, and lemon wedges. Drizzle with raw sunflower dressing (if using).

Tip: To prepare the rice noodles, separate the amount you need from the rest of the pack (you'll have to break them apart), put into a large bowl, and cover with cold water. Let soften for about 30 minutes. Drain and proceed with the recipe. The soaking makes them pliable and easy to work with, but they still need to be cooked.

ninja

The Ninja bowl was a staple on our menu for many years. It was the first hybrid between a bowl and a salad, combining warm rice or noodles, cold dressed lettuce, and crispy tofu cubes. It has many very passionate fans out there who are sad that it's not currently on our menu. While it may reappear one day, until then you can make it at home!

serves 2

16 Marinated Tofu Cubes (page 272)

1 batch Crispy Tofu Coating (page 266)

Oil, for frying (sunflower, canola, neutral-flavoured coconut oil)

2 cups (500 mL) cooked brown basmati rice or soba noodles

1½ cups (375 mL) Wasabi Dill Dressing (page 175)

8 cups (2 L) spring mix lettuce

2 tbsp (30 mL) Ninja 2 Sauce (page 258)

6 ready-to-eat sun-dried tomatoes, sliced

1 cup (250 mL) sunflower sprouts

1. Remove tofu cubes from marinade and toss in crispy tofu coating until completely coated.

2. Heat ½ inch (1 cm) oil in a frying pan over medium heat. Cook tofu for 1 to 2 minutes per side, turning so all sides are evenly browned.

3. Divide cooked rice or noodles between 2 large bowls. Drizzle with equal amounts of wasabi dill dressing.

4. Combine lettuce and remaining wasabi dill dressing in a bowl and toss until well coated. Divide into 2 even portions and pile on top of rice or noodles in each bowl.

5. Drizzle each bowl with ninja 2 sauce.

6. Over each bowl, scatter sun-dried tomatoes, sunflower sprouts, and crispy tofu.

Tip: There are many different types of sun-dried tomatoes available. The type we use at the restaurants comes to us nice and soft, and ready to eat. But if you can only find the really dry ones, you will have to reconstitute them. Just bring some water to a boil in a small saucepan, remove from the heat, and add the tomatoes. Let sit for 10 minutes or until softened, then drain and use right away. If you want to keep some in the fridge, place them in an airtight container and cover with olive oil; they will keep for up to 2 weeks.

high raw thai noodles

"High raw" is a new concept in the world of raw food, meaning almost all raw or as raw as possible. I think it's a great development, since eating all raw all the time is difficult, and this makes it easier to embrace the parts of raw food that I love—tons of raw veggies and highly flavoured sauces—without making it impossible to use things like peanut butter and tamari, which are not raw. It also allows you to add a warm element to the dish, like the tofu steaks, which really makes it feel satisfying in the winter months. You can also warm the sauce a little before serving, if you like.

If you don't have a turning slicer (Spiralizer) to make the spiralized zucchini, either use a julienne peeler, a regular peeler, or a knife to cut long, thin strips. If you have any of our Peanut Lime Dressing (page 172) left over, it also works well here.

serves 4

red curry peanut dressing

1 cup (250 mL) coconut milk

¼ cup (60 mL) gluten-free soy sauce or tamari

3 tbsp (45 mL) coconut sugar or sweetener of your choice

¼ cup (60 mL) natural peanut butter

1 tbsp (15 mL) peeled and minced fresh ginger

1 tsp (5 mL) red curry paste (we prefer Thai Kitchen)

bowls

8 cups (2 L) spiralized zucchini

¾ cup (175 mL) Red Curry Peanut Dressing

1 cup (250 mL) chopped red bell pepper

1 cup (250 mL) chopped English cucumber

16 grape tomatoes, halved

2 cups (500 mL) bean sprouts

2 cups (500 mL) micro arugula

12 Marinated Tofu Steaks (page 272), grilled

Sliced red chilies, to taste

8 lime wedges

1. **Make red curry peanut dressing** Combine coconut milk, soy sauce, sugar, peanut butter, ginger, and red curry paste in a blender. Blend on high speed until smooth. Set aside.

2. **Assemble the bowls** Divide spiralized zucchini evenly among 4 serving bowls and top each with 2 tbsp (30 mL) of dressing.

3. Top each with equal amounts of the following: red pepper, cucumber, grape tomatoes, bean sprouts, micro arugula, and grilled tofu steaks. Drizzle with an additional 1 tbsp (15 mL) of the dressing. Garnish with red chilies and lime wedges.

red river rock

Our Tex-Mex-inspired BBQ tofu bowl was named after the Johnny and the Hurricanes song of the same name. When I was little, on the rare occasion when my mum would go out for the evening on her own, my dad would put this song on the record player as loud as it would go and we would dance in the living room.

This bowl can be served on a base of rice, soba noodles, or steamed greens. The Mexican BBQ Sauce (page 257) is best if left to sit overnight for the flavours to meld.

serves 4

8 cups (2 L) cooked brown basmati rice or soba noodles, or steamed greens (bok choy, kale, Swiss chard)

½ batch Jalapeño Lime Sauce (page 254)

1 cup (250 mL) grated carrots

1⅓ cups (325 mL) canned black beans, drained and rinsed

1⅓ cups (325 mL) frozen sweet corn, thawed and rinsed

1 cup (250 mL) chopped tomato

1 avocado, chopped

12 Marinated Tofu Steaks (page 272)

½ cup (125 mL) Mexican BBQ Sauce (page 257)

4 tsp (20 mL) raw hemp hearts

1. In each bowl, put 2 cups (500 mL) of rice, soba noodles, or steamed greens.

2. Top each bowl with 2 tbsp (30 mL) of jalapeño lime sauce and equal amounts of carrots, black beans, corn, tomato, and avocado.

3. Arrange 3 tofu steaks in each bowl and drizzle with 2 tbsp (30 mL) of Mexican BBQ sauce.

4. Sprinkle hemp hearts over top.

tiger bowl

This decadent bowl is the staff favourite for a reason. It is the ultimate in vegan comfort food, providing a nice combination of savoury and spicy. The crispness of the red peppers complements the sautéed napa cabbage perfectly, and the crispy tofu cubes are a wonderful pairing with the cashews. We particularly like this one on a bed of soba noodles.

serves 2

4 tsp (20 mL) sunflower oil or neutral-flavoured coconut oil, divided

20 Marinated Tofu Cubes (page 272)

1 batch Crispy Tofu Coating (page 266)

4 cups (1 L) thinly sliced napa cabbage

2 tsp (10 mL) tamari

4 cups (1 L) cooked brown basmati rice or soba noodles

½ cup (125 mL) 3-6-9 Dressing (page 173)

2 tsp (10 mL) Chili Oil (page 264)

½ cup (125 mL) chopped red bell pepper

20 whole raw cashews, toasted (see page 274)

1 tsp (5 mL) raw sesame seeds

2 tbsp (30 mL) thinly sliced green onions

1. Heat 1 tbsp (15 mL) of oil in large frying pan over medium heat.

2. Remove tofu cubes from marinade and toss with crispy tofu coating until fully coated.

3. Cook tofu for a minute or two per side, turning, until all sides are browned. Transfer to paper towels to drain. Set aside.

4. Wipe out pan and add 1 tsp (5 mL) of oil. Heat over high heat. Add napa cabbage and tamari, and quickly sauté until wilted and slightly browned (this should take less than a minute if your heat is high enough). Remove from heat and set aside.

5. Divide cooked rice or noodles between 2 large bowls.

6. Top each bowl with equal amounts of 3-6-9 dressing and napa cabbage. Drizzle with chili oil, and then top with red pepper, cashews, crispy tofu cubes, sesame seeds, and green onions.

inside out
summer roll bowl

inside out summer roll bowl

This bowl is basically a deconstructed Vietnamese summer roll atop hot brown rice or soba noodles. It is light and extremely flavourful. This one is also great on shirataki noodles.

serves 4

4 cups [1 L] cooked brown basmati rice or soba noodles

12 cups [3 L] spring mix lettuce

2 cups [500 mL] shredded or spiralized carrots

2 cups [500 mL] chopped English cucumber

12 Marinated Tofu Steaks [page 272] or 32 Marinated Tofu Cubes [page 272]

4 cups [1 L] bean sprouts

½ cup [125 mL] chopped fresh cilantro

¼ cup [60 mL] chopped fresh mint

½ cup [125 mL] sliced green onions

½ cup [125 mL] chopped unsalted peanuts

1 avocado, chopped [optional]

4 lime wedges

1 batch Vietnamese All-Purpose Sauce [page 261]

1. In each of 4 large bowls, put 1 cup [250 mL] of rice or soba noodles.

2. Top each bowl with equal amounts of spring mix, carrots, cucumber, tofu steaks, bean sprouts, cilantro, mint, green onions, peanuts, and avocado [if using].

3. Garnish with lime wedges. Serve with Vietnamese all-purpose sauce on the side.

smart bowl

I developed this bowl to showcase the fabulous combination of Miso Gravy (page 256) and House Dressing (page 169). It's the pairing that those of us who work at Fresh never tire of, and I wanted to make something that automatically came with these two sauces so that our customers could discover it, too.

serves 4

6 cups [1.5 L] cooked brown basmati rice or soba noodles

1 batch Miso Gravy [page 256]

8 cups [2 L] finely sliced romaine lettuce

1 avocado, chopped

4 cups [1 L] assorted sprouts and microgreens

32 Marinated Tofu Cubes [page 272]

1 cup [250 mL] grated carrots

1 cup [250 mL] frozen green peas, thawed and rinsed

1 cup [250 mL] chopped tomato

½ cup [125 mL] Fresh Salad Topper [page 275]

½ cup [125 mL] House Dressing [page 169]

1. Divide rice or soba noodles evenly among 4 serving bowls.

2. Top each bowl with about ½ cup [125 mL] of miso gravy and equal amounts of romaine lettuce, avocado, sprouts and microgreens, tofu cubes, carrots, green peas, and tomato.

3. Garnish each with 2 tbsp [30 mL] of salad topper. Drizzle house dressing on top.

SAUCES

I think everyone will agree that the sauce is what makes the meal. No one wants to eat a bowl full of plain rice, noodles, and veggies, but add an exquisite sauce and you keep coming back for bite after bite. Our sauces range from light to creamy, and spicy to sweet. However, all are delicious and simple to make. And even though we do use some classic French culinary techniques, don't be intimidated—our recipes are designed to be simple. We don't have time to fool around with complicated recipes, and we're sure you don't either.

bbq sauce

This is the sauce we use on our ever-popular BBQ Burger (page 218). It also makes a nice glaze for baked tofu or grilled portobello mushrooms.

makes 3 cups (175 mL)

¼ cup (60 mL) olive oil

1 cup (250 mL) diced onion

2 cloves garlic, minced

2 tsp (10 mL) ground allspice

1 tsp (5 mL) cayenne pepper

¾ cup (175 mL) apple cider vinegar

¾ cup (175 mL) water

¾ cup (175 mL) ketchup

½ cup (125 mL) organic vegan sugar

4 tsp (20 mL) sesame oil

3 tbsp (45 mL) Bragg Liquid Aminos or tamari

3 tbsp (45 mL) blackstrap molasses

1. Heat olive oil in a saucepan over medium-low heat.

2. Add onion, garlic, allspice, and cayenne. Cook, stirring occasionally, until onion is softened.

3. Add vinegar, water, ketchup, sugar, sesame oil, liquid aminos, and molasses. Bring to a boil. Reduce heat and simmer for 30 minutes or until slightly thickened (see Tip). Use immediately or transfer to an airtight container and refrigerate for up to 2 weeks.

Tip: If your sauce doesn't thicken enough to use on a burger, combine some of the sauce and 1 tbsp (15 mL) cornstarch in a little bowl, stir until smooth, and then add to pan with remaining sauce, stirring well to combine. Return to a boil and stir until thickened.

beach sauce

This versatile sauce is named for our most popular Fresh bowl, the Beach. Its simplicity is a surprise to many people who ask for the recipe, since it seems to add up to much more than the sum of its parts, flavour-wise. It transforms the simplest bowl of rice or noodles into a savoury treat, and seems to work equally well with any ingredient you can think of to add to it.

makes 1 cup (250 mL)

¾ cup (175 mL) extra virgin olive oil

¼ cup (60 mL) tamari

1½ tsp (7 mL) Mixed Herb Blend (page 271)

1. Whisk together all of the ingredients in a small bowl. (Alternatively, use a resealable jar and shake well.) Use immediately or refrigerate for up to 1 month.

buddha sauce

We've been using this sauce on our popular Buddha bowl for over a decade now. The flavour is decadent and rich from the peanut butter, with spice and zing from the chilies, ginger, spices, and lemon.

Be careful when heating this sauce: stir often as the peanut butter has a tendency to burn. If making ahead of time, the sauce will thicken, so you may need to whisk in some water to get the right consistency and to prevent scorching before heating. If you don't have a juicer, replace the carrot juice with some vegetable stock.

makes 6 cups (1.5 L)

3 tbsp (45 mL) olive oil

1 cup (250 mL) diced onion

6 tbsp (90 mL) minced peeled fresh ginger

6 cloves minced garlic

2 tsp (10 mL) curry powder

1 tsp (5 mL) cayenne pepper or freshly ground crushed red chilies

1⅓ cups (325 mL) carrot juice

1 cup (250 mL) water

¾ cup (175 mL) rice vinegar

2 cups (500 mL) smooth natural peanut butter

⅔ cup (150 mL) tamari

¼ cup (60 mL) freshly squeezed lemon juice

2 tbsp (30 mL) toasted sesame oil

¼ cup (60 mL) sunflower oil

1. Heat olive oil in a saucepan over medium heat. Add onion, ginger, and garlic and cook for a few minutes, until onion is softened.

2. Add curry powder and cayenne pepper. Cook, stirring, for about 30 seconds, and then remove from heat.

3. Add carrot juice, water, vinegar, peanut butter, tamari, lemon juice, sesame oil, and sunflower oil. Stir well and let cool.

4. Using an immersion blender or regular blender, blend on high speed until smooth.

5. Before serving, gently reheat in a saucepan over low heat. Stored in an airtight container in the refrigerator, this sauce will last for up to 5 days.

fresh "cheese" sauce

I tried so many ways to make a vegan cheese substitute. I soaked nuts, added probiotics, drained things overnight in cheesecloth, special ordered from Brooklyn, New York, and had to go pick them up … but nothing tasted good to me, and it just wasn't worth all the trouble. I was about to give up. Then one day I stumbled across this idea somewhere on the internet. It was so fast, so easy, and so tasty I almost couldn't believe it. You know how if you mash potatoes using a blade (like in a food processor), it turns gummy? Well, it's that effect that makes this recipe work. The potatoes take on a gumminess that perfectly replicates melty cheese.

If you want to make the prep even easier, buy cans of cooked carrots and potatoes. Just rinse and drain, and you can have this sauce done in about a minute.

To make it really easy to use, put it into a squeeze bottle! You can get squeeze bottles for a couple of dollars at kitchen stores, or just reuse an old ketchup or mustard bottle.

makes 3 cups (750 mL)

2 cups (500 mL) peeled and chopped potatoes

¾ cup (175 mL) peeled and chopped carrots

½ cup (125 mL) flaked nutritional yeast

⅓ cup (75 mL) sunflower oil

⅓ cup (75 mL) water

1 tbsp (15 mL) freshly squeezed lemon juice

1½ tsp (7 mL) sea salt

1. In a saucepan full of boiling water, cook potatoes and carrots until very soft, 10 to 15 minutes. Drain.

2. Combine cooked potatoes and carrots, nutritional yeast, oil, water, lemon juice, and salt in a container and, using an immersion blender, purée until smooth. If needed, add some more water to get a pourable consistency, 1 tbsp (15 mL) at a time. (Alternatively, use a regular blender.) Stored in an airtight container in the refrigerator, this sauce will last for up to 1 week.

hollandaise sauce

One of the ingredients in this hollandaise sauce is black salt, also known as "kala namak." It's actually not black at all, but a pink-coloured powder, and it's very sulphurous smelling. It really gives the sauce an authentic eggy flavour. You will probably have to purchase it at a spice shop. If you can't find it, don't worry. The sauce will still taste good without it. We use this sauce on Tempeh Florentine (page 116), Brussels Sprout Fritters (page 114), and Cauliflower Benedict (page 122).

makes 1 cup (250 mL)

1 cup (250 mL) vegetable stock

1 tbsp (15 mL) sunflower oil

¼ cup (60 mL) minced onion

¼ cup (60 mL) dry white wine

1½ tbsp (22 mL) apple cider vinegar

2 tbsp (30 mL) cornstarch

¼ tsp (1 mL) ground turmeric

2 tbsp (30 mL) flaked nutritional yeast

¼ tsp (1 mL) black salt (kala namak)

1 cup (250 mL) unsweetened plain soy milk

1 tbsp (15 mL) freshly squeezed lemon juice

1. In a saucepan, bring stock to a boil over high heat. Cook until reduced to about 2 tbsp (30 mL).

2. Meanwhile, heat oil in another saucepan over low heat. Add onion and cook for a few minutes, until softened (be careful not to let it brown).

3. Add wine and vinegar. Increase heat to high and cook until liquid is reduced by half.

4. Combine cornstarch, turmeric, nutritional yeast, and black salt in a bowl. Gradually add reduced stock and soy milk, whisking to avoid lumps.

5. Pour soy milk mixture into wine mixture, whisking constantly to avoid lumps.

6. Bring to a gentle boil, then whisk in lemon juice. (It will thicken rapidly as soon as it comes to a boil, so be sure to stay with it and whisk constantly.)

7. Remove from heat and either serve or let cool, transfer to an airtight container, and refrigerate for up to 1 week. If not using right away, before reheating, you may have to add a little bit of water and whisk vigorously to get it back to a smooth texture.

hot sauce

This hot sauce has tons of flavour, not just heat. It was invented by Stash, a long-time friend of Ruth's. He was nice enough to share the recipe with us, and we have incorporated it into our menu and serve it as a condiment. It's so popular that we make over 130 gallons (about 500 litres) of it a month!

The long ingredients list may seem a little intimidating, but the method is very simple, so once you have all the ingredients together, it's a very easy recipe to make.

Scotch bonnet peppers are really hot! You've probably heard the horror stories about people who worked with hot chilies and then rubbed their eyes, or even worse, went to the bathroom! This is all true; the burn can last for hours. Luckily, in this recipe, you won't even need to touch the peppers, except to remove stems if there are any.

Capsaicin, one of the chemical components of hot chilies, is addictive and gives a kind of high, which is why people who eat a lot of hot spices insist on always including it in their meals. The lemongrass stays in the sauce to impart its flavour; it's not meant to be eaten.

makes 1¼ cups (300 mL)

4 scotch bonnet peppers, stems removed

½ cup (125 mL) chopped red onion

2 green onions, roughly chopped

2 cloves garlic

½-inch (1 cm) piece peeled fresh ginger, roughly chopped

½ tsp (2 mL) fresh thyme leaves

1 tsp (5 mL) fresh rosemary

½ cup (125 mL) tamari

1 stalk lemongrass

¼ cup (60 mL) balsamic vinegar

¼ cup (60 mL) Dijon mustard

½ tsp (2 mL) curry powder

½ tsp (2 mL) cayenne pepper

½ tsp (2 mL) crushed red chilies

¼ tsp (1 mL) dried oregano

¼ tsp (1 mL) ground cinnamon

¼ tsp (1 mL) ground cumin

1. Combine scotch bonnets, red onion, green onions, garlic, ginger, thyme, and rosemary in a food processor. Process until smooth.

2. Transfer pepper purée to a saucepan. Add tamari and cook over low heat for about 5 minutes, or until mixture turns a darker shade of brown.

3. Meanwhile, remove outer leaves from lemongrass, smash it with the back of a knife to break it open a bit, and chop into 3-inch (7.5 cm) pieces.

4. Add lemongrass pieces, balsamic vinegar, mustard, curry powder, cayenne pepper, crushed red chilies, oregano, cinnamon, and cumin to the saucepan. Bring to a boil, reduce heat, and simmer for 30 minutes.

5. Remove from heat and let cool. Stored in an airtight container in the refrigerator, this sauce will last for up to 1 month.

jalapeño lime sauce

This sauce is so tasty, you could put it on almost anything! Make only as much of this sauce as you need, because the jalapeño takes on a bitter taste if stored overnight. Rick Hardisty, a former Fresh kitchen manager, taught me how to pick perfect juicy limes every time—just look for limes with smooth skin!

makes about 1¼ cups (300 mL)

1 cup (250 mL) Garlic Mayo (page 268)

2 tbsp (30 mL) freshly squeezed lime juice

¼ cup (60 mL) roughly chopped fresh cilantro

2 jalapeño peppers, roughly chopped

1. Combine all of the ingredients in a blender. Blend on high speed until smooth. (Alternatively, combine ingredients in a jar and blend using an immersion blender.)

shortcut taco sauce

Don't have the time or inclination to make our Garlic Mayo (page 268) as the base for this sauce? No problem, just use store-bought vegan mayo and you can have it ready in a couple of minutes! Make only as much of this sauce as you need, because the jalapeño takes on a bitter taste if stored overnight.

makes about 1¼ cups (300 mL)

1 cup (250 mL) vegan mayonnaise

2 cloves garlic

2 tbsp (30 mL) freshly squeezed lime juice

¼ cup (60 mL) roughly chopped fresh cilantro

2 jalapeño peppers, roughly chopped

1. Combine all of the ingredients in a blender. Blend on high speed until smooth. (Alternatively, combine ingredients in a jar and blend using an immersion blender.)

lemon garlic glaze

This glaze tastes good on almost anything. Toss with roasted vegetables or steamed greens, drizzle on rice or noodles, or use in our Leek and Mushroom Toast (page 121) or Sam Houston Burrito (page 212).

makes ½ cup (125 mL)

1 cup (250 mL) water

3 cloves garlic

1 tbsp (15 mL) olive oil

½ cup (125 mL) vegetable stock

2 tbsp (30 mL) non-dairy buttery spread (we prefer Earth Balance), 3-6-9 oil, flaxseed oil, or neutral-flavoured coconut oil

2 tsp (10 mL) freshly squeezed lemon juice

½ tsp (2 mL) tamari

1 tsp (5 mL) sea salt

1 tsp (5 mL) freshly ground black pepper

1. Bring water to a boil in a small saucepan.

2. Add garlic and boil for 30 seconds. Remove from heat. Transfer garlic to a small bowl of ice water to cool; discard cooking liquid. Once garlic is cool, slice thinly.

3. Combine garlic and olive oil in small saucepan over medium heat and cook until garlic begins to brown, about 2 minutes.

4. Add stock, bring to a boil, and cook for 5 to 10 minutes or until stock is reduced by half.

5. Reduce heat to low and stir in non-dairy butter until melted. Add lemon juice, tamari, salt, and pepper. Stir to combine. Stored in an airtight container in the refrigerator, this sauce will last up 1 week.

Tip: Non-dairy butter, 3-6-9 oil, flaxseed oil, or coconut oil will all work equally well in this recipe. If you have used coconut oil and you have leftover glaze, you may need to reheat the glaze before using it to make it pourable.

miso gravy

This sauce has been on our menu since day one. Its unique, rich, savoury, and pungent flavour is one that our customers crave. It takes hardly any time to make, and keeps in the fridge for a few days. Just gently reheat before serving. Sweet potato fries with miso gravy is a classic Fresh combination. Miso gravy is also particularly good when paired with our House Dressing (page 169), as in the Smart Bowl (page 247).

makes 2 cups (500 mL)

4½ tbsp (67 mL) spelt flour

¼ tsp (1 mL) garlic powder

¾ cup (175 mL) powdered nutritional yeast

1½ cups (375 mL) vegetable stock or water

⅓ cup (75 mL) sunflower oil

1½ tsp (7 mL) Dijon mustard

3 tbsp (45 mL) mild soy miso

¾ tsp (3 mL) sea salt

1. Combine flour, garlic powder, and yeast in a saucepan over low heat.

2. Whisk in stock to make a paste. Bring to a boil, then reduce heat and simmer for 30 seconds.

3. Add oil, mustard, miso, and salt. Cook, whisking constantly, until mixture is smooth (see Tip). Serve hot or let cool, transfer to an airtight container, and refrigerate for up to 5 days.

Tip: You can use a whisk to bring this sauce together while you're making it or, to make it even easier, just use an immersion blender to blend it right in the pot.

miso tahini sauce

This sauce is great as a salad dressing or enjoy it poured over any cooked or raw vegetable.

makes about 1 cup (250 mL)

2 tbsp (30 mL) mild soy miso

⅓ cup (75 mL) water

1 tbsp (15 mL) apple cider vinegar

1 tsp (5 mL) tamari

1-inch (2.5 cm) piece peeled fresh ginger, grated (about 1 tbsp/15 mL)

2 tbsp (30 mL) raw tahini

½ cup (125 mL) sunflower oil

1. Combine all of the ingredients, except the oil, in a blender. Blend on high speed until smooth.

2. With motor running, slowly drizzle in oil and blend until all of the oil is incorporated. Use immediately or transfer to an airtight container and refrigerate for up to 3 days.

mexican bbq sauce

This sauce was developed to go on the Red River Rock Bowl (page 244). It combines Mexican chili powder and smoked paprika with a traditional barbecue sauce for a novel and delectable taste. Try to make this 1 day ahead of using—the flavours meld together really well if allowed to sit overnight.

makes 2 cups (500 mL)

2 cloves garlic, minced

½ cup (125 mL) tomato paste

2 tsp (10 mL) onion powder

1 tbsp (15 mL) apple cider vinegar

1 tbsp (15 mL) gluten-free vegan Worcestershire sauce

2 tsp (10 mL) Mexican chili powder

½ cup (125 mL) raw agave nectar

1 cup (250 mL) water

1 tsp (5 mL) sea salt

2 tsp (10 mL) garlic powder

1 tsp (5 mL) smoked paprika

1. Combine all of the ingredients in a bowl. Whisk together until smooth. Use immediately or transfer to an airtight container and refrigerate for up to 1 week.

ninja 2 sauce

This sauce is called Ninja 2 because it is the second sauce that goes on the Ninja bowl. We like to keep things pretty straightforward in our busy kitchens! This sauce can also be drizzled on any rice, noodle, or vegetable bowl to add an intense flavour and spice boost. If you don't feel like making our hot sauce, just use Sriracha or sambal oelek.

makes about ⅓ cup (75 mL)

1 tbsp (15 mL) tamari

1 tsp (5 mL) sesame oil

½ tsp (2 mL) peeled and grated fresh ginger

1½ tsp (7 mL) freshly squeezed lemon juice

½ tsp (2 mL) Hot Sauce (page 253)

1. Combine all of the ingredients in a bowl and whisk to combine. Use immediately or transfer to an airtight container and refrigerate for up to 2 weeks.

pineapple cashew sauce

The combination of cashews and pineapple gives an almost tropical twist to this creamy sauce. It goes on the Emerald City Bowl (page 225), but would be equally at home as a salad dressing or topping for steamed veggies. If you can find only salted cashews at the store, omit the salt from the recipe, adding it at the end only if necessary.

makes about 1¼ (300 mL)

¾ cup (175 mL) raw unsalted cashews

1 clove garlic

¼ cup (60 mL) pineapple juice (fresh or bottled)

3 tbsp (45 mL) freshly squeezed lemon juice

¼ tsp (1 mL) sea salt

½ cup (125 mL) water

1. Combine all of the ingredients in a blender (see Tip). Blend on high speed until smooth. Use immediately or transfer to an airtight container and refrigerate for up to 2 days.

Tip: It's easiest to get a super-smooth texture in this sauce with a high-speed blender.

roasted mushroom gravy

This rich-tasting gravy is amazing with our Super Bowl (page 139) and the
Green Poutine-Style Sweet Potato (page 147).

makes 2½ cups (625 mL)

2 cups (500 mL) sliced button mushrooms

3 tbsp (45 mL) sunflower oil

⅔ cup (150 mL) finely diced onion (about 1 small)

2 cloves garlic, minced

2 tsp (10 mL) tamari

2 tbsp (30 mL) flaked nutritional yeast

¼ tsp (1 mL) freshly ground black pepper

¼ cup (60 mL) gluten-free all-purpose flour (we prefer Bob's Red Mill)

2½ cups (625 mL) vegetable stock

Sea salt, to taste

1. Preheat oven to 400°F (200°C).

2. Combine mushrooms and 1 tbsp (15 mL) oil in a bowl and toss until well coated. Transfer to a roasting pan.

3. Roast in preheated oven for 15 to 25 minutes or until mushrooms release their liquid. Remove from heat and set aside.

4. Heat remaining 2 tbsp (30 mL) oil in a saucepan over medium-high heat.

5. Add onions and garlic and cook for 3 to 4 minutes, stirring occasionally, until softened.

6. Stir in tamari, nutritional yeast, and pepper.

7. Add flour and just enough stock to make a thin paste. Cook, stirring, until the raw taste of the flour cooks out.

8. For a smooth gravy base, put immersion blender into pot and gradually add the rest of the stock while blending. Remove immersion blender. (If you don't mind a gravy base with chunks of onion, just stir the rest of the stock in gradually with a wooden spoon, going slowly at first to avoid getting lumps of flour.)

9. Add roasted mushrooms and stir to combine. Bring to a boil, reduce heat, and simmer for 5 minutes. Add salt. Use immediately or let cool, transfer to an airtight container, and refrigerate for up to 1 week.

vietnamese
all-purpose sauce

vietnamese all-purpose sauce

This sauce is used on the Inside Out Summer Roll Bowl (page 247) and as a dip for the Collard Green Spring Rolls (page 140). I'm sure that once you have some in your fridge you will find many other uses for it, since its spicy, garlicky, lemony flavour livens up anything it's paired with. Up the sambal oelek content if you like things really spicy.

makes 1¼ cups (300 mL)

½ cup (125 mL) tamari

½ cup (125 mL) raw agave nectar

¼ cup (60 mL) freshly squeezed lemon juice

5 cloves garlic, minced (about 2 tbsp/30 mL)

1 tbsp (15 mL) sambal oelek, or more to taste

1. Combine all of the ingredients in a bowl. Whisk to combine. Use immediately or transfer to an airtight container and refrigerate for up to 2 weeks.

lemongrass sauce

This sauce has a mouth-watering, subtle flavour. We use it in the Broccoli and Mushroom Noodles with Cashews (page 224), where it perfectly plays off the slight bitterness of the broccoli, the umami of the mushrooms, and the nuttiness of the cashews.

makes 3 cups (750 mL)

4 cloves garlic, roughly chopped

¼ cup (60 mL) roughly chopped peeled fresh ginger

2 stalks lemongrass, roughly chopped into ½-inch (1 cm) pieces

¼ tsp (1 mL) crushed red chilies

¼ cup (60 mL) dry white wine

2 cups (500 mL) water

6 tbsp (90 mL) tamari

6 tbsp (90 mL) raw agave nectar

1. Combine all of the ingredients in a saucepan and bring to a boil.

2. Reduce heat and simmer for 20 minutes.

3. Strain through a fine-mesh sieve; discard solids. Use immediately or transfer to an airtight container and refrigerate for up to 1 month.

SPREADS, MIXES, MARINADES, AND MORE

This chapter contains all the little recipes, marinades, and flavour accents that go into making our dishes. But just because we use them for a particular dish doesn't mean they can't be used in other ways and added to your usual repertoire. If you come up with other ways to use them, let us know at feedback@freshrestaurants!

marinated adzuki beans

These simple marinated beans are very versatile. We use them in the All Star (page 159) and Transformer (page 167) salads, but they would go equally well on any salad or rice bowl, in a wrap, or even just eaten as a snack with some chopped avocado, cucumber, or any vegetable you like.

makes 1½ cups (375 mL)

1 can (14 oz/398 mL) adzuki beans, drained and rinsed

1 tbsp (15 mL) extra virgin olive oil

1 tbsp (15 mL) tamari

1. Combine all of the ingredients in a bowl and stir well. Use immediately or cover and refrigerate for up to 3 days.

adzuki bean stew

The Japanese adzuki bean is a tasty small red bean packed with nutrition. It contains 25 percent protein and is high in soluble fibre, which helps to eliminate cholesterol from the body. This bean is also a good source of magnesium, potassium, iron, zinc, copper, manganese, and vitamin B3. Because it is high in potassium and low in sodium, it is said to help reduce blood pressure. The red adzuki bean also contains protease inhibitors, reputed to stall development of cancer cells. All this and it tastes great!

makes 6 cups (1.5 L)

2 tbsp (30 mL) neutral-flavoured coconut oil or olive oil

2 cups (500 mL) diced onions

2 tbsp (30 mL) peeled minced fresh ginger

2 tsp (10 mL) dried oregano

1 tsp (5 mL) cayenne pepper

¼ tsp (1 mL) ground cinnamon

4 cups (1 L) cooked adzuki beans (about three 14 oz/398 mL cans, drained and rinsed)

2 tbsp (30 mL) tomato paste

¼ cup (60 mL) tamari

2 cups (500 mL) vegetable stock

1. Heat oil in a pot over medium heat.

2. Add onions and ginger and cook for 3 to 4 minutes, until softened.

3. Stir in oregano, cayenne, and cinnamon and cook for 1 minute, until fragrant.

4. Add beans, tomato paste, tamari, and stock and bring to a boil.

5. Reduce heat and simmer for 10 minutes. Use immediately or let cool, transfer to an airtight container, and refrigerate for up to 5 days. (It also freezes nicely.)

chili oil

We use this spicy oil on the Tiger Bowl (page 245) and Ironman Salad (page 163). After sitting in the hot oil, the chilies develop a smoky flavour that adds a real depth along with the heat.

makes 1 cup (250 mL)

1 cup (250 mL) sunflower oil

⅓ cup (75 mL) crushed red chilies

1. Heat oil in a small saucepan over medium heat until a wooden spoon stuck into the oil releases a lot of bubbles (that's how you'll know it's hot enough).

2. Place crushed red chilies in another small saucepan. Carefully pour in hot oil and stir.

3. Set aside for 3 hours to allow chilies to infuse oil.

4. Using a fine-mesh strainer, strain oil into a clean airtight container; discard solids. The oil will keep in the fridge for a few months.

crispy onions

These yummy onions add a savoury note to our Phytosalad (page 160) and Ironman Salad (page 163), as well as our Falafel Tacos (page 209).

makes 1 cup (250 mL)

1 cup (250 mL) thinly sliced onions

¼ cup (60 mL) flour of your choice (spelt, all-purpose, gluten-free)

¼ to ½ cup (60 to 125 mL) canola or sunflower oil, for frying

Sea salt, to taste

1. Toss onions in flour until well coated.

2. Heat oil in a frying pan over medium-high heat. Add a few onions, making sure not to crowd the pan, and cook for 2 or 3 minutes, until browned

3. Transfer cooked onions to paper towels to drain. Immediately sprinkle with salt. Repeat with remaining onions.

4. Let cool and use right away.

chili oil

crispy tofu coating

We changed this recipe in the last couple of years to make it gluten-free. It used to have wheat germ in place of the cornstarch, so if you would like to use wheat germ, feel free. This mixture keeps indefinitely as long as you don't get any bits of tofu in it. When using it, just pour a little bit into a separate container to toss with the tofu and discard the leftovers from that container.

makes 1½ cups (375 mL)

1 cup (250 mL) flaked nutritional yeast

½ cup (125 mL) cornstarch

1 tbsp (15 mL) garlic powder

¼ tsp (1 mL) sea salt

¼ tsp (1 mL) freshly ground black pepper

1. Combine all of the ingredients in a bowl and stir well. Use immediately or transfer to an airtight container and store at room temperature in a cool, dry place.

dosa batter

We use this batter not only to make the Avocado Dosas (page 142), but also as an all-purpose batter for coating and breading other items like Fresh Onion Rings (page 221), Crispy Cauliflower Bites (page 144), and Crispy Oyster Mushrooms (page 206).

makes 1½ cups (375 mL)

1 cup (250 mL) light spelt flour

½ tsp (2 mL) sea salt

½ tsp (2 mL) baking powder

½ tsp (2 mL) curry powder

¾ cup (175 mL) water

½ cup (125 mL) plain unsweetened soy milk

1. Combine flour, salt, baking powder, and curry powder in a bowl and whisk to combine.

2. Gradually whisk in water and soy milk until a smooth batter forms. Transfer to an airtight container and refrigerate for up to 2 days. (It might go a little black on top due to the spelt flour, but don't worry: just stir it back together and it'll be fine.)

Tip: Spelt is an ancient grain related to wheat. It has never been hybridized, so it is more easily digested than other forms of wheat. Some people with wheat intolerances can tolerate spelt, although it is not gluten-free.

miso mayo

This mayo is the dip for our Crispy Cauliflower Bites (page 144) and the sauce for our Naked Sushi Bowl (page 234).

makes 1 cup (250 mL)

¼ cup (60 mL) unsweetened plain soy milk

½ cup (125 mL) sunflower oil

1 tbsp (15 mL) freshly squeezed lemon juice

1 tbsp (15 mL) mild soy miso

1 tbsp (15 mL) water

¼ tsp (1 mL) dry mustard powder

¼ tsp (1 mL) apple cider vinegar

¼ tsp (1 mL) raw agave nectar

1. Combine all of the ingredients in a large measuring cup.

2. Using an immersion blender, blend until thick. (Alternatively, use a regular blender on high speed.)

shortcut miso mayo

Don't have time to make mayo from scratch? Just use store-bought and you can have it ready in a minute!

makes 1 cup (250 mL)

2 tbsp (30 mL) mild soy miso

3 tbsp (45 mL) water

¾ cup (175 mL) store-bought vegan mayonnaise (we prefer Veganaise)

1. Place miso in a small bowl and, using a fork or small whisk, gradually whisk in water until mixture is smooth. Stir in vegan mayonnaise. Cover and refrigerate for up to 1 week.

fresh mayos

This method for making mayo works almost like magic. It goes from two separate liquids to a thick mayo pretty much instantly. But remember: it only works with soy milk, not any other type of milk. Why? Who knows, but I tried rice milk and almond milk and neither of them worked at all.

You can make these in a blender or food processor, but I prefer to put all of the ingredients in a container and then use an immersion blender—that way you don't have to dig the mayo out from the bottom of the blender.

If you don't want to make your own mayo, you can still make the variations below by blending the ingredients into 1½ cups (375 mL) of store-bought vegan mayonnaise (we prefer Veganaise).

This mayo base doesn't taste like much on its own, so be sure to choose one of the variations below and add the variation ingredients to the mayo base ingredients before blending.

makes 1½ cups (375 mL)

mayo base

½ cup (125 mL) unsweetened plain soy milk

1 cup (250 mL) sunflower oil

½ tsp (2 mL) dry mustard powder

½ tsp (2 mL) apple cider vinegar

½ tsp (2 mL) raw agave nectar

1 tsp (5 mL) sea salt

2 tsp (10 mL) freshly squeezed lemon juice

For curry mayo: Add 2 tbsp (30 mL) curry powder.

For garlic mayo: Add 1 to 2 cloves garlic, minced.

For wasabi mayo: Add 2 tbsp (30 mL) wasabi powder. If you are turning store-bought mayo into wasabi mayo, wake up the wasabi first by mixing it with 1 tbsp (15 mL) water. If you're making wasabi mayo from scratch using the recipe above, you can just add the wasabi powder to the ingredients.

For chipotle mayo: Add 1 to 2 tbsp (15 to 30 mL) canned chipotles in adobo sauce (or more to taste).

For lemon aioli: Add 1 to 2 cloves minced garlic and 2 tbsp (30 mL) freshly grated lemon zest.

For Korean mayo: Add 2 tsp (10 mL) gochujang and 2 tsp (10 mL) freshly squeezed lemon juice.

1. Combine all of the ingredients in a container and, using an immersion blender, blend until thick (this takes just a few seconds). Transfer mayo to an airtight container and refrigerate for up to 1 week.

chipotle mayo

garlic mayo

chipotle peppers

curry mayo

herb falafel balls

These delicious green-tinged falafel balls can be either fried or baked. We use them in the Falafel Tacos (page 209) and Ironman Salad (page 163). For a more traditional use, stuff them inside a pita with fresh veggies and Tahini Dressing (page 174).

makes 30 falafel balls

2 cloves garlic

½ cup (125 mL) chopped fresh cilantro

½ cup (125 mL) chopped fresh mint

½ cup (125 mL) chopped fresh parsley

1 can (19 oz/540 mL) chickpeas, drained and rinsed

½ cup (125 mL) light spelt flour

½ cup (125 mL) dried breadcrumbs or panko crumbs

⅓ cup (75 mL) finely diced onion (about ½ small onion)

¼ cup (60 mL) raw tahini

1 tsp (5 mL) sea salt

1 tsp (5 mL) coriander seeds, toasted and ground (see page 274)

1 tsp (5 mL) baking powder

Sunflower oil or neutral-flavoured coconut oil, for frying

1. Place garlic in a food processor and pulse to mince. Add cilantro, mint, and parsley and pulse until finely chopped, scraping down the sides of the work bowl as needed. Transfer to a large bowl.

2. Place chickpeas in food processor and pulse to chop finely (be careful not to overprocess or it will form a purée).

3. Combine chopped chickpeas, flour, breadcrumbs, onion, tahini, salt, coriander, and baking powder in a large bowl. Using your hands, mix everything together thoroughly.

4. Form into small balls (about 1 tbsp/15 mL each), and then press together between your palms to pack together and flatten slightly.

5. Refrigerate until ready to use (for up to 2 days) or cook either in the oven or in a frying pan.
   To cook in the oven: Preheat to 350°F (180°C). Arrange falafel balls on a baking sheet and brush tops with a little bit of sunflower oil. Bake in preheated oven for about 20 minutes or until browned and crispy on the outside and heated through, turning over and brushing with a bit more oil halfway through.
   To cook in a frying pan: Heat about ½ inch (1 cm) of oil in a pan over medium-high heat. Cook falafel balls 1 to 2 minutes per side, until browned and crispy.

herb-marinated tempeh

We started using this tempeh marinade just in the last year or so. It's so simple and so delicious.

You can cook tempeh any number of ways. We grill it at the restaurants, but at home you can cook it under the broiler, in a panini grill, on a barbecue, or in a frying pan with some oil.

makes 16 slices

2 cups (500 mL) water

½ cup (125 mL) tamari

¼ cup (60 mL) pure dark maple syrup

2 tbsp (30 mL) roughly chopped fresh rosemary

2 tbsp (30 mL) fresh thyme leaves

2 tbsp (30 mL) roughly chopped fresh sage

1 block (9 oz/250 g) tempeh, cut into 16 slices

1. Combine all of the ingredients, except tempeh, in a bowl and whisk to combine.

2. Add tempeh slices and turn to coat.

3. Cover and refrigerate for 1 hour, or up to 2 days.

Tip: To cut the tempeh into even slices, first cut the block in half, then in half again, then in half again, etc., until you have the desired number of slices.

mixed herb blend

This combination of dried herbs adds flavour to many of our recipes. The mixture will last for ages; just give it a little rub between your fingers before using to release the flavours and aromas.

makes about 6 tbsp (90 mL)

1 tbsp (15 mL) dried oregano

1 tbsp (15 mL) dried basil

1 tbsp (15 mL) dried marjoram

1 tbsp (15 mL) dried dill

1 tbsp (15 mL) dried thyme

1½ tsp (7 mL) dried rosemary

1½ tsp (7 mL) dried sage

1. Combine all of the ingredients in an airtight jar. Seal and shake to combine. Store in a cool, dry place for up to 1 year.

marinated tofu cubes

This marinade is the epitome of simple, but it takes tofu from bland to delicious! We use these cubes in salads, bowls, and wraps. They are great raw, but are also amazingly craveable when coated with our Crispy Tofu Coating (page 266) and turned into our ever popular crispy tofu cubes.

This marinade can be reused one time after the first tofu cubes come out.

½ cup (125 mL) apple cider vinegar

¾ cup (175 mL) tamari

¼ cup (60 mL) water

1 block (12 to 16 oz/350 to 450 g) extra firm tofu, cut into ¾-inch (2 cm) cubes

1. Combine vinegar, tamari, and water in a bowl.

2. Add tofu cubes and turn to coat. Set aside for at least 15 minutes, or up to 2 days, to marinate (cover and refrigerate if longer than 15 minutes).

Tip: Tofu comes in many different sized blocks. This marinade makes enough for blocks from 12 to 16 oz (350 to 450 g).

marinated tofu steaks

We serve thousands of these tofu steaks every month. They go well on everything: from salads, bowls, and tacos to wraps and sandwiches. At the restaurants we grill them, but at home you can cook them under the broiler, on a panini grill, on a barbecue, or in a frying pan with some oil.

makes 16 tofu steaks

½ cup (125 mL) tamari

2 cups (500 mL) water

2 tbsp (30 mL) ground coriander

4 tsp (20 mL) garlic powder

1 block (12 to 16 oz/350 to 450 g) extra firm tofu

1. Combine tamari, water, coriander, and garlic powder in a bowl.

2. Cut block of tofu in half lengthwise, then cut each half into 4 slices, and then cut those slices on the diagonal to form 16 triangular steaks. Add to marinade.

3. Cover and set aside for at least 1 hour, or overnight, to marinate (refrigerate if overnight).

4. To cook, either grill or pan-fry with 1 to 2 tbsp (15 to 30 mL) of oil over medium-high heat until browned on both sides.

Tip: Tofu comes in many different sized blocks. This marinade makes enough for blocks from 12 to 16 oz (350 to 450 g).

tempeh bacon

We use this bacon on our Chipotle Bacon Burger (page 217), in the Ace of Kales Salad (page 163), and as an optional side with our brunch plates.

makes 24 to 30 slices

2 tbsp [30 mL] smoked paprika

2 tsp [10 mL] garlic powder

¼ cup [60 mL] tamari

¼ cup [60 mL] apple cider vinegar

¼ cup [60 mL] water

¼ cup [60 mL] sunflower oil

¼ cup [60 mL] pure dark maple syrup

1 block [8 oz/250 g] tempeh

Sunflower oil or neutral-flavoured coconut oil, for frying

1. **Marinate tempeh** Combine smoked paprika and garlic powder in a measuring cup with a spout. Add a little of the tamari and stir to form a paste. Gradually add remaining tamari, vinegar, water, oil, and maple syrup, stirring to prevent lumps from forming. Set aside.

2. Slice tempeh very thinly.

3. Arrange tempeh slices in layers in a baking dish or plastic container, pouring marinade over each layer before adding more tempeh. Keep layering until all of the tempeh and marinade are used up.

4. Cover and refrigerate for 2 hours or up to 2 days.

5. **Cook tempeh** Coat bottom of frying pan with a thin layer of oil and heat over medium-high heat. Add as many tempeh slices as will fit in the pan and cook for a minute or so per side, until both sides are browned. Remove tempeh from pan and transfer to paper towel to drain. Repeat for remaining tempeh slices. Use immediately or let cool, transfer to an airtight container, and refrigerate for up to 2 days.

toasted mixed nuts

This mix is equally at home on top of pancakes as it is on a salad. Make a batch with this mix, or make up your own combination using your favourite nuts. Keep in the fridge or freezer and add it to whatever you're making.

makes 1 cup (250 mL)

¼ cup (60 mL) raw cashews

¼ cup (60 mL) raw walnuts

¼ cup (60 mL) raw pistachios

¼ cup (60 mL) raw pecans

1. Preheat oven to 350°F (180°C).

2. Combine nuts and spread over a baking sheet.

3. Bake in preheated oven until lightly toasted, 3 to 5 minutes.

4. Use right away or store in an airtight container in the fridge or freezer for up to 1 month.

toasted mixed seeds

This mix works well with almost any dish. It's nice to always have some on hand to sprinkle on soups, oatmeal, salads, and greens.

makes 1½ cups (375 mL)

¼ cup (60 mL) raw sunflower seeds

¼ cup (60 mL) raw pumpkin seeds

¼ cup (60 mL) raw sesame seeds

¼ cup (60 mL) chia seeds

¼ cup (60 mL) raw flaxseeds

¼ cup (60 mL) raw hemp hearts

1. Toast sunflower, pumpkin, and sesame seeds in a dry pan over medium-high heat, stirring often, for 3 to 5 minutes, until lightly browned. (Alternatively, spread on a baking sheet and bake in a 350°F/180°C oven.) Transfer to a bowl and let cool.

2. Combine toasted seeds, chia, flaxseeds, and hemp hearts. Stored in an airtight container in the fridge or freezer, this mix will keep for up to 1 month.

salad topper

We use this cute-looking and tasty mix to finish the Superfood Salad (page 156) and the Smart Bowl (page 247). As the name suggests, this goes well on any salad, but is also a great addition to soups and adds some interesting flavours and textures to morning oatmeal.

If you can't find puffed quinoa at your local health-food store, you can substitute puffed millet or amaranth.

makes about 1¾ cups (425 mL)

1 cup (250 mL) puffed quinoa

¼ cup (60 mL) dried goji berries

¼ cup (60 mL) dried currants

2 tbsp (30 mL) sliced almonds

2 tbsp (30 mL) chopped raw hazelnuts

2 tbsp (30 mL) chopped unsalted raw pistachios

¼ tsp (1 mL) sea salt

1. Combine all of the ingredients in a resealable jar. Seal and shake gently to combine. Use immediately or store in a cool, dry place for up to 1 month.

tofu sour cream

This vegan sour cream can be used wherever you would normally use the dairy version. Depending on the water content of the tofu you are using, you may have to add a bit of water to get a sour cream–like consistency. If using a food processor to make this, be patient: it may take a few minutes to achieve a really smooth consistency. While processing, the tofu will go through a grainy stage, but keep processing and it will turn velvety smooth, just like the traditional version. If using a high-speed blender, it will come together quite quickly.

If you are storing this in the fridge, it may solidify. You can either whiz it up again in the food processor with a bit of water or just stir it vigorously until it loosens up.

makes 2 cups (500 mL)

2 cups (500 mL) chopped extra firm tofu

3 tbsp (45 mL) sunflower oil

3 tbsp (45 mL) + 1 tsp (5 mL) freshly squeezed lemon juice

1 tbsp (15 mL) raw agave nectar

½ tsp (2 mL) sea salt

1. Combine all of the ingredients in a food processor or high-speed blender. Process until smooth, scraping down the sides of the work bowl or blender jar as needed. Transfer to an airtight container and refrigerate for up to 3 days.

IT TAKES A CITY

Thank you, Penguin Random House Canada, for making our fifth Fresh cookbook happen, and Andrea Magyar, our editor, for your knowledge and invaluable experience in shaping this book.

Thank you, Kyla Zanardi, for your precise and joyful way of capturing our food and juice in the natural beauty of daylight, and Dara Sutin, for styling the images in this book and making the process so much fun!

Thank you, Tracy Bordian, for the toughest copy edit we've ever known! Your attention to detail is unrivalled.

Thanks to our long-time partner Barry Alper, for your strength and guidance in support of this project. You are the key to it all.

Deep thanks to Gillian Mountney and Stephanie Weinz, for holding everything together on a daily basis. With you two taking care of all the moving parts involved in the day-to-day running of Fresh, we have the peace of mind to do projects like this. Your loyalty and dedication is appreciated more than you will ever know.

Thanks to Jessica Brousseau, PJ Loo, Nancy DeCaria, Seelan Thevarasa, and Celeste Percy-Beauregard, for keeping the infrastructure of Fresh strong.

There are so many amazing people outside of Fresh who dedicate themselves to giving us their best and sharing their time and energy to make it all happen. Thank you Debra Goldblatt, Dinah Dieff, and Haley Greenberg of Rock-it Promotions; Lisa Kiss; Jay Eckhart; Debra Fenwick; Ilana Kadonoff; Mark Kadonoff; Andrea Damon Gibson and Steve Gibson; Marni Wasserman; Rich Donsky; Andrea Bates; Roger Thompson; and Jay Ezard.

Thanks to some special friends of Fresh: Sian Owen, Jeffrey Sum, Ian Turner, Ralph Giannone, Pina Petricone, Dan Trinnear, Robert Weinberg, Lawrence Malek, Joshua Spagnoletti, Ryan Skene, Shawn Pinnock, Matt Jumper, Johnny Demetriadis, Andrew Richmond, Hassel Aviles, Ciaran Dickson, Carmel Oren, Jeff Coussin, Gail Brode, Donna and John Weinz, Spencer Butt, Rick Hardisty, Houston Mausner, Lynn Alexander, Mike Radojkovich, James Long, Henry Pak, Sarah Donaldson, Mogan Subramaniam, and George Guevara.

Thank you to our growing family of Fresh partners for aspiring to make a difference around the world: LOV by Fresh Global – Dominic Bujold, Katrine Scott, and Michael Duhamel; Fresh Mexico – Ricardo Morales, Renata Burillo, and Christian de León; and Fresh Moscow – Irina and Dmitry Azarov.

Thank you to our two young brothers in cold-pressed partnership, Omar Shaheen and Tyler Colford of Village Juicery—for your vision and for welcoming us into your fabulous organic, never HPP'd, raw juice world.

Thank you to 889 Yoga's Emily Ridout and Christine Russell, as well as Dark Horse Espresso Bar's Deanna Zunde and Edward Lyons, for loving us, jumping in first, and leading the way in offering our cold-pressed juices at their stores.

Thank you, Francesca Elliott and Mia and Eva Richmond, for making our smoothies and milk look so yummy by smiling with your eyes.

Thanks to our team of brilliant and dedicated managers at our four Toronto restaurants: *Bloor* – Beth Hamersma, Nancy Young, Megan Carriere, Leiney Chiang, Liam Crowley, Kathryn McArthur, and Pino Russo; *Crawford* – Sam Segal, Brandon

McNeill, Arianne Glavina, Kelly McNamee, Jennifer MacFarland, Paul Martin, and Michelle Kaczmarek; *Spadina* – Gertrude Lung, Meghan Pike, Lauren Sebanc, Joyce Leung, Kenny Craine, Vanessa Fuller, Courtney McLeod, and Adele Dicks; *Eglinton* – Lauren Ho, Ivy Lovell, Daniel Teagle, Shanna Belzile, Kevin Schoenfeldt, Olivia Yetter, and Caitlin Ellis.

Thanks to our friends and family, who have been there along the way—for the love, laughter, and encouragement.

Barry Alper would like to thank Sara Heller, Emma Cass, Susan Abramovitch, Joel Kwinter, B and Bro Giddy, and Phyllis Levine.

Ruth: André Wiseman, Omar Wiseman, Haile Wiseman, and Beatrice Wiseman. Ronnie Tal, Laura Ulrich, Carly Tal, Jeremy Tal, Ari Tal, and Jonah Tal. Iris Tal, Raphael Marrache, Adam Halbert, Naftali Halbert, Shalom Halbert, Leah Halbert, Adina Halbert, and Yoel Halbert. Christine Thompson, Janice Thompson, Al Wiseman, Michelle Wiseman, Felicia Wiseman, Renita Taylor, and Darryl Taylor. And all those friends who, just like family, continue to keep me safe in their loving arms.

Jennifer: Christine MacLachlan, Melissa Curcumelli-Rodostamo, Kim Thompson, Katie Luedecke, MaryLynn Turk, Fiona Paterson, Jason Maguire, Gabrielle Shaw, Rachel Metalin, Erin Best, Sarah Attwell, Heidi McKee, Sean Qayum, Jojo, Billy, Ruairidh, Sanna and Shuna Steele, Gianni Sabatino, and Jessica Manning.

Barbara, Wayne, and Elizabeth Houston; Penny, Gary, Jeff, and Amanda Warner; Phyllis White; Sharon, Leo, Dwayne, and Debbie Punnewaert; Keith and Dianne Houston; Richard, Bev, and Dana White; Brad Miller; Tim "Chewy" Turner and Lou Goodwin.

Thanks to my favourite kids: Callum and Cecilia Smith; Francesca and Claudia Elliott; Ava Luedecke; Jack, Abby, and Grace Walker-Mitchell.

Thanks to Jane Rodgers for showing me what a well-stocked pantry was, all those years ago.

To some people who made cooking so much fun over the years: James Binnie, Lori Kilback, Tara Mills, Quade Generoux, Chris Pirie, Maria Hutton, Andrew Field, Scott Murden, Sue Bruton, Marg Hitchcock, Benji Perosin, Therese DeGrace, and Josh Bush.

And to my boys, Sam and Tex Houston, for all the love.

INDEX